The Complete Guide to Careers in Special Events

The Wiley Event Management Series

Series Editor: Dr. Joe Goldblatt, CSEP

The Complete Guide to Careers in Special Events

Step Toward Success!

Gene Columbus

WILEY

John Wiley & Sons, Inc.

Copyright © 2011 by John Wiley & Sons, Inc. All rights reserved.
Published by John Wiley & Sons, Inc., Hoboken, New Jersey.
Published simultaneously in Canada.

For general information on our other products and services, or technical support, please contact our Customer Care Department within the United States at 800-762-2974, outside the United States at 317-572-3993 or fax 317-572-4002.

Wiley also publishes its books in a variety of electronic formats. Some content that appears in print may not be available in electronic books. For more information about Wiley products, visit our web site at http://www.wiley.com.

Library of Congress Cataloging-in-Publication Data:

Columbus, Gene.
    The complete guide to careers in special events : step toward success! / Gene Columbus
        p.   cm.
    Includes index.
    ISBN 978-0-470-46325-3 (pbk.)
        1. Career development—Vocational guidance. 2. Special events. I. Columbus, Gene II. Title.
    HF5381.C6848 2010
    394.2023—dc22

                                                                        2010026280

Printed in the United States of America

10 9 8 7 6 5 4 3 2 1

DEDICATION

This book is dedicated to an amazing trio, my wife Becky and sons Robert and John. They know well my journey.

CONTENTS

SERIES EDITOR FOREWORD

In my professional opinion, there is no one more qualified in the entire world to write the first book about career development in special events than my best friend, Gene Columbus. I am grateful to Gene, as you will soon be as well, for writing this important and most valuable book. There are at least three reasons I know why you will greatly benefit from *The Complete Guide to Careers in Special Events: Step Toward Success*!

First, as a result of his 38-year history with Walt Disney World®, Gene has had the opportunity to interview and counsel thousands of potential cast members for the Walt Disney Company. Therefore, he has seen, better than perhaps anyone else, what it takes to establish, develop, and sustain a successful career in the special events industry.

Second, Gene's professional experiences provide an endless fountain of unparalleled wisdom that he transmits through his "Gene-Gems." These gems not only inform but also inspire aspiring and established professionals in the special events field. His gems are multifaceted and offer the insights, tips, and tactics of a man who has had a front-row seat in the events and entertainment industry for nearly four decades.

Third and perhaps most importantly, Gene is devoted to helping others find gainful and enjoyable employment in special events everywhere in the world. He truly cares about his students at the University of Central Florida, his associates at the Orlando Repertory Theatre, and the thousands of young people that he mentors throughout the world. A wise person once told me that before the readers care how much you *know*, they want to know how much you *care*. Not only is Gene an expert in career development in the special events field, but also he is the most caring and sharing professional I know.

The Complete Guide to Careers in Special Events will provide you with an effective career road map whether you are a student, aspiring professional, or experienced event planner. If you are considering switching careers, this book will provide you with the essential navigational tools to make your transition easier, simpler, more successful, and certainly more fun.

The Merriam-Webster Dictionary (2009) defines the term *magic* (originating in the fourteenth century from the Latin term *magice*) as "the use of means (as in charms or spells) to have supernatural powers over others" or "an extraordinary power or influence from a seeming supernatural source" and finally "as something that seems to cast a spell."

Gene Columbus is arguably one of the most experienced and best-loved executives in the treasured history of the magic kingdom of Walt Disney World. In **The Complete Guide to Careers in Special Events**, he generously provides, for the first time ever, his secrets of special event career success so that you may now cast your own spells on the special events industry and create the future success you so richly deserve.

We must all be enormously grateful to Gene Columbus for opening wide his extraordinary magic chest and sharing his charms with us. I encourage you not only to experience this magic but also to share it with others by encouraging your professional colleagues, friends, and others to purchase this book and benefit from the magical transformations that are certain to occur as a result of this phenomenal and groundbreaking work.

PROFESSOR JOE GOLDBLATT, CSEP
Series Editor
Queen Margaret University
Edinburgh, Scotland

FOREWORD

There are days that change your life forever. That day, for me, was the day Gene Columbus interviewed and hired me at Disney. Gene Columbus has coached, helped, hired, and mentored more entertainment and event professionals than anyone else, anywhere. He is part psychiatrist, part attorney on cross examination, part best friend and uncle, and he is always a true professional willing to invest in someone else's future. He has the ability to see beyond a person's potential and then coach them to that successful interview, first job, and greater career.

When Gene asked me to write a Foreword for his new book, **The Complete Guide to Careers in Special Events**, I was honored and excited. I had asked him for years to write down and share his special event and interview secrets. Now, it's all here for you! Also, I get to share my appreciation for Gene. I get to shout out to the future leaders in the world of live entertainment and special events . . . HEY! . . . LISTEN to a true legend and luminary in your chosen field.

Gene has the gift and track record for seeing the possibilities and potential in aspiring and driven entertainment "want to be's." He takes the time to invest in others . . . and now he is sharing his wealth of knowledge and expertise in this terrific book. If you read and study, and then DO what Gene has shared and outlined in this instructive and enlightening guide to success . . . you will have a huge leg up in the industry and on your competition for that first job.

Walt Disney said . . . (paraphrasing) . . . *you can dream, imagine, and create the most magical places in the world . . . but it takes people to make your dreams come true.* Gene Columbus is one of those people. He likes, knows, and cares about people. He wants and encourages those he mentors to succeed and make a difference. And here, he has taken his years of knowledge and experience, research, and personal contact with thousands of interviewees and corporate executives and crafted this guide for you. Read it . . . devour it . . . use this primer as your handbook and doorway to the world of the entertainment and special event business.

For decades, Gene has been selecting and guiding people to that "right fit" job. That place where you can do and be your best. I was one of the thousands that Gene helped and inspired. Gene's belief in me led to a 27-year Disney career of 14 different entertainment management positions.

At Disney, we relied on Gene to find the brightest and best candidates to contribute to our expanding and demanding needs. After my retirement from Disney, I became the Dean of the Weitzenhoffer Family College of Fine Arts at my alma mater, the University of Oklahoma. What I learned from Gene helped me, once again, with my interviews for a role in higher education. Now, as an educator and dean, I so believe in the value of this book that I recommend it as a teaching and learning tool. This book can be your bridge from what education teaches to what the real world demands.

So . . . read and use this insider's guide to the special event business and the interview process. Gene will focus you . . . just like he focused me and countless others on how to get hired and succeed. Your opportunity awaits—read on.

Rich Taylor
Dean, Weitzenhoffer Family
College of Fine Arts
University of Oklahoma

PREFACE

Your Journey into the Special Events Industry

Planning a successful trip requires reviewing maps and getting direction from those that have traveled the road before you, rather than heading off and hoping you will end up where you want to be. Having much of the needed information before you leave greatly increases your chances of a pleasurable journey, with the added benefit of points of interest along the way.

This book, *The Complete Guide to Careers in Special Events: Step Toward Success*! provides you with that roadmap to your destination in the special events industry, offering great directions from those that have come before you, as well as a number of points of interest along the way.

Qualified special events individuals will always be in demand, and *The Complete Guide to Careers in Special Events* is meant to encourage continuous training and personal development before launching, and throughout, your career. To assist you, industry professionals provide insight and advice on gaining the appropriate skills, making contacts, networking, and using your knowledge to showcase yourself in job interviews and professional settings.

The people who implement and create special events are as special as the events themselves. These individuals wish to serve others, and are committed to doing whatever it takes to delight, surprise, captivate, inspire, develop, motivate, teach, and carry out any other mission that the event is devised to accomplish. Of course, becoming a special events professional takes time and effort. However, if this is your passion, it will be a most rewarding and fulfilling career.

The Complete Guide to Careers in Special Events focuses on how you can capitalize on your unique abilities, training, and knowledge of special events to find gainful employment in this inspiring global industry. You will find that planning your career steps is not unlike planning an event. In seeking employment opportunities there is the need to do the following:

- Research the opportunities.
- Develop a plan for interviewing tailored to the target company.

- Deliver the "pitch" to sell yourself.
- Negotiate the terms.
- Close the deal.
- Go to contract.
- Ultimately, do an outstanding job while listening to feedback on your journey to success.

This step-by-step process will help you create a unique and creative approach with a tried-and-proven plan for showcasing your skills in the special events industry. This book shares how you can plan your interview by doing the right kind of research, getting the necessary training and experience, and understanding the importance of learning from someone willing to guide you on your path in the special events industry.

For Instructors and Mentors of Future Special Events Professionals

For instructors using this as a textbook, this is a roadmap to guide and challenge students with practical applications. Various "Action Steps" are featured throughout the book, as well as exercises to be used in and out of the classroom.

Assignments in the "Practice Activity" featured at the end of each chapter can be used to help measure student progress and identify areas of individual focus.

You are encouraged to send your thoughts and recommendations to me at gene@genecolumbus.com for future editions. The goal is to do all we can to mold, guide, and assist our students on their journey to success.

Over my years teaching, I have learned this: While the class textbook provides students with a framework for learning, it should provide instructors with the chance to expand and personalize the material to suit the needs of each student. Therefore, this book is structured to assist with class preparation so more time can be devoted to engaging in discussion, practicing interview techniques, and reviewing students' progress while creating new challenges for them with emerging special events opportunities. It is true that "one size does not fit all," but *The Complete Guide to Careers in Special Events* provides an excellent framework for instructors to fit their students' needs based on their particular course.

Today, bookshelves are full of books with good career advice, but they are rarely industry-focused. In this book, readers will learn how hiring managers read résumés and cover letters, and discover what managers look for in interviews *specifically* for the special events industry. Additionally, *The Complete Guide to Careers in Special Events* features industry professionals who share their thoughts on interviewing and hiring, as well as on how candidates should prepare themselves for the interview and their future career.

Advance Your Career

The core of *The Complete Guide to Careers in Special Events* is a guide for future special events professionals on being effective in the job interview by taking the necessary steps to prepare. This is valuable not only to college students but also established professionals seeking a career change, or people fascinated by the possibilities, but unfamiliar with the industry or uncertain whether it is the right career choice. Regardless, each will find great value in these pages.

The special events industry is always changing and requires a commitment to life-long learning. Here, you will explore the continuously expanding training programs and industry accreditation programs available.

The Complete Guide to Careers in Special Events will teach you more than simply how to write a résumé or how to give great answers to interview questions. The mission is to have you assess your training, talents, and skills, and practice how best to communicate your abilities and qualifications in a job interview. In the final analysis, your being hired for the job will come down to how your knowledge and talents bring value to the company. As any good salesperson will tell you, it is all about finding a need and filling it better than anyone else.

What's Inside?

The Complete Guide to Careers in Special Events is organized into four parts, starting with preparing yourself for the industry and learning the necessary skills that make you a valuable addition to any company:

1. **The World of Events**: Confirm special events as your career choice.
2. **Training Factory**: Focus on planning and personal development using available resources.
3. **I'm Ready for My Close-up**: Address the nuts and bolts of creating a résumé, writing a cover letter, and preparing effectively for job interviews.
4. **Power Tools**: Look at a long-range career plan and how to help those that follow you by being a good role model.

Throughout the book, special event professionals provide tips and insight on how to be successful. There are samples of cover letters and thank-you notes, in addition to dining etiquette when interviewing over a meal. This is a workbook, and you should take the time not only to read it, but also to complete the assignments in each chapter. There is much to be gained from the effort. One of the most positive results is the confidence you will gain from knowing you are well prepared for your interview to enter the special events industry.

■ Gene-Gems

Distributed throughout each chapter are "Gene-Gems," which is a term that my students created for the advice I give in class. I learned of this while at the University of Central Florida (UCF) in the Department of Theatre, where students in the Stage Management office had posted my picture surrounded by some of my quotes. Of course, I was thrilled and honored that my students had found the information worthy of being placed in public so others could see

> ### Gene-Gem
>
> If an opportunity presents itself and you are not prepared, that's a missed opportunity! However, the act of preparation often times creates the opportunity.

and read it. These sayings were once passed down to me, and they are now being passed down through this book to the next generation of special event professionals.

■ Quotes

Many years ago I began collecting quotes for the purpose of sharing when speaking to groups or writing letters. At the end of staff meetings, I was often requested to share a quote. In the spirit of that tradition, you will find a number of quotes in this book for you to think about and enjoy.

> "Just follow the Yellow Brick Road."
> From the Wizard of Oz, screenplay by Noel Langley (1911–1980), Florence Ryerson (1892–1965) & Edgar Allan Woolf (1881–1948)

There is great wisdom in that simple statement. It is about getting started and pursuing a path; you may not understand why, but it is necessary to take those crucial first steps in order to discover the reason. Now read this book, follow the instructions, even if at first you do not understand why, and enjoy your journey with all of the wonderful and interesting characters you will meet along the way to the place where your dreams come true.

Instructor's Manual

An **Instructor's Manual** has been prepared to accompany **The Complete Guide to Careers in Special Events.** It includes a number of assets to and instructors in preparing course instruction, including:

- Chapter learning objectives
- Activities
- Key points to explore
- Web connections
- Assignments
- Test Bank

Qualified adopters can download an electronic copy of this **Instructor's Manual** at www.wiley.com/college/columbus.

ACKNOWLEDGMENTS

This book focuses on the journey for those seeking careers in special events. It is meant to assist as you go down that path. Writing this book required a great deal of assistance, and I was honored to have the wisdom and experience of my best friend, Dr. Joe Goldblatt, CSEP, for guiding me along the path. Joe has written numerous books and papers and continuously delights his friends with his lovely personal stories of family, friends, and experiences, always with a moral. My best friend (MBF) encouraged me to take on this project, and along the way offered guidance and assistance. Therefore, you are not just reading what I wrote but also what MBF inspired and often recommended me to write.

"Dr. Joe," as his students affectionately call him, also introduced me to his youngest son, Sam, who has served as editor, adviser, encourager, and Internet pal. As my best friend's son (MBFS), Sam took special care and I quickly learned that this brilliant young man was much more than a senior editor for *Special Events*; he was writing his own book while obtaining his graduate degree. In addition, MBFS is the Edinburgh producer of the highly successful "48 Hour Film Project," which he established shortly after arriving in Scotland. Without the dynamic father-son duo, I most certainly would have been lost on my journey.

A special thank-you goes to my dear friend and past colleague Rich Taylor, now dean of the Weitzenhoffer Family College of Fine Arts at the University of Oklahoma, for sharing his thoughts in the Foreword of this book. He and Dr. Joe honor me by contributing their thoughts on the value of this effort. Rich and I spent many years working together at Walt Disney World®, where Rich was the vice-president of entertainment, including some very special events. Rich is uniquely qualified to share his thoughts, as he spent the majority of his career in a leadership role specializing in large-scale special events and then took that experience to the world of education. He is a man that is equally at home in both fields.

There are so many people to thank—including all those individuals who I had the opportunity to interview and hire, as well as those I interviewed and didn't hire. The latter group often offered the same level of passion for the industry but lacked the ability to communicate their skills while interviewing. Many of the recommendations in this book are based on what I learned from those who were unsuccessful, so in the long term, their experience will help others to be successful.

Appreciation must be given to my good friend Rick Neely from Professional Recruitment, who worked side by side with me for years helping many individuals make it through the Disney hiring process. Don Staples, director of creative entertainment, supported my efforts to find the best and brightest candidates for consideration, which established a new level of talent for creating and managing shows and events. Wendy Abraham went above and beyond in supporting the Disney internships and made sure that each person had a positive learning experience.

A special thanks to my closest Disney pal Hugh Kincaid, HR manager, who shared his wisdom, understanding, and time as my mentor for so many years. Our lunchtime meetings became famous, as they were filled with much more than eating—they were enriching for all those who joined us.

Over the years at Disney, there were many who assisted me in helping candidates get their start. They include Mary Malys, my assistant for nearly 17 years, Rita Barreto, Katina Catron, Miki Goad, Leslie Ann (L.A.) McCord, and Rhonda Anderson-Robinson. In addition, Greg Bell, who also contributed to this book, worked hand in hand with me with Disney Entertainment Staffing, assisting in the development of many of the processes used in evaluating and recommending candidates for placement.

Many others contributed to this book and also in expanding my network of respected friends. Their words of advice are right on target, and I would not have been able to complete this book without their input so I am grateful to each of the special events industry leaders for their time and effort.

Andrea Michaels—President, Extraordinary Events
Alisa Schwartz—Production manager/stage manager, Freelance
Arnold Guanco—Manager, special projects, Philippine Basketball Association
Carolyn S. Baragona—Owner/vice president, *Event Solutions* magazine and tradeshow
Charlotte J. DeWitt, CFEE—President, International Events, Ltd.
Dave Peters—President, Event Mall
Donald Seay, PhD—Professor of theater/theater consultant
Frank Supovitz—Senior vice president, events, National Football League
Gabriel Ornelas—Director, Ragsdale Center, St Edward's University
Greg Bell—Talent relations director, Walt Disney Parks and Resorts
Gregory L. DeSheilds—Senior director of corporate relations, Temple University
John J. Daly Jr. CSEP—President, John Daly Inc.
Josh McCall—Chairman and CEO, Jack Morton Worldwide
Laura Schwartz—White House director of events, the Clinton administration
Lisa Hurley—Editor, *Special Events* magazine
Michael Goldman—Senior executive producer, ProActive, Inc./Freeman Creative Group
Richard Aaron CMP, CSEP—President, Bizbash Media
Rob Murphy—Chief marketing officer, MC^2
Steve Wood Schmader CFEE—President and CEO, International Festivals and Events Association (IFEA World)
Tammy Bowman—Executive producer, Automotive Marketing Consultants Inc.

My thanks to Mary Cassells, Senior Acquisitions Editor with John Wiley & Sons, Inc., for hanging in there with me. She and Kara Borbely, Editorial Assistant, remained positive through the process and continued to thank me for my hard work. I greatly appreciate Richard DeLorenzo, Senior Production Editor, for skillfully shepherding this book through the production process along with the copyeditor, Cheryl Ferguson. In addition, Susan Matulewicz, Senior Marketing Assistant, provided special attention to this book while Jenni Lee, Editorial Assistant, kept me on schedule. It has been an honor to be a member of this remarkable team.

Finally, I thank my wife, Miss Becky, for permitting me to have my weekends and many evenings to work on this project. She spent a lot of time and effort preparing a location in our home for me to work that would have limited distractions. She very much contributed to this book by making it possible for me to focus on writing.

INTRODUCTION

"A person should set his goals as early as he can and devote all his energy and talent to getting there. With enough effort, he may achieve it. Or he may find something that is even more rewarding. But in the end, no matter what the outcome, he will know he has been alive."

—Walt Disney

Welcome to the Excitement Industry

During my 38 years with the Walt Disney Company, I read tens of thousands of résumés from people hoping to join the Special Events and Entertainment Department at Walt Disney World®. Many came prepared, while others had knowledge of their craft but were ineffective at communicating the value they could bring to the employer. This book provides the opportunity to share what I learned from my many years of recruiting, hiring, training, and supervising individuals in the entertainment and special events industry. I did not start by knowing: it was the many candidates that taught me, with how they prepared their written materials and the manner in which they answered questions. We learned together, and over time it became obvious that I needed to help the candidates so that they could ultimately help our company as employees.

In those early days with Disney, it was my responsibility to hire people to fill open positions. I quickly learned that one of the most important duties of a manager is to select the best person for the role, as they will solve many future problems and contribute to moving the business forward. As you read this book, you will better understand what a hiring manager looks for in a candidate. On the other hand, it is your job to get the training and experience necessary for the position.

My approach is to share with candidates what the interviewer/hiring manager is looking for, and how they, as candidates, could best communicate that information. Over time, Disney managers would share with me the amazing differences between those who were "Columbusized" and those who were not. It was very amusing that my process took on a name. The goal of this book is to "Columbusize" the reader, or, as I view it, fully prepare you to take on the challenge of finding the perfect position and showcasing why you are the ideal candidate for the special events industry.

Over the years, I interviewed thousands of candidates for various roles in both creative and operational positions, assisted other department managers with filling their open positions, and helped many candidates showcase their skills. Many cover letters and résumés were written with too little or too much information, and it appeared that the candidate spent more time formatting than providing the needed information for the interviewer/hiring manager. Most candidates felt that they were at the mercy of the interviewer, and would project a lack of self confidence. It has been my quest to help candidates have a better understanding of the total process, starting with an investment in getting the necessary training in the many exciting areas of the special events industry. As you receive training and seek opportunities, this book will provide a road map on how to prepare for each step of the process.

We all start somewhere, and there will be many people that contribute to your training and education. My high school drama teacher, Mrs. Fouche, was a major influence on my life and career. She was the first to point out that you cannot ask others to believe in you, unless you believe in yourself. You will not go far without a level of self confidence, and confidence comes with having the knowledge and understanding of what is expected. You will find that there are many helping hands along the way, and it is important to know that you are not alone. Often the challenge for most people is knowing how to ask for help.

Ms. Fouche inspired me to join my high school drama club, and I became so passionate about theatre that, after graduating, I became a professional dancer. As a young man, I performed with celebrities like Bob Hope, Barbara Streisand, Bing Crosby, Lucille Ball, Jane Fonda, and even Elvis Presley. Everyone's career develops over time, and after years of dancing, one day the legendary Disney Producer Bob Jani called me and asked me to stage manage *Disney On Parade,* which I did for nearly six years, touring all over the world. This position lead to the opportunity to work at Walt Disney World, where I became Manager of Entertainment Staffing and coach young artists on their careers.

As you read this, you will better understand the process as a candidate, but also learn the vantage point of the interviewer/hiring manager. The many exercises in this book are meant to prepare you for the interview, but also to establish you as a valued employee. A key point of this book is to be a willing learner, as that characteristic will open up many opportunities. Consider the time you devote to the exercises in this book as an investment in your future. And remember: You cannot ask others to believe in you, unless you believe in yourself.

PART ONE

The World of Events

CHAPTER 1

Confirming Special Events as Your Career

"Special: Distinguished by some unusual quality—Being in some way superior."

"Event: Occurrence; a noteworthy happening—a social occasion or activity."

(Merriam-Webster Online Dictionary, 2009)

Special events come in many shapes, forms, descriptions, and sizes, whether it is a birth-day party, wedding, anniversary, holiday party, retirement party, awards ceremony, festival, a mega-event like the opening and closing of the Olympics, or even a presidential inauguration. What makes these events special is that they are unusual happenings and expectations of all of those involved are for their event to be extraordinary. No matter what type of event, you know that it requires planning and implementation, as well as follow-up. Every step, from concept to clean-up, as well as the measurement of success, is part of a successful event.

These same techniques can be used in the planning of your career and those special meetings called interviews. If you have done your research and have a strong plan you are far more confident of achieving positive results. When you plan a trip, you have a destination in mind, so you plan a route that will get you where you want to be. Along the way there may be problems with detours but you know where you are going so you con-tinue making adjustments along the way. That holds true with your career and the various interviews you will experience along your journey to where you want to be. Just as some detours take you on a more scenic route, your career adjustments could provide you with opportunities to see and experience things you might not have considered.

No doubt everyone has had the experience of having or attending a birthday party. I learned that birthdays come in all sizes. My son's sixth birthday party was pretty sim-ple, but there were many details for mom and dad. We were faced with assembling the elements: invitations, decorations, refreshments, party gifts, fun and games, hats, pictures, and, of course, the birthday presents. We made a list, only to discover just before bringing out the cake that we forgot to get candles. We ended up using three large candles off the dining room table and some others we found in the drawer. They were not the same color or the right size, but they were candles.

In thinking back, it was the candles I remembered most about his birthday because I hadn't done my homework of checking to see if there were candles. You will remember that interview when you forget a detail such as bringing a copy of your résumé because you thought the hiring manager had the original you sent earlier. The hiring manager might have passed it on to a member of the staff or misplaced it, or might be testing you to see if you are prepared. Often in an interview, I would ask for a résumé to see if the candidate had thought ahead, and then later I would miraculously find it. Do not assume the hiring manager has your materials and do not assume you have birthday candles unless you check first.

One of the goals in the special events industry is to make every event special and memorable. We are in the business of making memories. You will remember your job interview much more than the hiring manager will. The experience might serve as a model for how you will interview candidates in the future. If you have a positive experience, you are encouraged to recreate that type of experience for others in the future. Should your experience not be positive, promise yourself that you will never put anyone else through that type of negative experience. Steven Wood Schmader, Certified Festival and Event Executive (CFEE), president and chief executive officer (CEO) of International Festival and Events Association (IFEA), reminds us, "Never forget what business we are really in. At the foundation, we are all in the business of creating memories and milestones that families and friends will share for a lifetime. Everything else is a detail."

Schmader, the founding director of the Boise River Festival in Boise, Idaho, and the CEO of one of the world's largest associations of special event producers, emphasizes that it is important to "Have a 'Whatever it Takes' attitude about anything that you undertake. That should be the mantra for those entering our industry. If you need predictable hours, sleep, eating habits, or responsibilities, this is probably not the profession you are looking for. If you have ever said the words 'That's not my job,' this is definitely not the profession you are looking for." Schmader also said, "Never let anyone else tell you what is possible or not. Hurdles and obstacles are only put there to see how badly we really want something. And, do what you love. The money and success will follow."

For those of you unsure about the special events industry but seeking more information, read carefully the section titled "So Many Career Opportunities," which outlines the many jobs and positions that are available. Early in my career, I was a stage manager. I would announce to the performers just before the curtain went up, "Places, everyone!" Now I share with those considering a special events career that there are "Places for everyone." You will see that there are many types of jobs and positions available in this industry. People will always celebrate life's milestones, seek to become better at what they do, honor those who achieve, and inform and entertain by bringing people together, and so too will there always be roles for diverse event planners (see Figure 1.1).

If you have decided that the special events industry is for you, and you are attending a college or university, this book will prove helpful as it provides insight on career planning

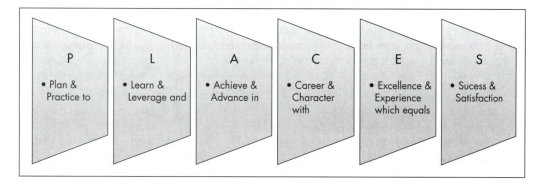

Figure 1.1   Gene Columbus Places for Everyone Special Events Career Model

and opportunities on how to present yourself to a potential employer. You will also have the advantage of a teacher to guide and assist you in your development. The instructors will blend their experience and knowledge with the industry trends to make sure that you are well prepared. As a teacher, my success is not measured by how well I do in the classroom but by how successful my students become once they leave my class. Keep in mind that those of us called to teach also have a responsibility to ensure that students meet the college or university degree requirements. We place demands on you as students, but often it is thought that you are doing the work for the teacher. Most students learn as they move forward in their careers that they are really making all this effort for themselves. The goal of teachers is to help students find and develop the skills that will provide them with a satisfying and successful career.

Schmader said,

> *Treat your life and career like a corporate mission statement. Define a personal mission statement and then define the best route to get there. Revisit your mission statement regularly. Participate actively in the industry. Never quit learning. Never let your ego lead. Always be part of the answer, not part of the problem. Always share with your peers and help to make others successful—you will need them to share with you often throughout your career and they will help you to succeed. Never let your success go to your head.*

Interviewing as Auditioning

My youngest son John, with the stage name of Nigel Columbus, is a professional actor who played leading roles in the national touring company of *Monty Python's Spamalot*, and his job is all about going to auditions and meeting with casting agents. Besides being a talented actor, Nigel is a fine singer and remarkable dancer. He understands that, in many auditions, he will not be cast in the show, but he keeps going back because if you don't audition, you will not get cast. His job is to audition and the casting director's job is to cast. If the show that is being cast is not right for Nigel, then he will not get the call, but the casting directors get to know him because he always comes with a positive attitude and a willingness to do anything.

Some people "play the role" of a successful interviewee. Dr. Donald Seay, former chair and artistic director of the University of Central Florida (UCF) Conservatory Theatre, says that, as a young actor, when faced with an interview, he had to play the role and rehearse. As a young professional actor, he dreaded the interview process. He knew he had talent and that he could perform, but the interview was always frightening. After a number of unpleasant experiences, he knew he would face the dreaded open-ended statement, "So, tell me about yourself." As a young actor with limited experience, he was fully aware that he did not have a wealth of professional credits, so in his mind he thought there was not a lot to tell. In fact, he would begin his answer by saying, "Well, there is not a lot to tell." It didn't take long for him to discover that this was not the way to begin your interview.

In Dr. Seay's experience, many young actors have problems with the interview process. They are trained to be outstanding performers but they are not well trained in how to get a job when the interview process is a very important component. These candidates sometimes learn their lines, rehearse, and then go to the job interview to play the part of a successful job seeker. It works for them, and it might work for you. It is possible that it will be the approach you might take with planning your interview, but you might find it restricting. Good actors learn not just their lines but also the meaning behind those lines. Like in a play, there is a text and a subtext, what is said and what is not said, that helps tell the story. You know your story and background better than anyone and are in the best position to deliver a great performance, but it must be your story, about your journey of learning that has brought you to that moment of connecting your past to what you hope will be your future.

Just as you would not go out on stage to perform without first doing a rehearsal, do not go into an interview without rehearsing. The interview should not be the first time you hear yourself talking about who you are, what you do, and what you have learned or experienced. Practice telling your story so that you have a comfort in talking about yourself. The secret is that it is not really about you, but about what you do. Companies hire you for the value you bring to an organization—and who you are emerges from the information you share, including your passion and excitement, as well as how well you communicate with others. Telling your story will be a key element to successful interviewing. As in theatre and special events, there is generally only one chance to get it right. The same holds true for your job interviews. Your investment in learning will pay off when you are able to talk with confidence about your skills.

Exploring the World of Events

For those seasoned professionals looking for new direction, this book is a chance for you to step back and look at the many opportunities available in the industry and reposition yourself for a new direction. The advantage you have is experience, even if it is not in the area that you are exploring. Proven work habits and being responsible for taking or giving direction are big assets. You can apply this understanding as you move toward the new, more desirable role.

You often hear that there is no substitute for experience, and your experience is a great asset. The process recommended to the students is very much the same for you. It will be all about the value you bring to an organization. If you have been in a leadership role, chances are that you will be looked at much more seriously because you have experience dealing with responsibility. You can sell your potential based on your strong foundational experience. If you are seeking a leadership role but have not had that level of responsibility, you can speak from the position of having been a very good follower, referencing the model leaders you have reported to and how they have molded and shaped you.

If you are unsure and find it challenging to step out of your current comfort zone, you need to establish a plan. The suggested steps outlined in this book will be most helpful to you. Change is hard for everyone, but if you are reading this book you are taking a step in the right direction—you are exploring.

"Twenty years from now you will be more disappointed by the things you didn't do, rather than the things you dzid. So throw off the bowlines, sail away from the safe harbor. Catch the trade winds in your sails. Explore! Dream! Discover!"

Mark Twain (1835–1910)

Sometimes it is necessary to take a step back in order to take many steps forward. That may be hard on your ego and even your paycheck, but think long-term. Ask yourself: Is there a bridge to where you want to be or must it be built? If you have a leadership background in setting up theme parties and you want to move into an area in which you have no formal training or experience, you might have to step down or step sideways into the new area to get the necessary exposure in the discipline before there would be confidence in your taking on a leadership role. Having said that, often it is our passion for doing something that gets us opportunities to do the things we love. At Disney, we called it "the burn," a great passion and knowledge that this is something you *have* to do more than just want to do (see Figure 1.2). My dad told me to find a job I loved and never work a day in my life. He was right about that!

Why are special events so important and continue to be important in the lives of people around the world? There are as many reasons as there are people, but perhaps the biggest reason is the chance to bring people together to laugh, cry, remember, celebrate, learn, mourn, and pray. The current trend is that people are connecting more and more electronically, over the Internet, via text messaging or by phone, with less and less personal, face-to-face experiences. We are communicating, but people are not really connecting. We keep up, but do not touch; we are up to date, but not up close. There are many opportunities to help provide those occasions to bring people together in special events. It is an important service to the world—bringing people together promotes better understanding and can change the lives of those who take part in events.

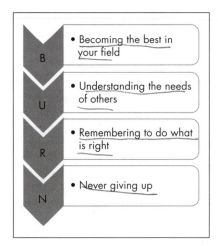

Figure 1.2   Gene Columbus BURN Special Events Career Model

My oldest son, Robert Columbus, is a musician and performing artist at Walt Disney World in Orlando, Florida, and he loves going to concerts. He can listen to the music on his top-of-the-line audio system in his studio, but he wants the experience of being there live and in person, along with people that have the same love for the music. It is that joint experience of seeing artists live on stage that attracts so many people to these types of special events. Someone has to organize those events, and if this is your calling, it can be a wild and enjoyable ride.

One day, Robert asked me, "Dad, do you enjoy watching the football games or basketball games on television?" Of course I love following some of my favorite teams and feeling the thrill of winning or the agony of defeat. Robert then asked if I enjoy going to the game in the stadium or the arena. Seeing a game in person is really special because I am with a large group that is caught up emotionally with the team. I never leave until the end of the game, even if my team is far behind. If we expect them to play the full game, we should stay out of respect for their effort, even when they are not winning nor have hope of winning. I understood his point about having the shared experience with others. As good as it might be on television or on a recording, there is something very special about sharing the live event experience with others.

People like to be around other people. Perhaps that is why sport bars are full even if the game is on television. Whether people are coming together, or they are being brought together, there must be a reason and purpose to justify the gathering. Special event professionals help make everything run smoothly. Understanding your role is important as you develop your career goals and the steps to get to where you want to be. Walt Disney once said, "You can dream it, you can build it, but it takes people to make it happen." I would add, people like *you*.

Learning How to Learn

For the college student focusing on this industry, try to broaden your studies to include a wide range of courses that could pertain to special events and entertainment. One of the best things you are learning is simply to learn—learning to learn is a great skill and will serve you well throughout your career. In seeking internships or entry-level positions, you will find that most companies want a willing learner. They will teach you their way of doing things because it has proved successful for them in the past. The number-one thing you have to offer is your potential.

Over the years, I would interview candidates that saw the glamour of the special events industry and thought it would be fun to be involved with the star talent, fancy meals and important people, because those of us in the industry are determined to make it look easy and making it look easy is really hard work. When seeking a position, keep in mind that there is the glamour but there is also every other part of the job that creates the glamour. While interviewing a well-educated young woman, I learned that she was only interested in being a coordinator working directly with the client. There is nothing wrong with this, but she made it very clear that she was did not want to deal with sales, had no interest in catering, nor had she taken time to learn about the technical support for events. She wanted to be there for the glamour and to take the bows. It is very hard to start at that level, and the person who has a diverse background and a willingness to do what was necessary for the overall success of the event has a much better chance of getting hired.

In your exploration of career opportunities, do not limit yourself to one area or aspect of the special events industry, but instead learn all you can about the various elements that make up events. As you move forward on your journey of learning, you will find that there are aspects that attract you and serve as a magnet. This book will focus on the primary areas, taking a somewhat generic approach to how to research areas of interest. You will use tools to prepare for making that strong first impression in your interviews, but the research will give you greater insight into the many opportunities available.

Your success will result from the hard work put into developing your skills and the research you do will make you more knowledgeable about the industry. It comes down to your ability to communicate with passion and energy that you know what you are talking about and can give great examples that show the hiring manager that you would bring value to their organization. In fact, I ask candidates: "What value do you bring to our company?" (See Figure 1.3.) Some candidates seem to think that their college degree is all they need to get their start and feel that the company should reward them for making it through school. The famous quote from the John F. Kennedy presidential inauguration speech, "Ask not what your country can do for you but what you can do for your country," may be adjusted to "Ask not what the company can do for you but what you can do for the company." You must communicate how your training has prepared you for continuing education and how you will bring value in the workplace.

Just as you learn in investment planning that it is best to diversify, the same things should be said about your career planning. Diversifying your training so that you have skills

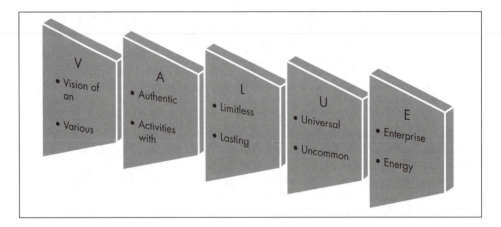

Figure 1.3 Gene Columbus VALUE Special Events Career Model

Figure 1.4 The Universe of the Special Events Industry

The circle of opportunities start at any point in that circle. It should be your task to ensure that you have prepared yourself to move where there is the need and opportunity. Leisure, entertainment, and corporate work often cross into the other areas.

in various areas will make you far more employable. During the economic crisis when Wall Street required a bailout by the U.S. government and banks were folding, businesses faced many challenges and those looking for work faced stiff competition. However, as the executive director of the Orlando Repertory Theatre, I had three openings and was holding out until I found the ideal candidates. Those selected were exceptional employees, as they brought great value to our company. None had a great deal of experience but each had shown that they had the discipline to learn various skills that made it possible for us to cross-train. These people were hired because they had potential and a great willingness to learn. Even in tough times there are opportunities; the key is to not give up. Hang in there and keep making contacts as well as building your network. It takes people to make the special events machine move. See Figure 1.4 and ask yourself, "Where do I best fit within this big universe?"

It could be said that there isn't a really good time or a bad time for those of us in the special events industry for finding employment. When there is a downturn in the economy, it affects the parts of our business that focus on high-cost productions. In downturns, the budgets tend to be smaller and the client expects to get more for less. The industry requires people to make that happen and understand the process of delivering great experiences on smaller budgets. The goal of most companies is to make it through the downturn and be ready to take advantage when there is an upswing. The special event professional keeps an eye on these trends so they are also ready to take advantage of opportunities.

Making a Good First Impression

Getting an interview and finding a position are only a small part of your special events professional journey. What is more important is the phase of taking what you have learned and applying it to your duties and responsibilities for the position you are assigned. This aspect of preparing for job interviews happens after you have gained understanding and are ready to showcase your knowledge and skills. Care should be taken not to jump in before being ready because it is true that there is only one chance to make a good first impression. However, during training, many people are willing to extend a helping hand to you, particularly while you are still in school. Every event industry person I know received help along the way and is willing to give back by helping others. Remember that part of this industry is helping young birds to fly, and once they are established they will do the same for others. It is very exciting to watch the next wave move up with new concepts and ideas on how to make special events even more special.

Many years ago, I learned that from time to time you have to dare yourself into doing something. For me, it was those first auditions when I was sure the casting directors were only looking at what I did wrong. I would hide in the crowd and hope to get hired with the crowd, which was a bad approach that led nowhere. Then there was the audition in which the choreographer asked if anyone had any questions. Up to this point he had shown us the dance routine with a slightly different count each time, but I could tell that it was his favorite combination of steps. I knew I could really perform the dance routine, so in asking my question, I danced it just like he showed it the last time. He replied with a smile, saying, "You got it!" In effect, I had a private audition and I got the job. Taking the risk—being bold—paid off in a big way.

"It takes courage to show your dreams to someone else."

Erma Bombeck (1927–1996)

One of the fondest memories of my early career was when I was working on my first motion picture at the Walt Disney Studios in the early 1960s and was not really sure what I should do. Mine was a very unimportant role and very little attention was given to me. Everyone was friendly, and I assumed that they thought I knew what I was doing because no one went out of their way to help me. Since I didn't know what to do, I would wait to see what everyone else did and then follow along. During coffee breaks, I would wait until the important people had their coffee before I would get in line.

On the fourth day, I waited until the coffee break was almost over before getting in line. Someone got in line behind me and, once I got my coffee and stepped aside, I looked back at the person who got in line behind me. He put his cup down and extended his hand to me, and said, "Hello, I'm Walt Disney!" He then started asking me questions about where I was from and what I was doing. To this day, I have no idea what I said to him except that I kept calling him Mr. Disney. The man whose name was on the gate I entered that morning did not presume that I knew who he was but extended his hand to introduce himself. I was determined to work with the Disney organization, and did for 38 years. Why? Because Walt Disney made me feel important. Think about how you have so many opportunities to make others feel important. If you make others feel important, they will make you important in their lives.

For some it will take practice to become comfortable reaching out, but you will find that it will create a new comfort zone for yourself as well as others. You become more approachable and valued as a member of the team, class, or group. Extending your hand should not be a passive move but done with purpose. Look the person in the eye, smile, take a moment to establish the connection, and call the person by name. Surprisingly, many people are not comfortable with this simple way of greeting another inhabitant of the earth. However, it is something that can be learned, and it is very necessary in the special events industry, and just as important in the interview process. Be happy to meet the other person so they will be happy to meet you. Choosing to be a positive people person will pay off. Abraham Lincoln said, "Most folks are about as happy as they make up their minds to be." It is much more enjoyable to be around happy people. In your career quest you will find that positive attitudes attract positive results, and I need not tell you about what happens with negative attitudes.

What are the qualities that set you apart? They are not just the attitudes you have in the interview but what you bring to the work force. A positive can-do attitude with a problem-solving approach needs to be the foundation for your work ethic. Always look for the best solutions to problems and make the team effort full of pride and purpose. Make it a nice day for others and it will be a very nice day for you. Make it a great event for others and it will be a great event for you and that will lead you to having a great career.

Gene-Gem

Do not ask others to be excited about you and what you do unless you are excited about what you do.

Career Connections

 ## Practice Activity

Attend a professional meeting of a special events industry trade association such as the International Special Events Society chapter near you or any other related group and introduce yourself to everyone in the room. Position yourself by the front door where people enter the event and try and meet as many people as possible. Be sure to smile, have a firm handshake, make eye contact and use people's names when speaking to them as you find out something about them, such as where they are from or where they are employed.

 ## Tool Kit

Friedmann, Susan (2003). *Meeting & Event Planning for Dummies*. Hoboken, NJ: John Wiley & Sons.

Goldblatt, Joe (2001). *The International Dictionary of Event Management*. Hoboken, NJ: John Wiley & Sons.

Lore, Nicholas (2008). *Now What? The Young Person's Guide to Choosing the Perfect Career*. New York: Fireside.

Roane, Susan (2007). *How to Work a Room: Your Essential Guide to Savvy Socializing*. New York: HarperCollins Living.

 ## Web Connection

Visit LAUNCH, the student program of Meeting Professionals International (MPI), at: www.mpiweb.org/Community/Students.aspx

CHAPTER 2

So Many Career Opportunities in the Special Events Industry

The special events industry requires many different types of skills and talents, so almost everyone can find an exciting niche. As for long-term opportunities, there will always be a need for people with a passion for this industry. It requires people with natural or developed leadership skills, but most of all it requires people willing to be part of a team that provides memorable experiences. The special events business is not for everyone, as it requires a major commitment of time. Many professionals will tell you that it is not a nine-to-five job but often 24/7. Make sure you have an understanding of the industry before going in that direction. You will not want to look back in a few years wishing you had done more investigation before jumping into this industry with both feet. However, no matter where you are in your process of researching and choosing a career, this book will be helpful in understanding the process of researching opportunities as well as preparing for job interviews.

Most industries have similar overall goals of providing exceptional products or services, creating loyal customers. It could be banking, legal, health care, training, dry cleaning, electrics, grocers, sales, service, automotive, and even theme parks—any business that deals with consumers seeking products or services. The vast majority of jobs in the service sector look for many of the same qualities in employees as what the special events industry requires. This book will help you first explore opportunities in the special events industry, and if you decide to explore other industries, the interviewing template will be extremely helpful as well.

> **Gene-Gem**
>
> It is acceptable to say "I do not know" in an interview. Never make up an answer if you don't know. Just because the interviewer asks the question does not mean they do not know the answer.

Making the right choice for you is what is the most important. Since you are reading this book, there is a possibility that there is something about this industry that has attracted you to seek out more information about the types of career opportunities available. Many times it is the fear of the unknown that prevents us from moving forward with a task or project. When it comes to a career choice, many young people feel that once they choose, they are locked in for life. That is not the case. Many of us end up in places we would have never thought of at the beginning of our careers. You might start in one direction and then adjust your course until you find the perfect position for yourself. That is why the special events industry is so wonderful; there are so many different roles and a countless number of different types of events for a wide variety of clients.

Years ago, I learned that people introduce themselves by what they do. Think about how you introduce yourself right now. Normally, it sounds like this; "Hello, my name is Elaine Event, and I am a student at State University!" or, "Hi, I'm Carl Candidate, working temporarily as a salesman for a big retailer but want to do something different, hopefully in the special events industry." Think about what would make you most proud to say in your introduction. Would it be; "I am the events coordinator with Exceptional Events"? What would sound good to you? You should start right now making a list of what you would like to say when introducing yourself. As you continue to read this book as well as others, make your list of roles you think you might like in the special events industry. Review the list and arrange them in a priority list, with the most desirable on the top. This will help narrow your search and help you organize thoughts that you can share with a teacher or trusted friend.

> ### Gene-Gem
>
> "We never do the same thing once!" (Heard many years ago about Disney events)

The Elevator Speech

The "elevator speech," as it is called, is a greeting in which you have only a few moments to introduce yourself and share what you do, as well as open the connection to the person you are meeting. This is a great exercise and should be well thought out, making sure that it does not sound self-serving. If you are in a classroom setting or in an industry networking event, this is good place to start practicing and getting comfortable with what you say. Choosing the words and then speaking them will build confidence and even clarify for you what you want to do. The following are examples of elevator speeches.

The teacher: Good morning, my name is Paul Professor and I teach a group of remarkable students at State University, and you no doubt would have something wonderful to share with them. May I call you to arrange a time for you to visit our class?

The speaker: Good afternoon, my name is Sally Speaker, and as a speaker and consultant, I help organizations find, lead, and keep outstanding employees. I do that often by learning about the needs of organizations. May I call you to learn more about your recruiting and retention plans?

As executive director: Greetings, my name is Darla Director, serving as executive director of the City Family Theatre. Perhaps you could be of assistance in offering recommendations on how we can make an even greater impact in our schools and community. I will not be asking you for anything but for you to tell me how you can help this wonderful organization.

As a volunteer: Hi, I'm Vince, and I am one of the volunteers having fun and making a difference. We are always looking for others to join us—we learned that many hands make for light work. May I share of bit of information with you?

Four steps in developing an elevator speech
Step One: Who I am by giving my name and using their name
Step Two: What I do by sharing my current position
Step Three: Using a question to make a connection
Step Four: Establish a continued opportunity for communications
Results: The person knows your name, what you do, and has a possible connection, and an opportunity to continue the communications

Like most things in life, it is best to practice until you feel comfortable sharing information about yourself and finding a way to engage the other person to take interest in what might be of benefit to both of you.

As you read, you should be making notes on how you are going to personalize your greeting. Review the suggestions offered in this book, reading other books to help you on your quest—particularly, stories about industry professionals. This provides more insight regarding the duties, and responsibilities of various roles plus great career advice. Write, review, and rewrite your greeting, and then practice saying it. Many people have told me their rehearsals took place in their car while driving to work or school.

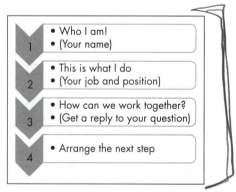

Figure 2.1   Four Steps in Developing an Elevator Speech

With so many exciting facets of the industry it would be impossible to cover them all; however, the following list of categories is a cross-section to help you understand the various areas and types of positions available.

Creative Development versus Operations

If you have an artistic flair or a talent for creative writing, there are wonderful opportunities in creative development. These positions are very exciting and attractive. Imagination is the key in this position. Writing creative concepts, designing scenic elements, creating exciting videos, making center pieces, decorating a room, providing graphic designs, composing original music, designing lighting, developing marketing materials and so on are very demanding and yet very rewarding. The creative director guides the team and the client in achieving the end result.

Dealing with the logistics and operational demands of events can also be challenging and rewarding. The conceptual and the operational aspects must both have a strong creative component, as there will always be creative adjustments made on-site to adjust for the unexpected things that can happen while producing an event. This is a role where

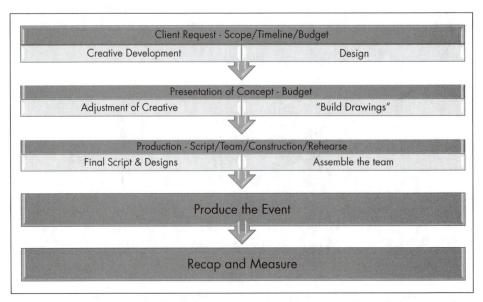

Figure 2.2 Serving the Needs of Clients Creatively, Developmentally, and Operationally, Interconnecting with a Common Goal

attention to detail is most important. Every aspect of the event must be reviewed and a plan in place to make everything run smoothly. All the work of the creative team is realized at that event. Making sure that everything is presented and sold to the client is very important. Often members of the creative team are present but the event production manager makes sure that everything is on time and on budget.

It is important to learn and understand both the creative development and the operational aspects of the Special Events industry, as knowledge of the challenges in these aspects will pay off in the long run and open doors for more opportunity. In fact, learn all you can about the industry so that you are able to step into various roles even if the one you want is not available.

Full-Time, Part-Time, Project, and Volunteer Work

Early in my Disney career an executive said to me, "We cannot build a church just for Easter Sunday," meaning that it is not possible for a special events company to hire all full-time employees or own all the equipment necessary for the largest possible events. Rather, they hire the least number of people and add employees as needed and own the basic equipment and rent for those once in a while larger events. Since you are considering this industry as a career, you might explore gaining experience being on a team rather than just reading or hearing about it. Begin by checking the local newspaper to see what is in the calendar section, as well as checking the volunteer opportunities online. You really do not have to look much beyond your school as there are numerous opportunities to get involved. There are class reunions, proms and after prom activities, as well as graduation. In addition there are local parades, school carnivals, and other city or county events which are good and safe places to observe what goes into doing events, as well as making a contribution—the other part is that it is a credit to put on your résumé.

Good event organizers do all they can to ensure that the volunteers have a good time and feel valued. It is nice to understand what it is like to be a volunteer so that you will remember to make sure your future volunteers are well taken care of and appreciated. Volunteers are an important resource in both the for-profit and nonprofit industries. Think how many volunteers fill the stadium for the Super Bowl or the number of bands that march in parades, or cheer on the runners while giving them water in marathons. The volunteers are often the life-blood of events, and if you take care of them this time you will be able to get them the next time.

One of best win-win situations is working part-time or on projects to learn more about the process as well as make great contacts in the industry. For instance, the Orlando Repertory Theatre uses undergraduate as well as graduate students in a variety of roles, most of which are unpaid. The eager students still feel that they are getting something much better than a paycheck: experience. They are working in the marketing department doing research on how to get the best return on investment in advertising. Some volunteer part-time workers focus on contract administration, dealing with performance rights to present shows or riders that outline the conditions a performing group must have in order to be appropriately showcased. Others work in front of house, learning about box office procedures and dealing with concessions and merchandise. They are also involved in the important duty of hosting patrons, ensuring that they are seated and dealing with any issue that comes up. The volunteers get the chance to assist in every area, from the parking lot to hosting guest artists. Volunteers work with box-office personnel, assisting in getting tickets into the hands of the guests in the shortest amount of time while also greeting them and answering questions.

This situation is typical at universities and community centers, and there will be many opportunities in your community to get involved in events. It is important to know what is expected of you so that, in the future when you are leading a team, you will understand what every position does as well as that every person, paid or unpaid, is important. Your goal is to gain understanding as well as experience in being part of the team that makes events special.

Career Sectors in Special Events

Destination management companies often serve as client representatives on site and take part in the planning and implementation of the event. There are so many elements that go into assisting a client to ensure a successful event. Just think about the enormous number of details involved with the travel aspects of getting a group to a location. It could be as simple as a local groups traveling by luxury bus or an international groups traveling by train, ship, or air from various locations around the globe. The mission is to get all guests from one place to another with little or no trouble. However, the travel is only the first step, as there are also the meals, business and break-out meetings, social events, recreation such as golf and tennis, room gifts, and on and on. Destination managers deal with challenges such as lost luggage or missed flights. Someone must think about every little detail and lead a team to make sure it all happens in a timely manner. That person could be you if you are well organized and able to multitask, or you can be an on-site person dealing directly with the guests. Both positions are important and require committed individuals.

Hospitality management is often a central part of the event if dealing with a group coming from outside the area. This position makes sure that rooms are ready and information is easily available for hotel guests. Conventions or association gatherings use host hotels, and with them come many opportunities in various areas, including catering, floral, décor, coordination, lighting, audio and AV support, and so much more. Entertainment and event themes have to work together in a seamless experience for the audience. Training in all aspects of hospitality management—from front desk, housekeeping, room service, recreation, banquet management and much more—are all part of the hosting opportunities available to you.

There are so many different types of events for which *party planners* provide their talents. It is about creating a memorable experience no matter what the event. When thinking about a party planner, one assumes birthdays and anniversaries, but there is so much more. The theme, décor, food and beverage, and entertainment blend together to free up the clients so that they can enjoy the experience.

Wedding planners have become a major part of the special events industry. This is a very demanding role, as this is a once-in-a-lifetime experience and it must be perfect. Often, there are many agendas at work with the wedding: the bride, her mother, the traditions of each family, the scope of the event, including where and when the ceremony takes place. Budgets that are limited and expectations that are high are part of the challenge. If you love the emotional experience of being part of pulling all the elements together, this is the role for you. You are the one that helps arrange all the details and instills confidence that all will go as planned. Weddings should be about the couple. The wedding planner, with a great deal of diplomacy, keeps everything on track.

We have all at one time or another had some dealing with *sports*. In my career I have been involved with football-themed parties, including one in which the center of a ballroom was covered with Astroturf with goal posts and benches and the background music was fight songs. There was the baseball theme with real sod covering a large portion of a ballroom. There were grandstands with hot dogs, peanuts and Cracker Jacks, along with other amazing dining. The hoop party changed the ballroom into a basketball court with opportunities to shoot free throws. Cheerleaders were always a hit and it didn't matter if they were from a pro team, a college or high school, everyone really enjoyed having a good cheer, particularly if it was customized to that group. Many professional teams have special events focused on the fans to increase season subscriptions.

Music is another wonderful element that can make an event unique. It is more than the musicians playing on the stage; it requires negotiating fees, selecting what is to be played, obtaining the rights to use the music, rehearsals, on-site management, and so on. *Audio and lighting support* is a key element in presenting live performances. That might be just for a small local band, but it is a very different scope to deal with a famous act or recording artist as a *talent buyer*. Hosting the group and dealing with *security* and the *production management* is demanding but yet very exciting. The artist's contract rider often outlines the requirements of the group, and since it is part of the contract, there is an obligation to provide all that is listed on the rider. There are opportunities to negotiate items but you will find that the artist will want to protect their image and the client will expect to see the production at the agreed level.

Just as music creates an atmosphere, *floral arrangements* warm up a room. The creative design in flowers and plants has risen to amazing heights over the past two decades. Nothing sets off a table more than a beautiful centerpiece. At a banquet table, the guests sit in a circle and all eyes will look to the center. Often, I have reduced the décor around the room to ensure that the item that will be viewed the most is exceptional. Floral designs are an art, and if you love the beauty of nature, explore this opportunity.

Many companies specialize in providing *equipment* necessary for events. Items such as tents, tables, chairs, linens, generators, air conditioning, heating, sound, lighting, staging, décor and much more are essential in producing special events. You should explore opportunities in this area as it could be a great way to learn about all the pieces that are necessary when creating an event, as well as providing you with needed experience.

Someone must ensure that all the *legal* issues have been addressed with proper documents, should there be any questions. The fire department is really your best friend in doing events, and their regulations are to keep your guests, your staff, and you as safe as possible. It is always in your best interest to work closely with your local fire department.

Events also require *security* to make sure the company's equipment is safe from being damaged by curious guests or being taken by someone that is not authorized to have those elements. This is an important part of event management and one in which there may be opportunities for you to get your foot in the door. You will also understand how critical these elements are to the event.

Many events book motivational *speakers,* and there is a need often to have someone coordinate with these speakers. This is a wonderful way to get experience and meet some remarkable people in the process. Your role may be as simple as waiting to bring an executive or a speaker to the stage when the event coordinator or stage manager gives you the cue, then waiting to escort them backstage.

A number of years ago, I filled in as host for a guest speaker who was to be the surprise guest at a big event at Disney. For about an hour I had the honor of speaking with the legendary George Burns. He had me laughing so hard that it hurt—he was as funny offstage as he was onstage but he also proved to be a very sweet man. It is one of my favorite memories of inducting stars into the Television Hall of Fame.

In the theatre we say that there are no such things as small parts. Every role in special events and every position is not a small part and each is very important. Show that you can handle the small responsibilities and that will prove that you can handle the big assignments.

Event Solutions Magazine

Carolyn S. Baragona, owner and vice president of *Event Solutions* Magazine and Tradeshow suggests that aspiring event managers "develop new relationships while keeping and cherishing the 'old' relationships. Develop habits for a lifetime of learning. Develop a reputation for following through on all of your promises. Develop an 'I can do that . . .' attitude and back it up. Be ethical . . . if you do something unethical, your reputation will precede you in your further networking and contacts. It will come back to bite you." She points out that "In our magazine, *Event Solutions,* we have a feature called "Plan B" in which event professionals share their stories of meeting unexpected challenges in their events. Their Plan B saves the day. And, Plan B almost always depends on having strong relationships with others in the industry who can rise to the occasion of your challenge and help you succeed in your event."

Baragona believes that employers are looking for "reliability, loyalty, attendance, ethics, talent, and education, demonstrated experience in the use of talent, energy, positive attitude, listening skills, and people skills. This may seem like asking a lot, but when working with members of teams from highly successful companies, they all exhibit these attributes. For example, over the years I have seen talented but unreliable people disappear from the event scene. I have seen people who lack loyalty move from one firm to another, with each move reflecting less credibility. Talent and education may get you in the door, but the other attributes and qualities keep your star rising."

The 2007 *Event Solutions* magazine "Annual Forecast" listed the positions in the special events industry shown in Figure 2.3. Some are full-time staff, more are part-time or

- Administrative Assistant: a dedicated office worker who can multi-task and operate various office tools
- Assistant Director of Events: assist and represents director with events, focuses on details and follow-up
- Assistant Director of Meetings: assist and represents director as well as doing follow up on all details
- Assistant Meeting Manager/Meetings Assistant: provides assistants to manager and serves as their representative
- Assistant Trade Show/Conference Manager: assist and represents manager as well as being the central communications hub
- Bartender: a friendly and efficient mixologist, who can mix drinks on request
- Brand Manager: responsible for appropriately marketing corporate brand
- Catering Manager: manages details of catering including manpower and schedule
- Catering Sales Director (commissioned): a convincing marketer who sells catering services through advertising and tastings.
- Catering Sales Director (uncommissioned): a convincing marketer who sells catering services through advertising and tastings.
- Cook: a disciplined kitchen artist who can work under pressure and follow strict direction from the head chef and sous chef
- Creative Director: concept design and development leader responsible for meeting the expectations of the client
- Designer: creates how something will look before it exists
- Director of Catering: manages and supervises catering management staff
- Director of Convention Services: a customer-oriented marketing manager at a convention center
- Director of Entertainment: responsible for coordinating all entertainment production both on and off stage
- Director of Events: leading authority on events, from galas to meetings
- Director of Exhibits: designs and implements exhibitions and tradeshows on the floor
- Director of Marketing: the head of sales and manager of all marketing staff and brand management
- Director of Meetings: conference design and development leader that often focus on seminars
- Director of Sales (commissioned): responsible for marketing and selling— establishes the high expectations
- Director of Sales (noncommissioned): manager of the sales team for both long and short term results
- Director of Sponsorships: manages and expands donor sponsor relationship
- Director of Public/Media Relations: develops and presents information concerning the public image of a company, ensures company is living its mission statement

Figure 2.3   Positions in the Special Events Industry

- Director of Trade Shows/Conferences: overall coordination of space usage and resources
- Entertainment Producer: executive director of a performing arts show
- Event Coordinator: arranges the various elements associated with events focusing on the smooth running of the event
- Event Manager: manages the details and smooth running of events
- Event Planner: works closely with client on details for events and follow through with supplier and vendors
- Event Producer: a well-rounded leader who assembles the team to create and manage events
- Exhibits Manager: leader of the team assigned to operate exhibits ensuring that both the exhibitor and the attendees needs are met
- Exhibit Sales Account Executive (commissioned): oversees finances for exhibitions and tradeshows to the industry or organization
- Exhibit Sales Account Executive (noncommissioned): client primary relationship contact and communicator to vendors
- Exhibit Sales Manager (commissioned): responsible for sales at exhibitions and tradeshows to exhibitors
- Exhibit Sales Manager (noncommissioned): ensures all contract and commitments are met by all parties
- Executive Director: responsible for both operational and creative activities and reports to a Board of Directors or owner
- Finance/Administration/Purchasing Manager: tracks all financial transactions and planning
- Floor Captain: an energetic member of the operations team who works well under pressure, managing crowd control, customer experience, and event operation
- Food and Beverage Director: responsible for all catering and bar staff, sales and operations
- Head Chef: the big cheese in the kitchen; makes all the recipes, calls all the shots, and manages the entire kitchen staff
- Internet/IT Manager: deals with all aspects of technology related to computers
- Lighting Designer: uses lighting to create a mood and audience focus as well as establishes cues—creates magic
- Marketing Assistant: an ambitious marketer who coordinates marketing campaigns under the direction of the marketing manager
- Marketing Manager: buys advertising and other collateral materials working closely with all department to ensure a unified message
- Meetings Manager: leader of the team assigned to meeting operations for both manpower and schedule
- Meeting Planner: works closely with client in developing programs and events and then works closely with suppliers and vendors to ensure execution of the plan

Figure 2.3 *(Continued)*

- Operations Manager: responsible for practical duties such as security and crowd control.
- Owner/General Manager: responsible for all business and creative operations (the buck stops here)
- Pastry Chef/Baker: department head responsible for managing pastry prep and presentation for the sweetest part of the meal
- Proposal Writer: a savvy marketer who sells event ideas to clients
- Public/Media Relations Assistant: a dedicated member of the marketing team who can deal effectively with press and media.
- Public/Media Relations Manager: serves as a representative for the company for information being presented to the public including press releases
- Senior Designer: an experienced production artist who can oversee designs for lighting, sound, scenery, costumes, and so on
- Senior Event Producer: proven event specialist with track record of success
- Sous chef: number two in the kitchen, manages the cooking operations according to the head chef's direction
- Technical Director: manager of the technical stage crew, including lights, sound and electrics with great ease
- Technical Producer: executive director of all technical stage production (lights, sound, electrics, special effects) for a large show
- Trade Show/Conference/Show Manager: manages and leads team assigned to events focusing on communications and detail planning
- Training Manager: develops and implements training and re-training programs to staff and volunteers
- Vice President Operations: director of all practical aspects of business, from cleaning to human resources to payroll
- Vice President, Sales (noncommissioned): directs marketing efforts both short- and long-term vision
- Vice President Sales (commissioned): director of existing and expanding markets focusing on long-term relationships
- Video Director: a production coordinator responsible for all video creation and projection
- Waitstaff: friendly and courteous waiters and waitresses with customer-service skills

Figure 2.3 *(Continued)*

project staff, and many are consultants who work for a commission based on their sales. Which of these roles might you like to take on?

Figure 2.4 lists the highest—paying jobs in special events, from the same Event Solutions 2007 Annual Forecast:

The salaries reflect a level of high responsibility, and often the individuals in these positions have a great deal of experience. However, this is a good reference for you as you look to the future.

Title	Average Salary
Director of catering	$87,951
Owner/general manager	$85,229
Executive director	$82,538
Senior event producer	$80,693
Director of sales (commissioned)	$80,200
Director of meetings	$75,448
Director of convention services	$71,909
Director of marketing	$71,865
Director of events	$68,918
Operations manager	$65,972

Figure 2.4 Highest-Paying Jobs in Special Events

Gaining Experience

If you are still in school and wondering if special events are right for you, you might look at the upcoming graduation ceremony and see if you can volunteer to help with the planning and coordination of the event. If there is not a graduation-style celebration, organize one and get classmates to help. This is a great time to practice leadership. It will be a lot of work and could really answer that question regarding if this is really what you want as a career.

Baragona says, "For a new college graduate, I would look for involvement in school or community events, and documentation of the success of their events. The job candidates just out of school should be able to demonstrate that they were part of campus organizations and played a role in the events of the organizations. Conferences, internships and event-specific classes would also be included on the résumé."

For those without school opportunity, there are many ways you can try your wings. Birthday and anniversary parties are wonderful and they give you a chance to explore how creative you can be with these types of events. Take on the task to find an event to honor a parent, grandparent, or a teacher. Not only would you learn from the experience, you would make someone feel very special.

Baragona points out that, "many pioneers of this industry seem to have started with one main passion and talent, and developed that talent with experiences, added to it, and evolved into an event professional: education through experience! There were no classes. No degrees. No professional organizations or publications . . . the event pros that emerged just had that desire for excellence . . . and where they saw a need, they learned to become excellent and rise to that need." Baragona states, "Young people interested in the event industry can become educated through colleges, universities, conferences, trade shows, internships, professional organizations, conferences, certifications. This is so valuable and contributes so much to the growth and professionalism of our industry. Today's entry-level event professional has the option, through education, to enter with information that the pioneers had to compile and consolidate on their own, through years of work and learning by experience."

Tammy Bowman, executive producer with Automotive Marketing Consultants Inc., says, "I cannot say enough about the importance of 'on the job training' and getting to know people in the industry. In the beginning, take any job and learn something new every day. Be flexible, stay informed and engaged in new technology, and always be willing to take a chance. Sometimes you have to venture into the world of the unknown and do something that is outside your comfort zone. In doing so, you will grow, learn and will build your knowledge base. If you are not doing something from time to time that makes your palms sweaty, then you are playing it too safe!"

If you enjoy seeing people enjoying themselves or learning something new or being acknowledged or rewarded, then this is an industry for you. You will see people laugh with delight or be moved to tears. There is an amazing rush of adrenaline when it all comes together and a feeling of pride knowing that you helped make it happen. If you like the excitement of detailed planning and implementing, you will love special events. Learning how to plan and dealing with many complex issues is the key.

As you learn, you will be also adding to your interview template, one that is as detailed as a well-thought-out special event. You would plan out the special event by researching the company, the type and scope of events it does, its competition in the marketplace, the individuals leading the organization, its client base, the company reputation, and even the word of mouth on what is being said about your target company. These are powerful factors that can arm you with information that will set you apart from your competition— and the same holds true for your job interview.

I encourage you to create a detailed profile of various companies. Before the Internet, we relied on industry trade magazines, which are still available. *Event Solutions,* for instance, is available both in hardcopy and online, at www.event-solutions.com. Today your target company uses the Internet to sell to clients, giving you an incredible amount of information on its Web site. Often there is a mission statement, long- and short-term goals, profiles of its leadership team, past successes, and current projects. There is a wealth of information to provide you with the cornerstone for your preinterview contact as well as great information for your face-to-face interview.

Also, many organizations post career opportunities, and if that is the case, mark your calendar to remind yourself to check their Web sites every couple of weeks. If you check a Web site today and there are no openings, the fact that the company posts its job opportunities would indicate that it is worth sending your materials on to them. Most companies want to have a stack of résumés should there be an opening. They often bring in additional staff to deal with those large-scale events, but once the event is over, these employees move on. Most companies want to have a large file of people they can call on to fill their staffing requirements, and you want to have your name and contact information in their files.

Where to Start

If you are at the beginning of your career, you might think you know exactly what you want to be and what you want to do, but few of us end up where we think we are going. Baragona suggests, "The best places to network are tradeshows, conferences, volunteering on nonprofit projects, participating in professional organizations, sponsorships, targeted advertising—anywhere that you have the opportunity not only to sit down and have a conversation with a colleague face to face, but also to see that colleague in action, demonstrating what he or she can do. Get involved. Participate. Showcase."

Baragona says, "Networking is one of the most important aspects of finding employment in the industry. That refers not only to individual "job hunting" but also putting your company into the awareness of those whom you wish to work with or for. Most events are a one-time-only opportunity . . . so when contracting with individuals or companies, the planner/producer will select those whom they know and whom they trust to follow through and deliver as promised. There are very few second chances—and members of an event team are selected with as much information about them as possible, especially reputation." Today, with training programs, certifications, and networking opportunities available to assist in career and personal development, you can develop short- and long-range plans for your career. The key is to commit to continuous learning.

For years I have volunteered, and many of my management friends from Disney, students, and individuals with interest in joining Disney would volunteer and get to spend time with established professionals who could be internal champions to help the volunteer get involved with the company. Seek out opportunities to be involved and the net result is that you will end up with more experience and possibly some great contacts.

Those who are not attending a formal educational program and are on a self-directed quest are on journeys with interesting challenges. It requires a great deal of determination and perseverance. It will be all about hanging in there and not letting setbacks discourage you. Throughout the book, there will be those recommendations that will focus on you and your quest. Dr. Goldblatt's book, *Special Events, a New Frontier for the Next Generation* (sixth edition), is highly recommended, as this book is intended to complement his publication.

Knowledge of the industry is the key to your success, and membership in professional organizations would give you the opportunity to interface with professionals and provide opportunities for seeking mentors. This is a very exciting way to learn the craft and develop skills under the watchful eye of a master craftsmen, as well as a chance to build a strong network.

Baragona says that the best way to position oneself for a long-term career success is in "keeping your company, yourself, and your talents in the forefront of your past, current, and potential clients." She outlines the following strategies for long-term career success:

- Targeting advertising
- Networking

- Maintaining relationships in the events industry
- Attending/exhibiting/participating in conferences and tradeshows
- Educating, learning, staying on top of the trends
- Speaking at conferences or meetings
- Participating actively in professional organizations
- Writing for professional publications

Review Baragona's list, asking yourself how you are going to implement each point. Some items, such as speaking at conferences or writing for professional publications, may be above your current abilities, but others you should begin on immediately. Your résumé is a form of advertisement. Networking and relationship building should be already well established, and attendance at conferences and tradeshows should be scheduled, in addition to keeping up with industry trends and getting involved with professional organizations.

Career Connections

 ### Practice Activities

- Read three articles in *Event Solutions*, (www.event-solutions.com), and for each article, write down three facts that you have learned that you can share with other event professionals in conversation. In addition, share that information with your mentor and have an open discussion about what you learned.
- List three areas of interest in the industry and look online to see how many positions are listed and what are listed as the job duties and responsibilities. Do a self-assessment of areas for your professional development and place that in a journal with an action plan on how you are going to go about achieving the necessary learning opportunities.

 ### Tool Kit

Goldblatt, Joe, and Kathleen S. Nelson (2001). *The International Dictionary of Event Management*. Hoboken, NJ: John Wiley & Sons.

Monroe, James, and Robert Kates (2005). *Art of the Event*. Hoboken, NJ: John Wiley & Sons.

Silvers, Julia Rutherford (2003). *Professional Event Coordination*. Hoboken, NJ: John Wiley & Sons.

Supovitz, Frank, and Joe Goldblatt (2004). *The Sports Event Management and Marketing Playbook*. Hoboken, NJ: John Wiley & Sons.

Sonder, Mark (2003). *Event Entertainment and Production*. Hoboken, NJ: John Wiley & Sons.

All of these titles are available from publisher John C. Wiley at http://www.wiley.com. A full list of recommended readings is available in the appendices of this book.

Professional Organizations

Following are several professional organizations, along with their Web sites and a brief description quoted directly from their respective Web sites.

International Special Events Society (ISES), www.ises.com: The Mission of ISES is to educate, advance, and promote the special events industry and its network of professionals, along with related industries.

Meeting Professionals International (MPI), www.mpiweb.org: Meeting Professionals International (MPI), the meeting and event industry's largest and most vibrant global community, helps our members thrive by providing human connections to knowledge and ideas, relationships, and marketplaces. MPI membership comprises more than 24,000 members belonging to 70 chapters and clubs worldwide. Check out the Launch Student Community at http://www.mpiweb.org/Community/Students.aspx.

International Festivals and Events Association (IFEA), www.ifea.com: Founded in 1956 as the Festival Manager's Association, the International Festivals and Events Association (IFEA) today is *the premiere association supporting and enabling festival and event professionals worldwide.*

Professional Convention Management Association (PCMA), www.pcma.org: PCMA represents approximately 6,000 meeting industry leaders, including planner professionals, suppliers, faculty, and students. Aside from students and faculty, members are categorized as either a professional or supplier, based on their position.

CHAPTER 3

What's So Special About the Special Events Industry?

As a staffing manager for decades at The Walt Disney World, it is impossible to say how many résumés found their way to my desk or how many thousands of candidates I met face to face. It has been an amazing opportunity to talk to many wonderfully talented people and give many of them a chance to share what value they could bring to the Disney organization.

My mission was to ensure that everyone had a positive experience, even if it did not lead to a position within the company. After all, these were "Disney guests," and it was my responsibility to provide them with a positive as well as memorable experience. Often, my relationship with a candidate went beyond the initial interview. It has been said that I have never met a stranger, and that may be true, but I saw it as my opportunity to meet people and learn from them as well as about them. I believe that if the candidate did not become an employee, he or she should continue to be a valued guest. I tried to make sure that everyone left with something, even if it was not the job offer.

Will all those hiring managers interviewing you have this type of attitude? It is unlikely, but since you cannot predict what type of person you will meet in the interview, you need to be prepared to deal with many different personalities. You should be like many of those well-prepared candidates who came to the interview like a bright light in a dark day. They were well prepared, and they helped me to help them. In other words, they took the responsibility of preparing to share what I needed to know about them to help get them placed in a position they were seeking. For many of these candidates I became their "internal agent." These candidates understood the importance of providing the needed information on their areas of interest, training, and experience.

With so many people seeking positions in Special Events, there must be something that attracts individuals to the industry. For the most part, Special Events are positive events that are celebratory in nature. There are festivals that celebrate music, art, dance, theater, film, food, wine, flowers and even lights during the Holiday Season all of which require planning and organization. There are large-scale parades such as the fantastic Macy's Thanksgiving Day Parade, which is a must-see event every year at my house, but there are also hometown parades welcoming the local hero, which require planning and organization, as well as a team to implement the plan. Basically, all these events are the same, with the biggest difference being the number of zeros in the budget and the number of people needed to make it work.

Special people like you are needed in Special Events, but this industry is not for everyone, as it requires a strong passion, drive, and commitment to pull off events. You are not like the typical nine-to-five worker: you might be doing an event at an odd hour of the day or night in good or bad weather. You do it because it is exciting and you love it. Special Events require special people.

Early on in my career I learned that everyone sells, and each event you do is a sales pitch for the next event for that company or clients they speak to about you and your service. The better the event, the better the chances of getting the business next time. There is no question that word-of-mouth recommendations are the best form of advertisement. On the other hand, if small things do not go as expected, it becomes more of a challenge getting a client to sign up for the next event. Figure 3.1 shows some of the benefits of using the theories of marketing in creating events.

Each person working on the event becomes the most important person on the project. The parking lot attendant who sends attendees to the wrong location will no doubt complain, and it reflects on the organizers and their ability to provide people to give correct information. But "recovery" is when you as a team learn that something less than positive has taken place and you take action to change the course of negative feelings. For instance, an attendee arrives late for a session because of wrong directions and is upset. You might provide a complimentary recording of the session plus early seating for the next session in which they pick their seats. Things will go wrong with events, and team members need to be empowered to address the problem and turn things in a positive direction.

The following are key reasons for the marketing strategy:

- An opportunity to provide face-to-face connections
- A way to involve media and get publicity
- To engage consumers at a deeper level
- To provide a three-dimensional brand experience
- A way to demonstrate products
- The bottom line of stimulating sales

Figure 3.1 Key Reasons for Marketing Strategy
Source: 2007 Event Solutions Annual Forecast

I have been called upon by a great many people to guide them in their career quest, and most of those have been in the area of entertainment and events. Often, I would ask why they wanted to be in this industry, and most said that they loved the excitement and the opportunity to be involved with experiences that are really special. I did it because it was challenging and very exciting, and hopefully, it would be something that would be long remembered as being a very special event. My change of direction was to help find the next generation that would take events to the next level.

> ### Gene-Gem
>
> The time comes for each of us to step aside, letting the next generation step forward: to encourage, not discourage, be available, but not imposing, and to support, not undermine.

Coach, Counselor, and Mentor

As part of your career development you must seek a coach, a counselor, and a mentor—and you can have more than one in each category. There are some individuals that can serve in all of those roles, and once you understand how they help you, the greater the value you will receive from those who will guide, mold, and shape you. For those in the classroom, you have a built-in coach and counselor in your teacher, and once you read the following material it will become much clearer.

With many Disney interviewees, my role was their career-coach, and I would show them step-by-step how to best present themselves in an interview or to a leadership team. This book contains many of the suggestions I would give to candidates and which I now give to you. The advantage you have is that you can go back and review the materials as well as get other points of view. The goal is to get positive results from your effort, and you must feel comfortable with your approach.

There were many times I gave direction not to seek a position with Disney, but for the candidate to pursue other opportunities to get experience elsewhere. I saw this as a long-term investment in which the candidate gained the needed experience so that they could come back much better prepared. The fact is that there were a couple of people that went out and became very successful—so much so that they were too busy to come work for Walt Disney World.

Many candidates considered me to be a career counselor besides being the interviewer/evaluator. If there was potential, I would continue to work with candidates and often become their counselor and even their mentor. Let me define what I believe to be the roles of the coach, the counselor, and the mentor. Often these get confused or lumped together as just one task by one person, when in fact they are three specific roles.

Coach

I stated earlier that as a "coach" I would take a person step-by-step, ensuring that there was a complete understanding of how to accomplish an objective. "This is how you do it, and there is an expectation that you will follow these precise directions."

Counselor

When counseling there is a shared responsibility for finding the best way to achieve the objective; it is more of a discussion on how to achieve the best course of action.

Mentor

Very different from the others, the mentor is like a good friend taking a nonjudgmental position, asking questions, being objective, challenging you on what you are considering and why, as well as looking out for your best interests.

■ Confessions of a Mentor

As their mentor, I never have a real personal stake in the outcome except my desire to see a positive outcome for the person being helped. Also, there is a moral obligation to challenge the candidate to be honest with themselves as well as others. If they were taking a questionable direction, as a mentor, I would have had to make sure that issue was addressed. I would not always tell a person what they wanted to hear, but rather, what they needed to know, suggesting consideration of various options. Those options would often begin with, "What is the worst thing that could happen with this course of action?" This is a good starting point, but can often be too negative. So many times the candidate has written a dialogue about all of the bad things that could happen. One thing I have repeatedly said over and over to candidates: "You are writing the dialogue and you really do not know what play you are in!"

So often, the candidates would focus on not wanting to say or doing anything wrong but they were approaching the interview with a negative mindset. Typically, it sounded like this: "I don't want to say the wrong thing so I'll say very little—because if I don't get this job I will have to live under the highway, lose my car, disgrace my family, starve and ultimately die!" Of course, we all have some level of negative self-talk, but if left uncontrolled it creates what I call *seepage*. Seepage creeps out during the interview as lacking in confidence and not believing in yourself. The goal of this book will be to help you develop a game plan for interviewing so you can go into an interview with a level of confidence. Will you still be nervous? Of course! Few of us are able to become the focus of attention without feeling a bit nervous. Those nerves can be used to your advantage by turning them into positive energy.

> **Gene-Gem**
>
> Control yourself so you can control the situation.

■ It Is Acceptable to Not Know

Through the years I have also seen the other end of the spectrum, including candidates who are cocky and arrogant. I need not waste your time sharing those stories, as I spent very little time with these candidates. If an individual is that way in an interview, how will he or she act on the job and with peers? Yes, we took chances on people with a great deal of talent, hoping that they would change their attitude, but too often, that did not work out for us or for them. A willingness to learn is important in this process, so it is all right to say that you don't know but are eager to learn.

Having spent most of my life in this very exciting entertainment industry as a performer as well as within the many levels of management, it has been possible for me to provide advice and guidance to those seeking help. Those experiences in many different job positions have provided the foundation in making assessments and judgments on the qualifications of individuals. So often, candidates misunderstand that when the interviewer asks a question, it is not because they don't know the answer but sometimes because candidates feel they must enlighten the interviewer, even if they are making up the answer.

In looking back, I recognize a number of major milestones that have shaped and affected me, even if I did not realize it at the time. There have been many people that influenced my thinking and helped direct me in a positive direction. I believe that I owe it to them to do for others as they did for me. You, too, will have many people to thank in a couple of decades, as they will provide you with direction, ideas, suggestions, and help. Your key is to be open to what they have to give, and often you will have the opportunity to provide them with what you have to give.

> **Gene-Gem**
>
> Arrogant candidates seem to have all the answers but know none of the questions.

Communications

Interviewing candidates for roles in this industry is very exciting, as the people are very interesting and often exceptional, with well-developed communications skills and an ability to share creative ideas. As individuals move forward in planning their career, it is recommended that a great deal of attention be paid in the development of communications skills. Making sure you are understood is a key to good communications. Begin now to be selective and careful with words, taking time to listen to others before speaking. Too often, people are thinking about what they want to say rather than what the other person has said.

> **Gene-Gem**
>
> We were given two ears and one mouth—guess that means we should do twice as much listening as talking.

We can learn from everyone we meet. Just think about how a little bit of each person you interact with will stay with you and a little bit of you will go with them. When you are part of making a special event, a piece of that experience goes with those participating, but a piece also stays with you. Listen carefully to how others speak about their experience and you can learn a great deal about how to get better at your craft.

An Apprentice Craft

You will learn quickly that there are many things that can and will go wrong with a special event, and working with someone that is a Certified Special Events Professional (CSEP), you have the advantage to see a master in the craft of special events. Because of experience, the master craftsman understands how to deal with challenges. The master craftsman could very well be your classroom teacher who is guiding you through the process of learning. This "educational" approach provides you, the apprentice, with a safe environment containing little risk to a client's budget, to expectations, and to your reputation.

In the classroom, the apprentice can learn about the interconnecting pieces that make up an event. Through case studies, there are many opportunities to take "snap shots" at any given point to explore the process. By comparison, the apprentice in the "heat of battle" attending the "School of Hard Knocks" might be doing an event under the watchful eye of the master craftsman. One way or another, it is important to learn and understand the interconnecting parts of an event, and there are advantages in both situations. If one is lucky enough to have a master craftsman willing to guide, empower, and hopefully forgive, if necessary, then you are experiencing on-the-job training, and it is an excellent way of learning. In the classroom you will learn and gain experience in a somewhat different but excellent way to learn your craft. Whether you are learning from a professional manager or your professor, you will need to impress them with your learning ability in order to succeed.

Gene-Gem

Earn a wage or earn a grade—pretty much the same thing.

Try as much as possible to blend the best of both worlds—training in a classroom environment as well as on the job. Learning the craft in an educational setting is a great way to "learn the language" and the "rules of the road" for the special events industry. Yes, there is a big difference between the classroom and being out in the field, producing events, but if you are prepared, there will be far fewer surprises.

The next step in the process is the internship. Generally, the internship provides you with a view of events from many different angles with real firsthand experience.

It is amazing how your first experiences serve as a foundation for your career as well as great material for your interview. "Never ask anyone to do something you wouldn't do" is one of the first leadership principles one learns, but keep in mind that it is not possible for you to do everything well. Play to your strengths, and above all, do not be afraid to say you do not know.

One of the biggest mistakes made by new team members is the fear of saying they do not know how to do something. Most people are more than willing to assist in helping you learn and understand. If you say nothing or pretend you know, there is a problem. If something should go wrong, the first question will be, "Why didn't you say you didn't know?" In job interviews, it is much more impressive when the candidates use examples of how they learned certain skills by seeking out help and assistance, rather than claiming to have figured it out on their own.

Remember that special events does require a level of independent thinking and action, but it is essential to be a team player and make sure that your actions are consistent with how the team planned and expected things to be implemented. Making it up as you go could get you, your team, and the client in trouble, and impact the overall results of the event.

When I started out, I learned from a master craftsman in the business and, as an apprentice, was guided, mentored, coached, and molded by a number of wonderful people. The late Bob Jani from Disneyland Entertainment was a creative role model with impeccable taste and understanding on how to exceed guest expectations. Peter Bloustein, who established and ran Convention Entertainment in the early days at Walt Disney World, taught me how to use and reuse, produce and reproduce, sell and resell events.

Each event was an opportunity to sell the next event. Providing an exceptional experience from beginning to end made it far more possible to get the client to sign up for the next one, even before you finish the current event. My friend and colleague Jack Cudworth would claim he was not in sales, although he is an excellent salesman, but that his goal was instead to help clients successfully achieve their goals.

The late Scott Powhatan reported to me when I first came to Walt Disney World, and some years later I proudly say that I reported to him. Scott was remarkable in planning large-scale events, including Super Bowl halftime shows as well as major Disney Theme Park openings. He knew every detail of the event and would guide the team to accomplish amazing things. He started at the bottom and learned each step along the way.

I learned from so many amazing people, including those who reported to me, and I have been told that many people have learned from me. There is Dr. Joe Goldblatt, with incredible successes in the special events industry, who has been my mentor and best friend for many years. He has many connections in the industry, and rather than continuing to focus on special events, he redirected his amazing energy to educate others. In the creative industry of special events, we learn from each other because we all come from different backgrounds, and so we each bring something unique to the industry. Everyone has something to contribute in this collaborative venture. Always remember to listen to others.

> ### Gene-Gem
> Remember to make sure your voice is not the only one you hear.

Patience Is a Virtue

Over the years, I have witnessed individuals who were impatient and continuously pointed out that if they had more responsibility they would be more successful. In fact, some were given that chance. Others never got that opportunity at Walt Disney World because they believed they were overqualified for the roles we had available and they were holding out for a more senior position.

> **Gene-Gem**
>
> Do enough to get by, expect only enough to get by!

There were a few individuals that got higher level positions and for the most part were reasonably successful. Most did a good job but not necessarily an exceptional job. They worked very hard learning the job but also learning the company and building a network all at the same time. They were regarded as competent in their roles and often stayed at the same level for a long time.

On the other hand, there were those who started off in lower-level positions and did excellent work because they were really overqualified. Those overqualified people quickly got the reputation of being exceptional, and that reputation tended to stay with them as they moved up the ranks, often jumping ahead of those who insisted that they start at a higher level. It comes down to having a "can do—make it happen" attitude, no matter what the task or level.

A few years ago, a production assistant worked on a fundraiser with corporate tables that required the name of the company on a stand to make it easy for the guests to find their table. As a member of the younger generation, she was well equipped with knowledge of the Internet, and she made a card not just with the name of the company but also with its logo. She also took responsibility for doing the master seating chart and having a copy posted at each of the doors into the ballroom. Because she took ownership of that small task and made it something special, she was viewed as someone who goes above and beyond with her assignments. It was easy to see why she was so quickly promoted and now is in a leadership role, but people still talk about her card stands and seating charts.

Throughout history, it has been the master craftsman who has taken on apprentices and taught them the skills they needed to become a *journeyman*, meaning that they had served the apprenticeship and were qualified to work at the trade. That has been the tradition from the earliest times and continues in many trades even today. Of course, there are now "basic training" programs in schools that give both the master craftsman and the apprentice a head start by teaching the fundamentals. More and more, we understand that time is money, and for the craftsman to have to take the time to explain the basics takes away from doing work that provides a return. It is a good investment to take time to train your people, but to the craftsman it is much more desirable to have someone that "speaks the language" and knows the fundamentals.

> **Gene-Gem**
>
> Another term for people that are overqualified is promotable!

In selecting an individual for an entry-level position or for an internship, the master craftsman will most often select the person with the greatest understanding of the business. The selection will be based on the potential value the candidates bring to the organization. Therefore, as a candidate, be sure that you focus on what you can do for the organization and not what the organization can to do for you.

At Walt Disney World, you would continuously hear how clean the parks are, but I share with you that it was everyone's job to make sure they stayed that way. I remember walking in the Magic Kingdom with Dick Nunis, former president of Walt Disney World. As we were walking and talking, without missing a beat he bent down and picked up trash that was on the street. It was second nature to him and to all of us. Attention to detail is the key to the success of special events or running any company. Dick was and is a master craftsman, and he showed by example his commitment to Disney and to the guests coming to enjoy one of the world-famous parks.

The master craftsman trains the apprentice on the details, and the training you receive in the classroom or on the job all become part of the standard you will live by in the industry. If you were a woodworking apprentice making picture frames, you would sand the wood endlessly to make it as smooth as possible. All the seams and joints would be tight and strong. Perhaps you would stain and seal the wood, followed by more sanding. Two or three layers of varnish would be applied, with sanding in between each coat. The master craftsman would have you clean the area between each layer of varnish to ensure dust would not ruin the next layer of varnish. Your work would be checked, and only when the master craftsman believed that it was to his standards would you get the nod of approval. Up to that point, there could be a level of criticism, which would be feedback on your progress.

Special events are somewhat like a picture frame. There are so many running inches or feet of framing and so much paint or varnish to make the framed picture. Think of the frame and materials as the budget for the event. Creatively, you can make the picture frame in many shapes but you have a limited amount of framing and paint. If you make it an odd shape, you might have a lot of wasted framing as well as a smaller picture. The buyer of the picture would like you to use the resources wisely without a lot of waste.

The goal is to make a work of art with the materials you have available, and the experienced master craftsman will guide you in how to use the materials in the most successful manner possible. What makes special events so special is that each one is tailor-made, and you are the artist creating the work of art with the available resources. Ordinary effort will produce ordinary results and ordinary events are not special.

Jim Carr, production stage manager of *Disney on Parade*, served as a master craftsman to me. I was the newly hired assistant stage manager, and it was his task to train me to call show cues in a very large touring show with hundreds of cues. Jim was my coach, and he set the standards for how I was to perform my role. The show was very demanding, with ten follow-spot operators getting no rehearsal and relying only on the cues the stage manager gave them. The cues happened quickly, and many of them were based on subtle visual cues on stage.

Jim would admit that he was not a man with a great deal of patience, although he was a remarkable stage manager. He would sit beside me, and he had the nervous habit of tapping a pencil on the table. Jim insisted I have at least 12 sharpened pencils on the table during the show to take notes. He would take one of the pencils and tap it, and if the cue was not called perfectly, Jim would break the lead on the pencil then grab the next pencil and return to tapping. One time I missed a cue and he shouted at me; "When are you going to learn this show?" while breaking my pencil in half and throwing on the floor. I worked very hard to learn the show so I would not have to deal with this situation. Needless to say, there was a great deal of pressure.

Jim had a mission, and that was to get me to his level of the operation of the show so that there would be no drop in quality when I was responsible for calling show cues. I was a bit nervous when he told me, "You're on your own this next show!" meaning he had confidence I would do an acceptable job. Not long after that, Jim announced that a new assistant stage manager would be joining the show. My first reaction was that, as hard as I had tried, I had been unable to live up to his standards. Then he added that I was being promoted to stage manager and would be responsible for training the new assistant stage manager. He followed that with a comment that was very true: "Heaven knows, I don't have the patience to train anyone else!"

I went from being the apprentice to journeyman and took on the duties of passing on what I had learned from the master craftsman to the new apprentice. My relationship with Jim also changed, and he became more of a counselor, spending time discussing issues and the best ways to deal with them. He valued my opinion and wanted my input. Before long, he became my mentor, guiding me in a number of ways even beyond my professional life. Jim is a great example of the master craftsman being a coach, counselor, and mentor.

I suggest you be very respectful of the time you request of your mentor and come prepared. Create an agenda and take notes. Many times someone would come seeking advice from me, not write anything down, and then come back later to ask the same question. You will get out of your relationships what you put into them.

How Do You Want to Be Remembered?

As varied as job candidates are, the interviewers are equally as diverse. There will be all levels of understanding regarding the interviewing process by the "hiring managers," and each will be very different. Some might be very skilled while others might not be as comfortable with the process. There seems to be little training in this very important management task, and often times it is left to the manager to figure it out.

I am not comfortable when hiring managers say they were casting or selecting based only on a gut feeling. Yes, there is that feeling, but being able to back it up with a valid reason for accepting or rejecting a candidate is more professional, and more importantly, it's fair. Part of the goal of this book is to help the candidate help the hiring manager get the correct gut feeling if they have no other basis on which to make a decision.

You will remember the interviewer, but your real focus should be on how you want the interviewer to remember you. The preparation and planning you do before the interview will really make the difference. For the inexperienced interviewer, you will be able to provide the necessary information for your evaluation. The experienced interviewer will see that you are well prepared and have done the necessary research to showcase yourself in a positive manner.

The Interviewer's Responsibility

In my staffing role over the years, I carried the heavy burden of knowing that I was dealing with a candidate's livelihood and, at times, their long-term career. If I was unsure of a candidate, a second opinion was requested from one of my trusted associates with a "tie" going to the candidate. In these "tie" situations, arrangements were made for short-term assignments, providing opportunities to demonstrate the candidate's skills. In this trial process, it was also very important to provide the necessary training to ensure the candidate was set up for success.

I cannot claim the credit for the success of some of these individuals; they earned every bit of success on their own. I was only a part of helping many people get their start. Since I am both a teacher and a staffing manager, there are a lot of opportunities to combine both of these activities. A good teacher wants his or her students to succeed in the professional world.

> ### Gene-Gem
>
> The true measure of a teacher is not how successful he or she is in a classroom but how successful his or her students are after leaving the classroom.

Why Is a Special Event Special?

The 1987 Twenty-Fifth Anniversary of the Special Olympics at the Walt Disney World Resort in Epcot was an event never to be forgotten. It could only happen once, and had to be special. Dictionaries define *special* as distinguished by unusual qualities, being superior and holding particular esteem. This organization was begun in 1962 by Eunice Kennedy Shriver, who had no idea how important it would become in the lives of so many. Celebrating 25 years was a major milestone and one in which I am proud to have been involved.

In the special events industry, you will be part of the planning and execution designed for a particular purpose or occasion such as a noteworthy happening, social occasion, or activity like contests, pageants, or sporting events. To make it special requires professionals to ensure that it takes place in a successful and memorable manner for all involved, including you.

Applying and interviewing for a position in special events is also special. By now you understand the uniqueness of the industry and wish to take part in making events special. As you meet industry professionals, ask them how they got their start and what effect it had on their lives.

Also ask about a time in which they didn't get the job, when they were turned down or rejected. Ask if they know why they were not hired and what they learned from that experience. Many times the answers will be that it was not the right timing or the company wanted someone with more experience. Often, professionals will tell you that it worked out best because another opportunity became available for which they were much better suited.

If you are not selected for a position for which you have interviewed, do not get mad or upset at the interviewer/hiring manager. You might have been almost hired and could be strongly considered for future opportunities or even recommended for other opportunities. It is best not burn the bridge by showing a negative attitude. I have had candidates tell me that I had no idea of what the company was missing by not hiring them and, in one case, a candidate said he needed to go to a higher-level company that would appreciate his talents. This is not such a good idea because it indicates that if this person does not get his way, he would become difficult. Even if these candidates had second thoughts about what they said, I am sure they were far too uncomfortable or even embarrassed to check back with me to see if anything had changed.

Experience is a hard teacher because she gives the test first, the lesson afterward.

Vernon Law (1930–)

It is best to request feedback on what areas you might focus on so that you are better prepared for the next time. Ask, "What do I need to focus on for the future, and can you make any suggestions on how I might gain the needed experience?" This demonstrates to the hiring manager that the candidate is a willing learner and will do what it takes to succeed. Not all interviewers or hiring managers will be willing or able to assist you, but it does leave a much more positive impression of you with the company.

There are organizations that will not give suggestions, as there are concerns that it might be perceived as leading you on or setting false expectations. Nevertheless, it could be that the hiring manager is very impressed with your skills and talents but does not have a position available for you at the time of the interview. The hiring manager may thank you and give you the standard line about keeping your information on file and contacting you should there be any future opportunities. You should request feedback, but take care that you are not too aggressive. Say thanks for the time, keeping the door open for you checking back with the hiring manager from time to time. Keep it positive and upbeat. Remember that this person took time to speak to you but is under no obligation to hire you. There is something about you that sparked interest for them to be willing to meet you, so take that as a positive first impression and then assess this impression.

Special events are special because of the individuals in this industry doing their work with pride and passion. They are committed to performing their duties skillfully and creatively, continuously challenging themselves to find ways to surprise and tantalize their guests. Special events is a demanding career, but if you love this business you will find it a rewarding, fulfilling opportunity, to create lots of memories for your guests, as well as for yourself.

Career Connections

 ### Practice Activity

Who have been coaches, counselors, or mentors in your life? It could be your sports coach or a teacher you admire. How have these people helped your personal or professional development? Make a list of how they shaped you into who you are today and request their guidance on ways you can continue in a positive direction.

 ### Tool Kit

Cohen, Norman H. PhD (1999). *The Mentee's Guide to Mentoring.* Amherst, MA: HRD Press.
Maxwell, John C. (2008). *Mentoring 101.* Nashville, Thomas Nelson.
Wellington, Sheila, and Betty Spence (2001). *Be Your Own Mentor: Strategies from Top Women on the Secrets of Success.* New York: Random House.

Web Connection

www.social.macys.com/parade
www.nfl.com/superbowl/history/entertainment
www.specialolympics.org/volunteers

Ask the Pro

MICHAEL GOLDMAN, SENIOR EXECUTIVE PRODUCER FOR PROACTIVE, INC. AND FREEMAN CREATIVE GROUP

What is the best career advice you have ever received?

Rise above your own point of view and look at everything before making a decision. Even as the event producer, my point of view is certainly not the only one that matters.

What career advice would you offer aspiring event employees?

Attitude is everything. It matters little to me, or anyone else for that matter, if you are a genius but you're impossible to get along with. Your attitude is the only thing in life that you truly control. Problems come and go, but how you deal with adversity on the event (and I have yet to produce a perfect show), will determine if you are truly successful in this business.

What do employers want to see on a résumé?

We are in a relationship business. I ask for referrals. Experience matters, so list as succinctly as possible what you've done. All a résumé should do is convince me that I need to meet you. Then it's up to you to sell me on your abilities.

How important is education and training?

I look at producing special events the same way I look at fighting in karate tournaments

(I do both). You can learn how to fight from the best in the world, but until you actually get in the ring, you are not a fighter. Education is the best when it has practical implications. If you want to be a producer—produce. And, for the record, a good one-word definition of producer is "gatherer."

What do you want to hear from a candidate you are interviewing for a job?

I survived the Gene Columbus "What if . . . Scenario" interview at Disney in 1989, which is a special events version of *Star Trek's* Kobayashi Maru training exercise. I like to place candidates in a hypothetical situation and see how they respond. I have never forgotten that exercise.

What is your advice for long term career success?

Never bring your problems to work with you, and learn to say, "Sure, I can do that." Become good at doing everything, and do it with a smile on your face. If the client wants an elephant to fly around a field sneezing fireworks, make it happen. I've always felt I can do anything until someone proves me wrong.

PART TWO

Training Factory

CHAPTER 4

Your Career Planning Strategy: What Do You Bring to an Organization?

Hiring managers look for the value the candidate brings to the company. Your value to the company might be your creativity, your organizational skills, or your commitment of quality service. You, in turn, could be rewarded with the opportunity to be part of the team, continuing to develop your skills. Your additional reward might be the wage you earn or the assignments you are given. The focus of your job interview should be to demonstrate to the company that there are advantages to having you on their team.

The Interview Stage

In the interview, articulate your values and what is important to you in a concise manner, to show the company how you will be a valuable asset to them. You must explore what is important to you in order to understand how your philosophy is consistent with that of the company. Your career should focus on the opportunities to learn, grow, practice, and develop your craft as part of a special events team. In most interviews, your personal goals emerge as you talk about your training, past experiences, and why you want to be a part of their company. You should know where you are most passionate well in advance of the interview. When discussing what you offer a company, Albert Einstein said it best in this quote:

> *Try not to become a person of success. Rather become a person of value.*
> —*Albert Einstein (1879–1955)*

As you plan your career, ask yourself eight questions to determine how strongly you feel about issues:

1. *What is really important to me?* The answer might be that family is on the top of your list, and a location in which to live and work must be close to family. Your target companies must then be restricted to that area.
2. *What does success look like?* Measuring success is different with everyone, but over time, you will come to understand that doing something you love will make you far more successful than doing something you dislike.
3. *What is my responsibility in this business relationship?* If you are reflecting the mission and goals of the company and always doing what is in the best interest of the organization, then the company tends to look on you with favor.
4. *Who are my role models?* Most role models are highly successful, but they spent a long time developing their skills to get to where they are. Most started at the bottom and had to work hard to get to where they are, and that is what you should be emulating.
5. *How do I solve problems?* You should go to work not to avoid problems or create problems; your mission is to be a problem solver. Solution-oriented people go to work to fix problems.
6. *What are my immediate goals?* If your goal is to complete your education and find that first position, challenge yourself to do everything each step of the way as if you are being measured. If you take the easy way, it could be very hard to find a company that will trust you with that first position.
7. *What are my long-term goals?* Aim high but be patient—drive yourself and continuously look at where you are and where you want to be.
8. *Where do I see myself five years from now?* This may well change but, as the old saying goes, if you don't know where you are going, any road will get you there. Keep a journal, and as you move forward, look back at what you thought you wanted to be in the future. You might be right on target, but you will see there are many exciting alternatives available—and one might even take you down a path you had no idea you would ever discover.

Consider carefully how you are going to answer these questions when someone else is doing the asking. If your answers tend to be focused on what is in it for you, then you might find it challenging to find a connection to an organization that is committed to serving others. A company will hire you more for what you can do for them rather than what they must do for you. The hiring managers are looking for a return on investment, and you must demonstrate that you would be worth the investment. What do you bring to the table?

Recap of Questions

1. What is really important to me?
2. What does success look like?

3. What is my responsibility in this business relationship?
4. Who are my role models?
5. How do I solve problems?
6. What are my immediate goals?
7. What are my long-term goals?
8. Where do I see myself five years from now?

Companies want people who will solve problems and deal with issues that come up in the production of an event. Richard Aaron, president of Bizbash Media, advises the following:

Always be prepared to improvise a crisis into a solution. Situations will arise no matter how much planning you have executed. The ability to think on your feet and create a solution separates the great planners from the pack. I've seen it happen over and over: the need for a quick action. So learn to think on your feet and evaluate rapidly and get a new plan moving. Get involved with the numerous industry associations to accelerate your learning curve and expansion of your resource network. After all, it's who you know that will count in the end. Most importantly, find a great mentor and learn from him or her. Andrew Carnegie did just that, and look where it got him.

What Is Success?

Perhaps you have a unique skill such as graphic design that could improve efficiency, making the company more profitable. You might also have connections to current or future clients that might bring increased sales to the organization, or it may be that you bring a very strong work ethic and willingness to learn. Keep your focus on how to make the organization successful.

In my journey, there were many options available. As a member of the chorus, performing in films and television, I made the commitment to no longer perform in the chorus after my thirtieth birthday. As I proceeded, the opportunity to stage manage in theater became available. In my planning, this was not an area I had considered, but it turned out to be exciting, demanding, rewarding, and fulfilling. You will also find many options available as you proceed in your journey to success.

> **Gene-Gem**
>
> The best way to be successful is to make others, including your company, successful.

If success for you is about having lots of the free time, money, a great place to live, a cool car, taking long vacations, and wearing the latest fashions, then hopefully you are independently wealthy. If you were not born into wealth and have not won the lottery, you will have to earn these perks. Moreover, being rich does not mean that you are automatically happy and fulfilled. The true measure of success for a man or woman in the special events industry is a complex set of variables. First and foremost, success is measured in finding rewarding and meaningful work. However, success is also measured by the positive reputation you establish in the industry. Regardless of how you measure success, it is important to remember that success is a journey rather than a destination.

We all know people who seem to have everything they want but are unhappy because they are not fulfilled; they feel empty because happiness is not something that can be purchased. I have also had the opportunity to work with wealthy people who were involved in community or educational causes, using their influence and position to make a difference in the lives of others. Consider the number of wealthy people that go into public service because they need a cause greater than themselves. The quest for fulfillment could lead you to wealth, but it is very likely that a quest for wealth will not lead to fulfillment.

It has been my privilege to work with some remarkable individuals at Disney who did not make a great deal of money but who loved their jobs. You would see the pride they took in making sure that Disney guests had a wonderful and memorable experience. These people found fulfillment and were very happy as they enriched the lives of others, even if they were not becoming wealthy in the process. Perhaps Benjamin Franklin said it best when he observed the following.

A person wrapped up in himself makes a very small bundle.

— *Benjamin Franklin (1706–1790)*

John J. Daly Jr, president of John Daly, Inc., shared with me that "Attitude is everything—with passion for your work! No passion—no good in this business. It is important to be flexible, with a can-do attitude. Live by good, honest ethics to both the clients and suppliers."

A Personal Cause

Do you have a cause greater than yourself? Evaluate your personal goals and seek to help others reach their goals. Make a list of what you want and what is important, and then prioritize the list with what is more important at the top of the list. Use the eight questions as a starting point, with a goal to establish your personal mission statement. Once this has been accomplished, create a list of goals that will provide you with a list of action items to achieve your mission.

Some years ago I attended a workshop in which we were asked to write ten words that best describe you. I made my list and thought everything was pretty well covered

My Personal Mission Statement

Continuation in leadership role of providing quality experiences to audiences, students and employees, utilizing skills in managing, motivating, training, and developing for the next generation. To give time willingly in support of enriching the community and to share my many years of experience.

—Gene Columbus

(see Figure 4.1). We were then told to cut it down to five. This was a bit of a challenge to reduce to only five, but I found I could not just select the top five, I had to look at each one and pick the ones that best described me (see Figure 4.2).

The next step was to reduce the list to three. However, I found that it took soul-searching to reduce to three. Just selecting the top three left out much of what I do and

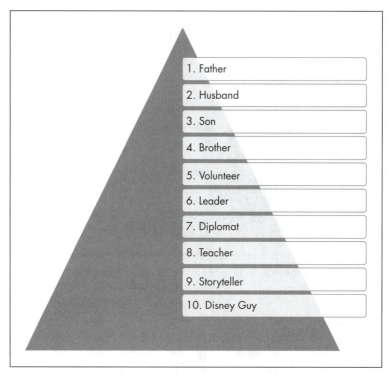

Figure 4.1   Gene Columbus List of Ten Words He Believes Describes Him

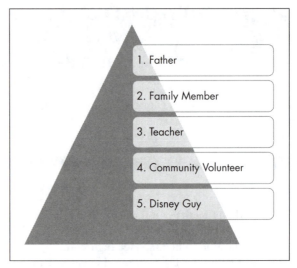

Figure 4.2   Gene Columbus Reduced List to Five That Best
Describes Him

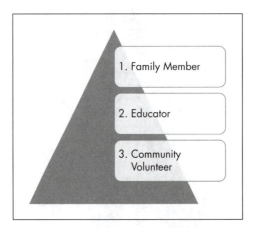

Figure 4.3   Gene Columbus List of Three Words
That Best Describe Him

became more about who I was as a person. I thought I had it covered when I picked family
member, educator and community volunteer (see Figure 4.3). But that wasn't the end of
the exercise. We were asked to find one word that we felt best described us. I looked
to the members of my group that I had worked with for a long time. I asked for assistance

Figure 4.4   The One Word That Best Describes Gene Columbus

from them to describe me, and they said I was a "helper." When we announced to everyone our one word that best describes us, the room erupted in applause when I said I was a helper (see Figure 4.4).

Being a "helper" is how I bring value at work, in the community, at the university, and at home. That conclusion came after looking at where I am most passionate. I truly love volunteering in the community and helping candidates become successfully employed. As a teacher, I assist students who, in seeking to learn, are making an investment in their future. Now I am investing the time writing this book to help you successfully find gainful employment in the special events industry.

In the classroom, I share my goals with the students with the following Gene-Gem.

> **Gene-Gem**
>
> I don't just teach stage management, I teach students—one at a time, if necessary.

Armed with a Mission

Once you have created your mission, made a list of your goals, established what is important to you, truly defined what success means to you, embraced who you are and what you do, then it is time to create a list with priorities and an action plan. "This is where I am and this is where I want to be." Next to each item, write what you must do to get where you want to be. This will give you a clear understanding of who you are and how you will present yourself. To check if your are on track, ask your teachers, coaches, counselors, mentors, and those that know you best to see if you are headed in the right direction. A timeline is an important part of this process, and you may need to make adjustments but establish deadlines for yourself and try to accomplish each item on your list ahead of schedule.

Feedback is important because we often look at aspects of ourselves that may or may not be important. In my days as a dancer, we would practice in front of a mirror to see what was wrong. A wonderful teacher said one day, "Why don't you start looking for what you are doing correctly?" Take time to identify what you do well and commit yourself to doing it even better: that's progress.

> **Gene-Gem**
>
> Most of us look in the mirror for what is wrong—try looking for what is right.

Explaining your personal values in addition to how you would "bring value" to the company should be one of your interview goals, and is less challenging if you invest time before your interview. Your examples will help the interviewer determine if you would be a right fit for their company. Examples of your involvement helping to bring about success tend to be the most powerful. It is suggested that you write out the example and practice sharing your story before interviewing.

Reporting the Story

As you are writing, think back on events at school, the community, on the job or with family, what you did, or even what you observed. Do not underestimate sharing in an interview what you learned by watching and listening. Talk about examples of behavior that demonstrated the qualities and standards you have established for yourself and your work ethic. Sharing how you served others on a large or small scale is a good indicator of your commitment in the future. If you have had the opportunity to work in the industry, share the examples of how your role fit into the overall objective of the project.

> **Gene-Gem**
>
> When does an interview begin? It has already started—your reputation will precede you!

In assessing the positive characteristic of a special events candidate, hiring managers look at your leadership style and qualities, as well as being a good team player. Responsibility and accountability are basic qualities, but there is so much more. Sharing examples in your interview of your responsibility and how you solved problems is a successful approach in the interview.

> **Gene-Gem**
>
> We hire people to solve problems—fact is, if there were no problems then there would be no need to have people to fix things!

Honesty and the ability to build trust are part of the foundation of building relationships. Give examples that show that you care for others and will treat people professionally, whether they are reporting to you, a peer, your leader, or the

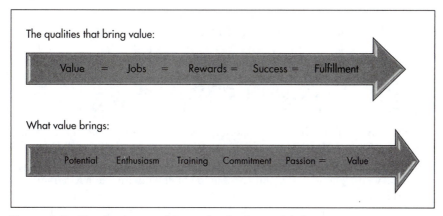

Figure 4.5 The Qualities and Rewards of a Successful Career

client. Talk about how you respect others and you are a caring person with a commitment for the overall positive results of the team (see Figure 4.5).

Thinking Ahead

Project yourself into the future when *you* are responsible for hiring. You will understand that, in the long run, if you are doing a really good job hiring, many future problems will be solved. Putting the right people in the right job will solve many problems before they become problems. One of the more important duties you will have is the selection of team members. Think about the qualities you will want and expect in people that you would hire and then look at yourself and ask if you measure up to what you would want from those individuals you hire in the future.

Now think about the person you will be meeting in the interview and how committed they are to doing the very best job possible. Like you will do in the future, they are going to want the best person in the role because they will solve many future problems. It is up to you to show that you are a person who can and will address issues as they arise. The goal of the hiring manager is to employ someone who will be very successful. To do otherwise reflects on the manager's ability.

Some individuals falsely state that they care for others and have the company's best interest at heart but are really only saying this to get the job. Once hired and on the job, they reveal the real side of their personality that is less than what they portrayed in the interview. Yes, people slip though and find their way into the industry and unless they are really amazingly gifted they do not last long. Most companies have 90-day probation to make sure the person is working out. You will find that people that are hard to get along with are people that often find it difficult to retain a long-term position.

Communication Is Key

Communication is one of the most important issues on the job, and therefore it must be your area of focus in the job interview. Simply put, communication is the key between you and other people. When you are answering questions, the interviewer is evaluating your ability to deal with a client, and if you are able to obtain and provide needed information and support for their event. Like clients, hiring managers are seeking to know how you are going to support them and their business. Whether it is the interviewer/hiring manager or a client, it requires that you prepare so as to not be making things up as you go along. If you have prepared, you will be able to communicate with confidence because you have done your homework.

Look around and learn from the really good communicators. You will find they are continuously seeking to make themselves understood. No doubt you have heard some people say they expect others to communicate to them in the same manner in which they communicate—kind of a "one size fits all." The secret of the good communicator is for you to communicate to people in a way the other persons need to be communicated with so they understand what you are saying. Those who are not good communicators tend to get upset and blame others for not listening, but the fact is that after a while, people stop trying to decode what is being expressed from the poor communicator—they just tune out. If a person is not understood, look first at how the information is being presented.

Many years ago, I was giving show cues for *Disney on Parade,* and if something didn't happen as cued, I was told to look carefully at how I was giving the cue to make sure that it was understandable. It serves no useful purpose to get upset with a crew member that may not have understood what I was saying. From that experience, I made it a habit to apply that to all my communications. First and foremost, the goal is to be understood, and that is an ongoing effort. Make a commitment to improve your communication skills; you can start by recapping what was said to you and invite the other person to share what they learned from you.

Gene-Gem

The key is to represent yourself the way you will represent the company!

Professional

The dictionary defines *professional* as a term used to characterize the technical or ethical standards of those involved in providing something defined as special. The professional exhibits a courteous, conscientious, and generally businesslike manner in the workplace, participating for gain or livelihood in an activity or field of endeavor often engaged in by amateurs. The professional has a commitment to a permanent career, having been engaged in receiving financial return while following a line of conduct.

Even before becoming a professional, you can and must act in a professional manner. You must understand and embrace a businesslike code of conduct and a strong work ethic. It is how you dress and how you address others. It is about making sure you understand the expectations and exceed those expectations. It is about being on time and how you use your time.

> ### Gene-Gem
> Individuals should not declare themselves as professionals; rather, they must be embraced by those who already meet a standard of professionalism.

> ### Gene-Gem
> If you are not early, you are late!

Be Prepared

It takes more than a great résumé and a winning personality to land that great job. You must bring to the hiring organization a level of value and understanding that you know enough about the business. And it is a business and with so many capable candidates entering the field, the need for companies to hire people and then invest in training them is no longer necessary. If you are really serious about a career in this industry, you know that you will have to demonstrate that you have the passion and the willingness to do whatever it takes to get your start, including getting the necessary training.

If you are reading this to learn more about this special events industry, you must ask yourself, do I know what I am getting myself into? This is a very rewarding and exciting business, and the really successful people doing it make it look so easy. But each person will tell you that they had to "pay their dues" in their journey. For most, it is a journey of learning and adding experiences in your bag of tricks. The better you are prepared, the better the chance there is for you to be successful.

> ### Gene-Gem
> Each of us is destined to rise to a certain level in life, and the more education and training you have, the faster you will get there!!

As you move forward in your career, remember those that came before you established the level that is your starting point. Someday in the future, the next generation will come along, and their starting point will be at the level you and your generation established in your careers. Like all things in life, we should try to leave things better than we found them.

"Whatever we accomplish belongs to our entire group, a tribute to our combined effort."
Walt Disney (1901–1966)

Career Connections

 Action Steps

Answer the following questions from this chapter:

1. What is really important to me?
2. What does success look like?
3. What do I believe is my responsibility in a business relationship?
4. Who are my role models?
5. How do I solve problems?
6. What are my immediate goals?
7. What are my long-term goals?
8. Where do I see myself five years from now?

List the top ten words that best describe you.

1. Reduce it to five words.
2. Reduce to three words.
3. What is the one word you believe best describes you?

 Practice Activity

In your group setting, discuss what you have learned about yourself. Give an example by telling a personal story that explains how and why you answered the eight questions and why you selected the words to describe yourself.

 Tool Kit

Lore, Nicholas (1998). *The Pathfinder: How to Choose or Change Your Career for a Lifetime of Satisfaction and Success.* New York: Fireside.

Zichy, Shoya and Bidou, Ann (2007). *Career Match: Connecting Who You Are with What You'll Love to Do.* New York: AMACOM.

 Web Connection

Top Ten Job Interview Questions and Answers: www.jobskills.info/interviews/top-ten-questions.html.

Biz Bash: www.bizbash.com.

CHAPTER 5

Skills That Make You Marketable

"The best way to predict your future is to create it."

— Unknown

Getting the Necessary Training

Great performing artists must spend years learning and practicing their art. The pianist learns to read music, practices, and perfects technique to share his or her interpretation of a composer's masterpiece. The dancer takes classes throughout his or her career in continuous pursuit of excellence. Even after they have reached a high level, they must continue to train and stay in top condition. Top athletes will tell you that their success started with an intense training program that required discipline, sacrifice, and hard work.

Your quest in the special events industry requires the same level of effort to be in top form for you to win that great position that will lead to a successful career. There are many good training programs in the special events industry available to you around the world. Dr. Joe Goldblatt not only teaches at Queen Margaret University in Edinburgh, Scotland, but also speaks to students and industry professionals all over the world, from the Midwest to the Far East. Special events is a very large and important industry but is a relatively new industry, and only recently have there been educational programs devoted to meeting the ever-growing demand for training individuals in this business. Dr. Goldblatt recommends that you gain broad training through a university course or industry certification program and simultaneously gain specific experience through internships, work-study experience, and even observation. He says that, "Observing others develop and deliver a special event can be a most valuable learning experience. After all, the Greek philosopher Aristotle supposedly said to his students, 'If you wish to learn, just watch me.' Find your own Aristotle in the world of special events and watch them carefully."

Programs are being added in colleges and universities to provide training to those seeking careers in this exciting industry. In the United Kingdom alone, the applications for event courses have grown by over 450 percent in the past decade. According to Dr. Goldblatt, there are hundreds of event courses from Australia to North America, throughout Europe, Africa, and South and Central America. One of the fastest-growing areas for educational development is Asia, where countries such as South Korea and China are creating many new event courses.

After she retired, my mother learned that she had an exceptional talent in visual art, something she did not understand until very late in life. In the last month of her life she said the only regret she had was that she didn't discover art sooner. Once you discover your interest in special events, it is important to develop the skills and experience to practice your art as soon as possible so you won't look back wishing you had started sooner.

Gene-Gem

World-class talent without training and practice remains completely unknown.

As you consider your training programs, consider the training that those competing with you for jobs may receive. You must commit to investing in your training so that you will be prepared to compete in this competitive market. That means you have to train hard and push yourself to higher levels throughout your education. Challenge yourself to be involved with a program that is very demanding and that attracts highly motivated individuals like you. There is much to be learned from your peers in and out of the seminar or classroom. Attend local and national trade shows to meet professionals and people whose enthusiasm inspires you. If you are in a classroom setting, perhaps your group could establish a Special Events Career Fair, getting industry professional representatives to present an overview of their company and then meet with students one on one, reviewing résumés or portfolios. At the University of Central Florida (UCF) Department of Theatre, each year the Professional Advisory Board conducts a career day that connects students to individuals in their targeted area early in their education to guide and assist in the educational process. This is often how students get internships and entry-level jobs. It is a big responsibility to take on this task, but it is a great opportunity to learn and make strong industry connections. Therefore, look for educational programs that have strong industry connections to help you gain employment.

Alisa Schwartz, entertainment manager with The Disney Event Group and graduate from University of Central Florida (UCF), recounts her first job experiences:

I went to the UCF and received a BFA in Stage Management. While in school, I decided that I wanted to work in special events and conventions because I liked the excitement and fast pace. After graduation, I completed my internship at Disney Event Group, which led to my first job as a Production Assistant. I became a stage manager and production manager in special events and conventions at Disney and also as a contractor for multiple production companies. If special events are your goal, theatre is a great place to start. It teaches you how to create an organized production book as well as how to call show cues. Theatre also teaches you how to run a rehearsal. That becomes very important in special events when you have one chance to address everyone and it is up to you to conduct a rehearsal. Theatre helps you develop the language necessary for communicating during an event. A special event is similar to a theatre show, but in fast forward. During internships, you have the opportunity to meet and work with a variety of different people, which will only help develop your own style in your management career.

You must be able to speak the language and know the tools of the special events trade. It is strongly recommended that if you are in school you stay until finished, and if you are not in school, you consider going back or getting involved in a training program. If you are now in the industry and seeking better opportunities, get involved with a professional organization that recognizes the importance of training and accreditation. No matter where you are in your journey of learning, there are opportunities to learn and improve your skills (see Figure 5.1). Your investment of time will pay dividends over and over.

Andrea Michaels, president of Extraordinary Events, suggests that job seekers do this:

First, intern with a reputable company and then network and make them visible at every possible event. They must educate themselves constantly and do more than they are asked to do. They should think of what they can do to improve their company's positioning in the industry (without being asked). Furthermore, they must constantly think of new and unique things their company can do to improve their services.

Education and training tracks and options

High School Classes	College Courses	Industry Training	Graduate (Post Graduate) Programs
Drama/stage craft	Theater/stage craft	Volunteering	MBA
English	Creative writing	Internships	Technical design
Computer graphics	Economics	CSEP certification	Stage directing
Public speaking	Business—marketing public relations	CMM and CMP	Hospitality management
Business	Sciences	Entry-level position	Video production

Figure 5.1 Options Available to Reach Your Goal

The Value of Theater

A background in theater is useful because special events often require presentation on a stage with audio, lighting, scenic treatment, entrances and exits, video, music, and announcements. It is highly recommended that your special events training includes becoming familiar with the technical elements of theater. Although it would be an advantage, it is not necessary for you to know how to operate the technical equipment, but you should be familiar with how it is used and what it takes to make it operational. Theater also stresses "the show must go on," and every audience deserves the best possible experience, which is exactly the same in Special Events.

The Value of Stage Management

The stage manager is responsible for the smooth running of a show or event and typically manages the process of blending the technical aspects with the performing elements. The stage manager is often thought of as the hub of the wheel, or communications central. Your training touches most aspects of show or presentation, including costuming, scenic, lighting, audio, props, rehearsals, schedules, documentation, cast and crew management, and much more. Stage managers write and call show cues and work closely with performers or presenters regarding what they do on stage in addition to working with the crew controlling lighting, audio, scenic, pyrotechnics, video, or any other production element. This is a highly demanding role in the events business and one that requires great understanding of all the elements that go into event production.

The Value of Show Production

Training in production gives you a firsthand view and understanding of all the elements that a stage manager is responsible for. Learn the glossary of theater terms, as it is the language the technicians and suppliers use and will prove to be very valuable to you. Many events require the talents of the International Association of Theatrical Stage Employees (IATSE) to deal with the technical elements, including the set-up, operation, and strike of your event. This union covers employees in film, stage, television, convention centers, touring shows, concerts and many special events. These professionals have union guidelines that must be followed, and each area has a local union that establishes work conditions. Most IATSE members work in all areas of the industry but speak the language of the theater.

The Value of Verbal and Written Communications

Communication is one of the most essential skills in an industry that requires an understanding of what is requested and what is provided. Your written communications represent you when you are not there to represent yourself. Event managers must represent themselves in a professional and creative manner.

I took a creative writing class in college to complete my English requirement, and I had no idea how demanding and yet how rewarding I would find this class. It is strongly recommend that you take classes in writing throughout your college career. Most job descriptions require "strong verbal and written communications," and the stronger your written communications are, the better you will be at verbal communications.

The Value of Professional Writing

Besides creative writing, you should develop skills in basic writing, including business letters. You will spend a great deal of time corresponding with clients, vendors, suppliers, and coworkers in the special events business. Rather than showing great imagination, this style of writing is focused on providing facts and figures. In addition, you will learn how to read contracts and contract riders, followed by your writing revisions to these documents.

The Value of Public Speaking

According to the *Book of Lists*, one of the greatest fears that people have is speaking in front of a group, and the reason generally has to do with confidence. Presentations are very much a part of the special events industry, and this is an important skill. Event managers must be able to tell a story about what the client's guests will experience. You are encouraged to include speaking beyond the classroom with such organizations as toastmaster. This gives you opportunities to speak and receive valuable feedback from peers that help build confidence.

The Value of Technology Skills

A picture is worth a thousand words, and in this fast-paced world, getting attention and keeping it focused can be done in very creative ways if you have the skills. Learning the scope of these tools will put you steps ahead in your career. Furthermore, in addition to the basic Microsoft Office™ package, it is useful to have specialized training in computer-assisted design (CAD) and drawing (to create meeting and event diagrams), database software to maintain guest records, and even accounting software.

Two emerging technology tools are MeetingMatrix (www.meetingmatrix.com), a venue and computer-assisted drawing package, and MeetingMetrics (www.meetingmetrics.com), a meeting and event evaluation software system.

If you are particularly interested in event design, you should also become familiar with Vivien Event Designer (www.viviendesign.com). Vivien is a very sophisticated design tool that allows you to create full-color renderings of your meeting and event designs, including focusing the lighting throughout your event site.

Computer training is a must in special events, as the industry relies more than ever on computer technology. Software is being developed at a record speed, and individuals who can master those programs that make a company more cutting-edge, efficient, and effective will be in demand. In the meantime, become highly proficient in the day-to-day operation of computers with word documents, spreadsheets, calendar management and the Internet.

The Value of Business

Everything is a business, and all classes related to accounting, managing budgets, making projections, evaluating, and marketing will provide a foundation necessary throughout your career. You should also study basic project management, because corporations and government organizations increasingly use the principles of project management to develop and deliver their meetings and events. As you explore areas that provide greater insight into the business of the special events industry, training in finance is highly recommended. This training takes you well beyond reading a profit and loss (P&L) statement or an event budget. You will bring great value if you are able to maintain business records, preparing forms, and reports for financial review.

The Value of Marketing

The service and product of an organization will only be successful if there are clients buying what the organization has to offer. Branding is a key part of what the special events industry has to offer clients. One good basic source for marketing information for your career is the classic text *Event Marketing* by Leonard Hoyle. Included in your marketing training, be sure to explore the important area of public relations (PR), as many special events involve press releases and efforts to attract nonpaid advertising. You will learn the importance of brand management and of a company's mission statement. Companies invest many resources in their brand and their advertising, and you will benefit by understanding all that goes into presenting an image to the public.

The Value of Science

Dr. Joe Goldblatt states the following in his article "Tourism Experience Design in the Eventological Century":

Exploring the promise of tourism in the 21st century is an opportunity to provide the tools for people to make decisions in the real world and to design tourism experiences that transform individuals and groups. Using anthropological, psychological, sociological, technological, and even theological literature, it may be argued that the future of tourism will result in the development of a new field entitled eventology. . . . The linkage between an emerging scientific field of inquiry such as eventology (Higgison, Goldblatt 2003) and other established scientific disciplines is critically important as tourism seeks to advance from a craft and profession to an established field of scientific investigation.

Tourism and special events are closely related to tourist events such as The World Cup, The Olympic Games, a World's Fair, and other mega-events, which are often the primary catalysts for the regeneration of cities through tourism. Therefore, it is to your advantage to understand the interrelationships that converge in special events, as you are exposed to a wider range of understanding of the world and of the people you will be serving.

The Value of Anthropology

Anthropology is the study of human beings. Dr. Goldblatt said, "The anthropologist's use of ethnographics through extensive field research may provide tourism researchers with additional tools for multilayered scientific investigation." Event ethnography is the science of observation and participation in an event. As an event ethnographer, you may study, observe, and participate to learn how best to develop a future event. The more you know about how your fellow human beings interact through events, the better you will be able to lead and serve them.

The Value of Geography

Geography is the study of the earth's natural landscape. Dr. Goldblatt reminds us that it "is the field that is most closely aligned with the study of tourism. The study of tourism involves spatial relationships, and therefore it is necessary to understand the basic principles of geography in order to fully comprehend the essence of the travel experience." In the special events industry you might very well be taking your client and their guests to an exciting location or might be recreating that exciting place where you are.

The Value of Psychology

Dr. Goldblatt said,

The root word of psychology is derived from the word soul in the Greek language. Although consumer psychological research has been introduced through various symposia and monographs, there has only been a marginal attempt at linking tourism to its psychological roots. By applying these psychological theories to tourist behavior, researchers may be able to more accurately forecast future actions and responses to tourism phenomena.

Your guests will experience different human reactions, depending on the types of guests and types of events. If they are in a sporting event, you may witness the energy and excitement of a competition, but the mood and emotion created at a wedding may be far different.

The Value of Sociology

Sociology is the study of society and civilization. Dr. Goldblatt emphasizes that "Tourism is a social phenomenon that intrinsically involves social human action, often within highly complex social structures." For example, fundraising events often focus on the strong helping those that are not able to help themselves. Therefore, the social structure is very important when organizing these types of events.

The Value of Theology

Dr. Goldblatt says, "Most investigations regarding theology and tourism are linked to the study of ritual, or sacred, indigenous, religious pilgrimage. However, there has been little investigation of the spiritual motivations of tourists who seek the divine through a tourism activity." Religion is part of almost every culture, and deeply rooted beliefs are often included in special events. A personal understanding and respect of traditions is important in the special events industry. Many religious holidays and celebrations are a part of the special events industry, and the more you know and understand these traditions, the better you will serve your clients.

The Value of Eventology

Dr. Goldblatt observes, "The development of an eventological theory of tourism collaboration and analysis requires well-integrated teams from various established scientific disciplines who desire to use integrated thinking to identify patterns and models that will result in better tourism outcomes, one event at a time."

There are fields of study that might sound unrelated to the special events industry, but that can play a very big part in your personal development and the value that you bring to an organization.

If you are in an adult career transition or you are seeking the next step in your career development, explore the Certified Special Events Professional (CSEP) certification. Achieving this designation is demanding and requires a commitment of time and study, qualities that are warmly recognized and respected by members of the special events industry.

The Value of Time Management

It has been said that with enough time and money, you can do just about anything. In the special events industry, even with enough money you cannot make things happen without time. Therefore, time management is a skill that must be learned and practiced. I still use the skills learned more than 30 years ago in a time management class. I try to end my work day with a firm plan for the next day, considering all that must be accomplished that week, month, and quarter. The day begins with reviewing the plan, knowing that there will be many unexpected issues to develop during the day.

The Value of Management

The real goal of a manager is to get people to do things they would not otherwise do, or to get them to do better at something they are already doing. Risk management will demonstrate that the investment in safety training will reduce the number of injuries and therefore reduce absenteeism in the workplace. Compliance training will assist in learning about practices that discriminate, harass, or treat employees in an unfair manner. It is good business to have managers that understand their role and how they are responsible for providing a safe work environment. In small companies, often a member of the staff must serve as the human resource (HR) manager and ensure that all employees are treated fairly.

Many nonprofit organizations operate with the same management skills as a for-profit company. Within this area, fundraising is a very important skill. The special events industry is very involved with organizations that serve the interests of the community and rely on community support to keep their doors open.

The Value of Accreditation

Frank Supovitz, senior vice-president of events for the National Football League (NFL), says, "I speak at a lot of college and continuing education events and sports management programs at universities, and they run the gamut from marginally valuable to very good.

I have been impressed, however, with industry certification programs like the CSEP certificate, and believe they are increasingly valuable as one rises within the industry."

Just as you would go to a certified public accountant (CPA) for issues related to finance, an organization will seek an event professional to ensure that their event goes as planned. In the special events industry you will see designations such as CSEP, CMM, CEM, EFEE, CITE, CMP, and CMM. Each person with those letters following their name has earned that right by demonstrating knowledge and experience through demanding testing.

CSEP—Certified Special Events Professional

From the Web site: www.ises.org

The CSEP designation is awarded by the International Special Events Society (ISES) and its Certification Committee. ISES is the international umbrella organization representing professionals in all disciplines of the special events industry. The CSEP is a worldwide recognition of the special event industry and is an influential designation for education and the promotion of professional ethics and standards. Being a recipient of the CSEP demonstrates a continuous dedication to enhance individual and professional performance. To qualify as a candidate for the CSEP exam, you must demonstrate a broad range of experience in the special events industry:

- A minimum of three years employment experience in the special events industry
- Current full-time employment in the special events industry
- 35 professional industry points (see the CSEP points itemization list)

CMM—Certification in Meeting Management

From the Web site: www.mpiweb.org

Meeting Professional International's (MPI) Certification in Meeting Management (CMM) is an intensive learning opportunity designed for experienced and highly accomplished members of the global meetings industry community seeking career advancement and professional recognition. Management-level meeting and event professionals with a minimum of ten years experience in the industry. This certification is for leaders who have existing expertise in all aspects of meeting management including logistics, budgets, people, legal/contracts, and marketing and communications.

CEM—Certified in Exhibition Management

From the Web site: www.iaee.com.

The International Association for Exhibitions and Events (IAEE) created the Certified in Exhibition Management (CEM) designation to raise professional standards and provide a vehicle for certification for exhibition professionals. The certification is recognized throughout the exhibition industry as the premier mark of professional achievement. To earn the CEM designation, participants must complete a nine-part program within three years. The nine parts of the program are composed of seven mandatory courses and two courses chosen from five available electives. The designation is attainable through classes that are offered online by taking self-paced courses and through on-location classes at the IAEE Mid-Year and Annual Meetings.

CFEE—Certified Festival and Event Executive

From the Web site: www.ifea.com

The CFEE certification, created by International Festivals and Events Association (IFEA), is meant to enhance the professional stature of professionals that have gone beyond expectations in the industry by setting higher standards for our industry.

Prerequisites for certification:

1. You must be enrolled in the program and have completed all requirements.
2. You must have five years of paid, full-time festival or event-related industry experience at a professional level.
3. You must be currently employed in the festival and events industry.
4. You must be an active IFEA member in good standing before you can receive your designation.

CITE—The Society of Incentive Travel Executives (SITE)

From the Web site: www.siteglobal.com

Members of SITE are encouraged to pursue the CITE Certification, which recognizes the knowledge and experience in the Incentive Travel Industry. The SITE global network of meetings and event professionals focus on delivering business results and bring solutions, insights and global connections to maximize the business impact of motivational experiences.

CMP—Certified Meeting Professional

From the Web site: www.conventionindustry.com.

The CMP certification recognizes individuals who have achieved the industry's highest standard of professionalism. Established in 1985 by Convention Industry Council, the CMP credential increases the proficiency of meeting professionals by:

- Identifying a body of knowledge
- Establishing a level of knowledge and performance necessary for certification
- Stimulating the advancement of the art and science of meeting management
- Increasing the value of practitioners to their employers
- Recognizing and raising industry standards, practices, and ethics
- Maximizing the value received from the products and services provided by Certified Meeting Professionals

Through the CMP program, individuals who are employed in meeting management pursue continuing education, increase their industry involvement, and gain industry-wide recognition. The requirements for certification are based on professional experience and a written examination. Currently, more than 13,000 individuals in 35 countries and territories have earned the CMP designation.

"We are what we repeatedly do. Excellence, then, is not an act, but a habit"

— *Aristotle*

Laura Schwartz, White House director of events under the Clinton administration, said, "You should take the opportunity to be certified, but I do not believe in that alone. I believe that education in the fields of communications and public relations and advertising is an incredible background. What you learn through school on branding and messaging will be the basis for every event that you propose and create. Every event sends a message, and the ability you have to communicate engaging messages through events will set you on the right path for a job."

Your special events training program should include a finance component, as understanding budgets is a key requirement and an asset you bring to an organization. Most organizations measure their success by their financial results, as well as client satisfaction. Some special events students say they want to only produce events and are not comfortable dealing with the business aspects. However, classes in business, economics, finance, accounting, marketing, contract administration, and business law will open the door of understanding the interconnection between customer service and business results. Most of all, this training teaches you where to go to find answers to your questions. Not knowing the answers but knowing where to find the needed information is half the battle. Getting training and developing your understanding of special events will place you in a favorable position with your target organization. The company is always measuring you, starting in the beginning with your potential, and then with how successful you are at dealing with the clients and, finally, with the business results.

Walt Disney Parks and Resorts talent relations director, Greg Bell, stated the following:

Gene-Gem

If you can measure it, you can manage it, and if you can manage it, you can improve it.

Education, certification and experience are all important in the special events industry. From a leadership or project manager perspective, you cannot separate one from the other. However, in looking at individual team member contribution, the diversity of these elements within different members of the team will be of great help. Make no mistake that a diverse team may be cause for passionate discussions, but it will pay great dividends in the quality and delivery of the final product.

Without training or experience, it can be very difficult to even get a job interview. Over the years, I have been asked to meet with a number of people who would "like" to be in the special events business. Requests would come from senior management doing a favor for a relative or a friend of a friend, requesting me to meet with a candidate. Often, the inexperienced candidate expressed the desire to have a job so they could attend events. The lack of understanding of all the planning and coordination that goes into events would become apparent in the interview. My responsibility was to ensure that every member of the special events team made a contribution and did not drain the group.

Even with training you must have realistic expectations, and assuming that your degree entitles you to a more senior-level position can be very negative to the hiring managers. Having a long-term goal is very appropriate, but plan to invest time working your way up to that level. There are real advantages to working your way up. You not only learn firsthand how events come together, but you also have the opportunity to work with the team. There is the old saying, "Be nice to the people on the way up because you will meet them on the way down," which is true. However, if you are a nice person, people will do all they can to prevent you from falling.

> **Gene-Gem**
>
> People that start at the top always seem to work their way down—quickly!

Plan Your Work—Work Your Plan

Many years ago I met a craftsman working at Walt Disney World whose task it was to maintain the storefronts on Main Street, USA, in the Magic Kingdom. This committed professional worked after-hours in the Magic Kingdom to keep up "show quality." I asked what his secret was in keeping the quality at such a high level, and he replied, "You plan your work, then you work your plan."

This phrase sums up how we have to work most projects. It is all about planning, anticipating what needs to be done and in what order. It is impossible to build a budget without knowing the scope or elements of the event. The timeline is a key, and those of us that have done this for a long time understand that even with a lot of money and great ideas, without the time to make them happen, they won't happen.

> **Gene-Gem**
>
> Plan your work, work your plan—fail to plan, plan to fail.

There are three things your clients may want: fast, good, and cheap. You will learn that you can have only two:

1. Fast and good, but it won't be cheap.
2. Good and cheap, but it won't be fast.
3. Cheap and fast, but won't be good.

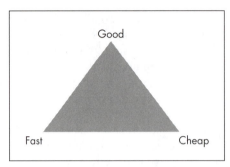

Figure 5.2 In Special Events There Are Three Possibilities but Only Two Available

"Even if you are on the right track, you'll get run over if you just sit there."
— *Will Roger (1879–1935)*

Your investment in getting the best possible training will not come without an expense, but the return on investment will pay off over the span of your career, so it will not be cheap. The "good" or quality of your education/training is equally important, but it will not be fast. Many special events professionals work and study for many years to get the desired education, and most will tell you that it was worth the effort because it was sustainable.

Volunteer

If you are in school or seeking to enter the industry, get involved in any way you can with the special events industry. Being a volunteer is one of the best ways to see how things are organized. Many programs offer opportunities for students to get involved. Look in your community for volunteer opportunities.

Here are some of the advantages to getting experience as a volunteer:

- Volunteering is a great way to prove you to be a willing worker.
- Volunteering is a great way to network.
- Volunteers can learn from observing.
- Volunteers are making a contribution.
- Volunteers are demonstrating they want to do this type of work.

When volunteering, explore areas such as guest check-in, seating, banquet, staff interface, speaker coordination, and even running lights and sound if you have the training.

Example found by Google: Hands on Orlando—Volunteer Central

List the following opportunities for the following:

- Group or club
- Yourself
- Employee team-building opportunities
- Youth volunteer involvement
- Becoming a volunteer coordinator

The volunteer coordinator attends, leads, and manages hands-on community projects. They are creative, caring, outgoing and know how to have fun. They leverage their time and talents to maximize positive results.

There were 569 Orlando volunteering opportunities listed, including:

- Folk festival
- Juvenile diabetes walk
- Neighborhood block party
- Children's art festival
- History center exhibit opening
- Special Olympics
- Relay for Life

Doing this while in school is a great way to learn the business. Remember that, at any given moment, any person can become the most important person in the entire special event. The manner in which a guest is greeted can make a big difference to the overall experience. When planning an event, anticipate each step and the type of reaction or response you will get, from the moment the guest opens the invitation to the moment we close the door to their car, saying "Good Night!" and all the interaction in between. We expect that attention to detail from each member of our team, and that is what we will be looking for when we are adding staff. At every point along the way there comes a moment in which each person can make or break the event. Experiencing those moments is very educational, as you see the importance of every member of the team. Each time you volunteer, you should request a letter of recommendation at the conclusion of your assignment. It provides you with more materials for your on-going effort of gaining more experience, and shows the level of commitment you have on the job. One more advantage is that the person writing the letter takes time to think about you and the manner in which you did your duties, which will be a much stronger memory since they are writing about you.

Charlotte J. De Witt, president of International Events, Ltd., says, "Never, ever give up, and never do less than the very best. Think creatively; think proactively; think outside of the box. If you are inexperienced, volunteer to work with a high-profile event. Give 200 percent—the competition is

Gene-Gem

Don't just let things happen, make them happen!

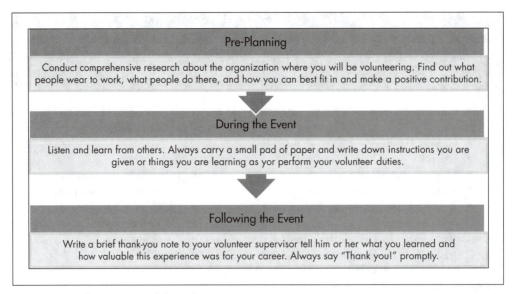

Figure 5.3   Three Stages of the Volunteer Experience

fierce, and the demands are intense." See Figure for the three stages of the volunteer experience.

If there is not an event available for you to gain experience, create one at your school, in the community, with a local charity, with a friend, or even for a family reunion. Apply the techniques as outlined in recommended books on special events. Perhaps you have a family member or a friend getting married who needs help. A wedding is a very sensitive special event and requires a great deal of expert coordination. The goal should be to make this one of the happiest days in the life of the family. The current trend is that couples are expected to have a big wedding, which makes it very important to have an event planner that is on top of each element. If you attend a wedding, perhaps a member of the wedding party will introduce you to the professional who is hired to produce the event. The wedding planner might be willing to provide you with insight into how they are approaching the project, and to permit you to job shadow.

Consider the many opportunities to create a win-win situation by working with a nonprofit organization or a school to help raise money by doing an event. For a number of years, students from the University of Central Florida have been assisting in the production of the annual fundraiser with the Edgewood Children's Ranch. Because this annual event is produced by volunteers, the students are able to step into roles with great responsibility and get firsthand experience in the production of an event. The organization gets your help and you get hands-on experience.

Volunteer and school experiences are ideal for sharing in your special events job interview, as you are sharing real experience. For example, college students may assist on a large-scale fundraising event, where the organization raises a lot of money as well as hosts a large number of guests. Students work side by side with other volunteers from the professional world, and these contacts lead to internships and entry-level positions. You are not just helping others with your time and effort, you are helping yourself. It will make a difference in your career and it will make a difference in the lives of others.

Learning to Learn

"Learning to learn" is a phrase we used at Disney when considering candidates, and could be a key ingredient to your employer of choice. Learning to learn requires first understanding what you do not know and then finding the resources, people, and programs to provide you with the knowledge and experience to improve your confidence and ability. Learning, of course, is a perpetual pursuit in the special events industry. Perhaps, one day, as a result of your learning and experience, you may find that you have an interest in teaching and will be sharing your knowledge, wisdom, and experience with the next generation of special events professionals as a college guest speaker, author of an industry article, or mentor to others.

Career Connections

 Action Steps

- Explore what other training programs are offering to their students—make a list of how your training program is better preparing you for your area of interest.
- Attend a performance at the campus or community theater and request a back-stage tour to learn about volunteer opportunities.
- List all the possible classes beyond special events training that are available and how each would enhance the abilities for employment.
- Create a list of possible events your class or group would like to produce. Examples:
  - Career fair for special events
  - Earth Day celebration
  - Book exchange to promote reading
  - Opening celebration of a show, sports season or back to school
  - Class reunions
  - Holiday celebrations
  - Fundraiser
- Once an event is selected, plan the scope, timeline, and budget.

Practice Activities

- Once the event or events have been selected, each member of the team should present his or her plan to the group, to practice public speaking and delivering a sales pitch.
- In the classroom, each student presents why the program he or she is in is the best suited to the student's long-term goals. Comparisons to other programs is recommended, but not in a derogatory manner.

 ## Tool Kit

Blaustein, Arthur I. (2003). *Making a Difference: America's Guide to Volunteering and Community Service*. San Francisco: John Wiley & Sons, Inc.

Rosenberg, Bob, and Lampard, Guy (2005). *Giving from the Heart—A Guide to Volunteering*. Lincoln, NE: iUniverse.

 ## Web Connection

Explore some of the ways you can network for job opportunities while making a difference in your community:

www.networkforgood.org

www.volunteeringamerica.gov

PART THREE

I'm Ready for My Close-up

CHAPTER 6

Target Companies: Where to Find Opportunities

Look for local Job Banks in your community or online. Study the various application procedures for different companies and compare.

Where I Started

Early in my career, the accepted manner of looking for a job was to make the rounds of possible employers and drop off résumés. This activity was called "pounding the pavement," and was basically going door to door, hoping the employer would grant a job interview on the spot or call you at a later time for an interview. Much has changed, but the one thing that has not changed is timing. It is still about being in the right place at the right time with the right training and skills.

Computer Advantage

Years ago, updating a résumé was a major undertaking, as you would go to a printing shop and the typesetter would create the document. Today, the computer is much more than a word processor, as it connects you to the world with Internet and e-mail. If you do not use these advantages, you may appear as someone out of step with the world. Since it is possible to continuously update materials and fix mistakes, there is no reason for you to submit anything less than a perfect document (see Figure 6.1). In addition, every résumé and cover letter must be tailored to your target company, and anything short of that could

Figure 6.1   Well Written Documents Are Examples of Work Skills and Habits

make you look like someone with limited computer skills. Whether there are typographical errors, punctuation mistakes or poor grammar, your writing skills can impact your chances of being considered for employment.

Computers and the Internet give you amazing tools for finding needed information on target companies as well as customizing your résumé to suit that organization. Many people send their materials electronically and follow up by going to the post office and mailing a hard copy of their materials. It is harder to delete a hard copy, since there is the action of opening and discovering what is inside. However, résumés are much easier to store and retrieve electronically as hard copies. In the past few years I have actually requested that candidates send an electronic copy of their résumé so I could share it easily as well as keep it in a file that I could access very quickly. Computers have changed life for the better in many ways, but in terms of your job search, do not overrely on them. Instead of pounding the pavement, make sure you are "pounding the keyboard."

The Internet opens many doors to companies as their Web sites showcase who they are and what they do. Companies want clients to learn about their services and products on the Web site, which can be quickly updated as new materials are available. Web sites have become sophisticated and artistically pleasing, and showcase the company in a spectacular manner. The goal is to captivate the audience, getting them to stay longer, which increases the chances of making sales. All of that information is available for you in our quest to learn about the company. It is surprising to me that many candidates come to the interviews without having done much research on the organization. Make this a top priority for your interviews.

The Internet is a major tool for special events companies, as it showcases what they have to offer and may include information about career opportunities with steps you should take in submitting your application. This is a great way to learn about the types of positions available and what skills are needed in the marketplace. Knowing what the company is looking for provides you with powerful information on what you need to do to qualify for a position. Looking at career opportunities within a number of companies is time well spent.

Within minutes you will be able to learn about a company and what services it offers to clients. Here are just a few samples:

Creative Services Event Business Solutions	Darren Johnson Founder & CEO	www.cseventco.com
Tillinger's Boston, Massachusetts	Dr. Martin (Marty) Tillinger Founder	www.tillinger.com
MC-2	Rich McAdam President	www.mc-2.com

Outsourcing Screening

It requires time and effort as well as staff to deal with candidates seeking opportunities, so many companies are using the services of job boards such as Monster.com or CareerBuilders. com to collect résumés (see Appendix 7). Candidates often feel they are sending their materials to a "black hole," but for the company it is a way to screen candidates. Under these circumstances, it is difficult for candidates to get feedback on what skills they need to develop to be considered in the future. However, if a company directs you to send your materials to a third party, follow its instructions. When going through third-party Web sites, be very selective in providing your personal contact information. Beware of scams or false companies offering fake positions.

When you apply through a third party, make an effort to get your materials in the hands of the people that hire, as that will greatly increase your chances of getting an interview. It is not always easy, and sometimes the company does not want to screen candidates, but there are various ways to address this issue.

If you are a working professional seeking to re-position yourself and are looking to move to the next step, you need to consider issues related to confidentiality and how and who will see your information. The ideal situation would be to have the help and support of your current employer, but that is not always possible. You will need to be discreet in your new job search. Identify an individual in the target company, and, in overnight mail, send your letter and résumé, stamped "personal and confidential." In your letter, you should be positive about your current employer, but say that you are now seeking to take the next step.

Your professors or mentors may have relationships with various special events companies. Perhaps they could introduce you to a professional, or invite a guest representative from the industry to speak in the classroom. If a professional is willing to take time to speak to a class, it is likely that the person would be willing to take the time to meet with an aspiring event professional.

Too often, these become missed opportunities, as the students may feel that they learned all they need from this person in the classroom discussion. That is only part of the connection. You need to make people like this part of your network. A follow-up thank-you note and a request for a short meeting to learn more about the company could secure for you a mentor who is well established in the industry. For the working professional, an informational interview is a good way to make a connection, even if there are no positions available. This opens the door to future opportunities as well as teaching you more about the company and the people who run it.

Creating Connections

Do a research project on a particular company of interest to you. It would also be part of your career development to learn more about the various positions and would include a report to the class. Companies are much more likely to help with this type of project, as there is only the commitment of providing information about their organization.

To help you stay focused, work with the following checklist:

- ☐ Request a meeting to learn about the company.
- ☐ Focus on the company's history and heritage.
- ☐ Find out how the person from the company got started in the industry.
- ☐ Discover what events the person is most proud of and what made them special.
- ☐ Learn what advice they give to students or others training for the industry.
- ☐ Research the long-term and short-term trends in the industry.
- ☐ Learn about career opportunities in the industry.
- ☐ Find out about opportunities in the company you are interested in.
- ☐ Find out if they use interns.
- ☐ Find out what this company looks for in new hires.

The best questions will come from what you learned about the company. Most industry professionals like to talk about their past successes and what they learned in the process. This meeting can be an opportunity for you to gain important information on shaping your own career, but can also be helpful in planning a formal interview with the company. This meeting could provide great insight as to how the company finds and hires their staff, as well as interns. If you were effective at establishing the relationship, you have an internal champion as well as a starting point.

Read what various event companies are looking for in a candidate so that you can assess your skills to make sure that you are getting the needed exposure to what companies are seeking. Also look at what types of events each company is doing to see if there might be a connection to your long term goals. This effort could introduce you to an area that you might not have considered. Make a list of each company and compare what type of events they are doing with the skills these companies require the most.

Even if you are unable to make connections with a person in the targeted company, one of the best parts of researching a company's Web site is that it provides a large

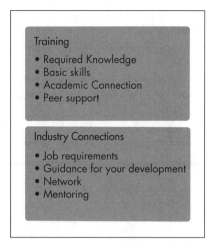

Figure 6.2   Training, Industry Connections and Company Knowledge Increases Chances for a Job Interview

amount of information not just about the organization but also about the industry. You may learn from the company's clients by reading testimonials about what makes the company exceptional, and often the names of key personnel and their contribution. This is valuable information, as it demonstrates the company's efforts as well as its achieved results.

Many companies include a mission statement of their philosophy, as well as goals associated with their mission. This is powerful information if you are seeking an opportunity with this organization. You will also gain insight about their leadership and what is important to them as a company (see Figure 6.2).

Making Contact

Try not to send a letter "to whom it may concern," since there are so many ways to get

names and profiles of key players. At Disney, my priority was to contact individuals who had written to me by name, followed by those who sent their materials blindly. For those who send to "whom it may concern," it is a challenge to send a follow-up letter.

Read every page of a special events company's Web site, including profiles of each member of the team, if available.

Gene-Gem

There is no way of telling how a letter addressed to nobody is going to reach anybody!

You might discover that a staff member is an alumnus of your university or has other connections that might make that person a possible internal champion. There should be a great deal of information about individuals from the Web site, but it is also suggested that you use a search engine such as Google or Yahoo! to find additional information. Besides being part of a targeted company, staff members might be involved with local organizations, as many special events professionals are committed to assist with community events. You might be surprised to learn of the connections you may already have or that could easily be established.

Most special events professionals worked their way up on a journey similar to the one you are taking. They needed experience, and many started off by volunteering and learned the importance of giving their time and talent. Most professionals I know do not give up being part of a worthy cause once they become successful in the industry, but rather, they get even more involved.

> *"Words are plentiful, but deeds are precious."*
> *Lech Walesa, former president of the Republic of Poland (1943—)*

Think of the impact if, in your interview, you spoke about the company's events and what you found to be most impressive. Many companies include photos of their events with details on the scale and scope of their involvement. If you were in attendance, then you can speak from experience, but if you are speaking from what you saw on the Web site or read in a magazine, make that clear.

On a company Web site, you might learn about an upcoming public event, and, if possible, you should attend, as this provides a good opportunity to look at how the company operates and to introduce yourself. If it is not open to the public, do not just show up, hoping you can meet staff members. If you do, it could backfire. It is appropriate to make a request to observe, promising to stay out of the way. If you are a student, companies tend to be more open-minded.

With any of these types of opportunities, be sure to have business cards, because generally, if you give a business card, others will give one of their cards. Note where you met and what was talked about so that when you contact that person later there is some bit of information that will trigger the connection back to you. Write down a note about the person on their business card so that you can remember them. Do not do this in front of them, as it will look like you are messing up their business card.

This is where your "elevator speech" is very important, and it needs to be clear and quick.

This should be practiced and said quickly, with the goal being to get the other party to ask a question. If they are asking questions, they are engaged. It then is up to you to judge just how far and how long you can take it. Be bold, but also request if there might be a time to meet and learn more about their company. The best setting for this is when special event professionals are doing volunteer work. They are always looking for more help, and this could be very much to your advantage.

As executive director of the Orlando Repertory Theatre, it is my goal to get people to come to our theater complex, because once they see what we do, they get excited and want to be involved. This is not a high-pressure encounter, but rather, an invitation to

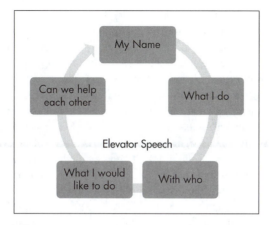

Figure 6.3   Gene Columbus Elevator Speech "Snap-shot"

have an enjoyable experience. Once they have toured the building, I do not ask for anything other than saying: "How would you like to help us?"

Sample: Hello, I'm Gene Columbus, executive director of the Orlando Repertory Theatre—we focus on family theatre. Have you had the chance to visit us? (answer) I would love to have you come down and see a performance, and I would like to take you on a backstage tour. Are you available next Tuesday? (answer) Well, what works best for you?

The difficult part is to ask a question that makes it hard for someone to say no, but does not put them in an awkward position.

Sample: Good morning, I am Sally Student or Adam Aspiring Professional attending Special Events University, where I am receiving training or exploring new jobs so I can specialize in weddings. Perhaps you could put me in touch with someone who would be willing to share advice to a student or young professional aspiring to be in that part of the industry. (answer) Would you be willing to make the introduction?

The person might answer: "I can't think of anyone off hand." You should say thank you, provide a business card (hoping the other person will give you one, too) and ask them to keep you in mind if they hear of anything. Follow up with a short note, thanking them for taking time with you, and once again sharing your request. That keeps you in their mind, and should they come across an opportunity, you will be the first person to come to their mind.

Volunteering

Make a list of community volunteer opportunities, starting at your college or university, focusing on those opportunities that will give you experience and résumé credit. Here are a few ideas:

- Charities need assistance from volunteers for all types of events, which could open the door to learning new skills such as setting up and taking down the event.

- Boys and Girls Clubs provide opportunities for young people to get involved and it can be very rewarding to be a volunteer leader.
- The YMCA or YWCA has many events each year to raise money or celebrate the success or introduce new programs, all requiring lots of help, mainly from volunteers.
- Museums often will do events in celebration of the opening of a new exhibit, and, like most nonprofit organizations, they need assistance with fundraising events.
- Health care organizations such as your local hospital, cancer society, or trust often produce fundraising events to bring about awareness concerning health issues.
- The American Cancer Society and the Susan G. Komen Race for the Cure (www .komen.org) try to get as many people as possible involved with the mission of awareness and support. Relay for Life (www.cancer.org) is an event that is done in many communities and requires a great deal of coordination. It is a wonderful event and a great way to gain experience.

Organizations are continuously seeking volunteers to assist with special events and that provides those looking for opportunities the chance to get involved, learn, build a résumé, and make contacts, while making the world a better place to live.

Personal Information on the Internet

Care must be taken when posting personal information on the Internet. Pictures that might not show you in the best light might become a factor in the hiring process. Comments you make can have a life well beyond what you intended. Funny photos of you pretending or actually drinking are not in your best interest. They may be fun now, but you will not be laughing if you do not get a position because of the company's concern about your character. The Internet works both ways: You can find out about the company, but the company can also find out about you. One measure of Internet safety might be to not put anything on the Internet that your parents wouldn't be proud to share with their friends and your grandparents.

Make your e-mail address professional, as companies could get turned off by partygirl@ college.edu or beer4breakfast@college.edu. This might be fun for you and your circle of friends, but it is unlikely that the company considering you for employment will find it amusing. I remember so well a candidate getting cut because the review team thought the e-mail address went over the line. When I approached the young lady, she thought we were very narrow-minded—there was no question that she was hurt that people thought ill of her by looking only at her e-mail address.

When Dr. Joe Goldblatt speaks to his college students about their professional demeanor, he asks if he might call them on their cell phone while they are in his office. He places the desk phone on speaker and dials their number. Invariably the phone answers as follows: "Hey, what's up?! I'll call you back. Later." They blush, and Dr. Goldblatt's point is made. Since the mobile phone is a key first point of contact now, make sure you have a professional answering message.

Your Past

Companies may do background checks, and if there are issues regarding your past, you should address them, as you will not hide them. I once had a candidate share with me that there would be issues in his background check, as he admitted, frankly, that he had made a big mistake in the past. He went on to point out that he had learned more from that mistake than all the successes he had ever experienced. The candidate displayed the correct attitude of honesty and determination. If you have these issues, hopefully you will find someone that will give you a second chance, but do not expect many people to give you a third chance.

Networks that Work for You

There are a number of services that claim to help you with your network. Facebook, LinkedIn, MySpace, and others have a place but there is no substitute for direct connection to people in the industry. These services are great ways to stay in touch with people that you have met and had an exchange with, but without having that one-on-one connection, they are limited. You will find the Internet does not replace the need for the person-to-person connection: you need to be more than a screen name. People like to work with people they know, and it is your job to be known. Face-to-face, you have opportunities to build trust and gain better understanding of another person. Once the trust has been established, the text message and quick e-mail message become in some ways like a continuation of real-life conversations.

Steven Wood Schmader, CFEE, the president and CEO of International Festivals and Events Association (IFEA), says this:

My philosophy says that if you need to use Linked-In, you probably aren't. Personal relationships are the most important resource you can have, but they take time and a dedicated effort to build and grow (beyond completing a personal profile in an online web program). You don't gain any credibility by being the friend of a friend of a person who doesn't know you all that well. Concentrate on building "one-degree-of-separation" human relationships. That allows you to sell yourself by being truly credible, one relationship at a time. From watching the job-hunt process by many different individuals in our industry, there is no question that the shortest route to a job in our business is networking. I always liked the statement, "It's not who you know. It's who knows you.

Frank Supovitz, senior vice president of events for the National Football League (NFL), says,

Networking is essential. It's a people-business, and you meet the same people over and over again, in one company or another, one hotel or another. To get a choice position, you have to be top-of-mind among those managers who are preparing to hire. Coming on too strong is a detriment. Selling yourself in a subtle, professional way is a plus. Make lots of friends and make sure the buzz about you and your work is always positive.

Frank makes a very good point about selling yourself but gives great advice even beyond getting your foot in the door:

> *Remember that you meet the same people over and over again. Engender respect as a professional among your colleagues and don't hold grudges. You will meet the same people at different stages in your career and at different stages in their career. You'd be surprised to learn how many people I interview for jobs or consider as contractors to whom I once delivered interoffice mail. I'll bet there were people delivering my email 10 years ago to whom I'll be responsible as a coworker, supervisor, or client in 10 years.*

Online Magazines

As a real Internet fan, I am connected to several trade publications such as *Event Solutions* and *Special Events* magazine with online subscriptions. These magazines are filled with great information about business trends and feature great descriptions on all types of events. You learn what is new in weddings, corporate events, catering, décor, entertainment, fairs, festivals, conventions, and much more. There are profiles on individuals that might even provide contact information. An article may inspire you to want to know more about a person or the organization with which he or she is associated. If you are inspired by the achievements of award-winning special events producers and they include their contact information, it would seem that they would be open to having readers reach out to them. I had a number of people send messages after an article appeared in a magazine. I was thrilled that these people took time to read the article and then to contact me. Some were looking for opportunities, and I was happy to help them.

Lisa Hurley, Editor of *Special Events* magazine, points out that "being a success in special events requires a remarkable mix of planning and on-the-spot decision making. True professionals stay flexible and stay informed, and are willing to give that extra bit of energy and effort to put an event over the top."

Nearly 9,000 special event professionals from around the world attend The Special Event annual trade show and conference where they attend seminars, discussion groups, explore emerging trends and, most importantly, network with other professionals. Innovative programs, including "The Special Events Gives Back Community-Service Project," are planned, where those seeking opportunities in the industry can find ways to get involved working with industry leaders. Beyond the annual meeting, professions stay connected to what is happening in the industry with the monthly magazine. As an aspiring special events professional, you need to be reading *Special Events* magazine.

In your interview, there might be an opportunity to reference how you were inspired by what you read and the standards that were established by the person you read about. You should be honest, as the skilled interviewer can tell when a person is fabricating interest in something to appear knowledgeable. The more you read about special events professionals, the more you will learn about the industry. If you can talk about issues within the special events industry with knowledge, energy, and excitement, you will surprise your interviewers and present yourself in a positive, self-confident manner.

A Tech-Savvy Résumé

Many companies request you send your information via the internet, which is quick and easy, but there are some issues to keep in mind:

- Make sure that your résumé and cover letter are technologically sound by sending it to yourself or your mentor.
- Plain-text résumés tend to have the advantage of being readable no matter what system the receiving computer uses.
- Plain-text résumés should avoid italics, unusual formatting, or fancy fonts—keep it simple.
- Portable document format (PDF) files ensure that your materials will not change when transmitted via the Internet and is most recommended.
- Résumés and cover letters are generally sent as attached files rather than in the body of the message.
- The e-mail message is extremely important, as it is the invitation for the reader to open and read your attached documents.
- Web site portfolio is a great way to showcase your design skills, photos, and documents you created; however, you must have high-quality images, or it will reflect poorly on you.
- Video portraits are for those who are not shy being in front of a camera. This can provide the target company with a "snapshot" of you and your skills. It shows how you present yourself. It is best to keep it short, as people watching tend to have short attention spans.

The old adage "Nothing ventured, nothing gained" rings true in the pursuit of career opportunities. It really is an exciting adventure, and part of the enjoyment is finding your pathway that leads you to that dream job in the special events industry. Each of us will have our own unique journey, filled with many advances, and perhaps, from time to time, a setback, but it will be a thrilling ride, so make it your goal to work really hard and have fun along the way.

Career Connections

 ### Action Steps

- Select five special events companies that you would consider as an employee.
  - Research the types of events, the size of the groups they serve, and positions they may have listed.
  - Include their staffing structure and accomplishments.
  - Select to whom you would address your cover letter.
  - List what skills or experience these companies might value.

- Attend an industry meeting in which there are many people you do not know and make it your goal to meet everyone and get their business cards.
- Write your "elevator speech" and practice with other members of your group.
  - Make it less than 30 seconds.
  - Use the other person's name, if possible.
  - Get them to answer your question.
  - Establish how to move on to the next step.
- From your profiles of companies, create an invitation to visit your class or group to talk about a person's company. Include a meal experience to give you additional quality time with the professional.

 **Practice Activity**

Go to *Special Events* magazine at http://specialevents.com and peruse the articles about various events. If you read a profile on someone and contact information is available, make the contact, thanking them for writing the article.

 Tool Kit

Levit, Alexandra (2008). *How'd You Score That Gig?: A Guide to the Coolest Jobs-and How to Get Them.* United States: Ballantine Books.

Schawbel, Dan (2009). *Me 2.0: Build a Powerful Brand to Achieve Career Success.* New York: Kaplan, Inc.

 Web Connection

Visit the ISES Career Center at http://careers.ises.com.

CHAPTER 7

Creating a Résumé and Writing the Cover Letter

Write your résumé and cover letter, then give it to a mentor to review.

How the Interviewer Will Read Your Résumé

Having received and read thousands of résumés over many years, I have a pretty good idea of what works and what does not work. In addition, while sharing résumés with members of the hiring team and watching as they scanned over the documents, I observed the order in which they read the document as they picked out items of interest. The conclusion was that the most successful way for a candidate to write a résumé is the way decision makers read them. The basic purpose of a résumé is to highlight your experience, training, and measurable progress you have been making in the best possible way to a prospective employer. You include accomplishments and skills the employers need from their team members; if you appear to be a good fit for the company, you could very well move forward with the next step: an interview.

Each prospective employer should receive an original, tailored résumé and cover letter, because one size does not fit all. You should closely review the job requirement, ensuring that your skills and experience match the needs of the employer. Generally speaking, there will be little if any adjustments to your résumé, but you should make it a practice of reviewing the position description/job outline/job posting, as well as your résumé to make sure there are connections. If you are a student, often times you will have covered materials in class or with class projects so that you will be knowledgeable about the duties even if you have not had firsthand experience performing them. There are companies that will hire manager trainees, so do not discount opportunities where you have limited training.

Carolyn S. Baragona, owner of *Event Solutions* magazine and tradeshow, has this advice about résumés:

I want to see a concise résumé that reflects education, plus experience to support it. I want to see a portfolio of work that can be discussed during an interview. I want to see documentation that demonstrates that the candidate is successful in accomplishing goals, including education in the field of interest and supporting areas. These résumé specifics would vary by position sought and by the skills and talents required to complete their job successfully. But documentation of successful previous performance is a must.

Interviewers do not read your résumé the way you write it, and often their eyes will glance at your name, but at that point, it is only to connect what they are really seeking from the document. This is the typical order in which most interviewers/hiring managers read your résumé:

1. Your experience is where they look first, and if there is no experience and/or training, it is unlikely they will continue to read the rest of the résumé. Include significant volunteer work when you list your experience. Volunteer work does more than help others: it helps you gain experience and often builds your network.

2. Your education and/or training are the foundation on which you will build your career, and if you do not have experience but have training/education there will be a level of interest to find out more about you.

3. You might want to include an objective. There are various points of view on this, and you need to make a judgment call. In this fast-paced industry, sometimes the hiring manager does not read the letter but only glances at it and then looks at your résumé. If there is nothing of interest in the résumé, it and the cover letter are placed in the pile of no interest. Knowing there is a strong possibility that your résumé will be reviewed before your cover letter is read, it might be wise to make sure that document can stand on its own, having the needed information that will cause the hiring manager to want to read your cover letter. As an example, if your objective is an internship, you might put that on your résumé, so that the hiring manager looks at your credentials in a very different manner. In a large company like Disney, often the cover letter does not accompany the résumé. The résumé is copied and forwarded on to those areas that have openings or might have a long-term interest.

4. Qualifications are often placed at the top of the résumé. Too often students use buzzwords. Buzzwords are key terms or phrases that immediately connect with your reader and promote him or her to read further as well as perhaps tell others about your talents. Here are a few résumé buzzwords:
   o *Strategic thinker and planner:* If there are good examples of how you were strategic with positive results in your planning, then by all means include them on your résumé, but if they are only there to make the résumé look good, expect the phrase to cause challenges in the interview.
   o *Engaging and inspirational leader:* Cite an example in your interview of your leadership of a group such as student government, community volunteers, or

any team in which there were positive results that made an impact in the community or in special events.

- o *Delivers exceptional results:* This phrase is used a lot, but there must be very good examples in the interview of what was done and for whom. In the interview you might very well be asked, "I see here on your résumé that you have delivered exceptional results. Tell me about that."

- o *Exceptional at problem solving:* Provide examples of dealing with challenges such as a class project where a guest speaker was unsure if he or she would make it to your event because of a snow storm. How did you solve the problem?

- o *Build and lead high-performance teams:* Think of how that will relate to the organization to which you are applying. Unless you are or have been in a senior level position, moving to another senior level position, this could be a challenge to the hiring manager. Your qualifications need to be strong and to bring value and dedication to the company.

Everything on your résumé must be considered as a possible item for being questioned by the interviewer. "Dynamic leader" is what was in vogue for a while, and when a candidate had that on his or her résumé, I would ask: "I see you consider yourself a dynamic leader; why?" Most of the time the answers were uncomfortable for almost all but the most experienced candidates. Of course, if that happened, I would quickly move to an area that the candidate would feel more comfortable with, but many interviewers will continue to dig, with follow-up questions like: "Then give me an example of a time when you demonstrated dynamic leadership." If you put anything on your résumé, be able to back it up.

5. Your address does not need to be on your résumé, but a phone number and e-mail address are necessary. If your phone number (such as a cell number) is from outside the area, that might be of concern to the targeted company, as they may believe you live in another town or city than the one in which they operate. You might then consider including information that would address that issue in your cover letter, such as: "As a student at Hometown College . . ." or "In my recent relocation to. . . ." This lets the company know that you are locally available.

6. Should you be seeking a position in a city you are not living, perhaps in your letter you could include a statement such as, "seeking to relocate to the Targeted Company's area," which is very helpful to the company. Larger companies are much more willing to consider relocating than smaller companies, because of the expense as well as the risk.

7. Your skills are a key part of your story for companies considering you for employment. It is important to share, in a nonboastful manner, what you do better than most other people. Your self-assessment will be most helpful as you prepare your résumé and cover letter, and then prepare for the job interview. Showcase areas of interest as skills, because you tend to develop in those areas you most enjoy. If your area of interest is music, you will go out of your way to be involved with anything related to music. Because you are so close to it, you become somewhat

of an expert. In most businesses, it is wise to get experts to accomplish what needs to be done.

8. Computer skills should be listed in terms of proficiency. Proficiency with basic word processing or spreadsheets is important, but if you do not have those skills, you can write "basic knowledge." The special event industry needs many people with different skills, and the more skills you have, the better the chances are of finding gainful employment. In your journey of learning, include such tools as PowerPoint for presentations, Excel for budgets, Word for written communications, Photoshop for sharing pictures, and graphic design programs to make images that are memorable. Computers are no longer just a nice thing to have, but rather, an essential tool in the special events industry.

> **Gene-Gem**
>
> If you cannot get someone to pay you for your services yet, then give it away and get experience, as well as having items on your résumé.

9. Sports are a very big part of the special events industry, and your experience, interest, and passion is a strong indicator that you want very much to be involved with these activities. Many sports are team-related, and experience being part of a team can work to the candidate's advantage in many ways.

10. Interviewers are often interested in community involvement:
    ○ Volunteer work does more than help others; it helps you gain experience and build networks.
    ○ Volunteering shows a willingness to do whatever it takes to get a job done.
    ○ Volunteering often connects you to members of the special events industry giving back, so there are many opportunities to network with those well-established professionals. These professionals appreciate seeing someone out there giving their time to help as well as to learn.

The Résumé as a Menu

Most hiring managers read résumés the same way that you and I read the menu at a restaurant. Your résumé is very much like a menu, but rather than telling us what the chef has prepared, it outlines your experience and education. Rather than looking to satisfy hunger, hiring managers are looking to fill positions in their companies.

The Entrée

The hungry patron scans the menu, looking for familiar items that can be depended on, but also looking at unfamiliar items for variety. The hiring manager pretty much does the same thing with your résumé, knowing what he or she wants, but scanning the résumé for other items that hold promise. Just as the diner looks first at the entrée, so too, does the hiring manager look first at your experience. This is one of the first steps in seeing if the candidate has what is necessary to fill the void in the organization.

Gabriel Ornelas, director of special events at Ragsdale Center, St. Edward's University in Austin, Texas, says that, when reading a résumé, she looks for "a progression of work, but also a body of work that is diverse in experience, that reflects an ability to take something on and be able to learn what is not known. Supervisory experience is always a plus, as it reflects the ability to deal with people and make hard decisions, which is necessary with special events."

The Beverage

Next, the hiring manager looks at education. Think about going to a restaurant that only serves soft drinks, ice tea, and coffee but has as an entrée Prime Rib. Expectation for that meal is not high if it is being served at a diner. However, let's say there is a little bistro that offers wine and beer, which on your résumé would be some level of education or training. This would mean that its Prime Rib might have an expectation that is a bit higher. Well, there is a very nice restaurant with a full-service bar and a selection of wines. As the beverage selection enhances the diner's experience, so does a college diploma impress the hiring manager. Like the finest and most expensive wines, graduate degrees will impress the hiring manager even more, although they will also be more expensive to obtain.

Greg Bell, Talent Relations Director for Walt Disney Parks and Resorts summed up his thoughts on résumés by stating, "It is my experience that an employer wants to see honesty. Basing a résumé on honesty and integrity will speak mountains to an employer. In fact, a good employer will look at those two qualities as a long term investment in a future employee, over a person that may list experience and talk a slick game." Greg says, "It is the responsibility of the applicant to list relevant experience which will help the employer to make the best decision, and to be able to cite examples that back-up those items on a résumé."

The Appetizer

Within the context of the menu, the appetizer is what starts out the meal, and on the résumé it is what starts out the relationship with the hiring manager. This issue of the "objective" has been discussed, but it is suggested that this statement establishes a mission of what the candidate can do for the company, not what the company has to do for the candidate. It is also suggested that the statement clearly lets the hiring manager know what the candidate is seeking. Too often it is: "A job in the special events industry with a company that will provide long-term advancement opportunities." On the menu, that might read: "Come here often and spend a lot so we can be in business for a long time."

The objective should speak to the mission and goal the candidate has in relationship to the company. Words in the objective like "seeking" and "pursuing" are better and stronger than "looking" and "wanting," as they show greater determination in making a connection to this type of position. Target the need but focus on using experience or training to serve the needs of the company that is fulfilling the needs of customers or clients.

Example of a Good Objective

Seeking an internship with Flag Ship Productions utilizing training and experience in show productions as a coordinator of talent and technical staff, to be a part of the team that engages and motivates clients and their guests.

Gene's Résumé Menu

1234 Career Path   Home: (123) 456–7890
Fulfillment, USA   Cell: (987) 654–3210
                   E-mail: gene@genecolumbus.com

Appetizers = Objective: (The third thing read)

(Your mission—first impression, and what you can do for hiring manager)

   Wonderful, tantalizing items prepared by well-trained chef for your taste buds served in a delightful and memorable manner.

Entrees = Experience (The first thing read)

(Company—then the position you held)   (Date)
   Note: We read from left to right. Start with most important, plus start with most recent.

- Beef (Company) The Finest Dining Experience Anywhere
   o Meatball Supreme Master Cook $9.99 (Position)
   o Tossed Green Salad and Baked Garlic Bread (Duties and Responsibilities)

   (Descending order of importance)

- Chicken (Company)   An Excellent $8.88
                       Place to Dine
   o Judy's Chicken Surprise Assistant Cook (Position)
   o Served the rice and vegetables (Duties and Responsibilities)
- Sea Food (Company) Sea The Best
   o Kat's Meow Seafood Platter $7.77
     Server (Position)
   o Served crisp lettuce and cocktail sauce (Duties and Responsibilities)
   o Volunteer experience is generally unpaid – this section is for paid and volunteer experience is under coffee below.

Gene's Résumé Menu (*Continued*)

BEVERAGES = EDUCATION (THE SECOND THING READ)

- Fine Wines (Graduate Degree) $7.77
- Full Bar (Degree) $5.55
- Wine and Beer (Some College) $4.44
- Soft Drinks, Coffee, Tea, and Milk
  (High School) $2.22
- Cool Tap Water (Needed Training) $1.11

DESSERTS = SPECIAL SKILLS (THE FOURTH THING READ)

(Rounds out the meal and leaves a wonderful taste)

- Mega Byte Pound Cake (Computer
  skills with programs) $3.33
- French and Italian Sorbet (Languages) $3.33
- Shakespeare's Bread Pudding
  (Other skills) $3.33

COFFEE = COMMUNITY OR VOLUNTEER ACTIVITIES (THE FIFTH THING READ)

(An additional way of gaining experience or giving back)

- Colombian Coffee (Children's
  Community Centers)   FREE

Dessert

Desserts round out the meal just like special skills round you out as a person. I must check out the desserts before making my selections for the meal and might forgo the baked potato so that there is room for the cheesecake. Desserts round you out (in more ways than one), and it is that final part of the meal that is ever so sweet. On your résumé, the desserts are those things that round you out as a candidate. It is where we find those language skills or other skills that others might not have. What are the special things you do that not everyone can do? Do you play the piano, speak a second language, write short stories, or work in watercolors? Many of those activities are done for enjoyment and often are overlooked for the résumé because they are things you enjoy and do not think of as skills.

"Interests" is another area that is open for discussion as to how appropriate it is on your résumé. You may be an experienced photographer, and most special events companies like photo documentation, so there would be a very good reason for including this as an area of interest. Favorite books and movies, on the other hand, are not of any interest to hiring managers, and are inappropriate for your résumé.

Tea and Coffee

Tea and coffee keep you awake at night, and on the menu/résumé of experience, the coffees are those things that you do as a volunteer. When unable to sell your services, give them away, and in the process, help others and learn first-hand how to manage events. This was covered earlier, but it is worth repeating. There are many opportunities to make an impact in the community and learn a great deal while performing a labor of love.

A "Summary" is sometimes recommended at the top of the résumé as an alternative to an objective. Once again, there seems to be a temptation to use buzzwords to fill this space. The summary seems best suited for a senior-level position where a capsule of achievements can be listed. However, the summary may also be very valuable to those with experiences that need to be highlighted quickly.

Steven Wood Schmader, president and CEO of International festivals and Events Association (IFEA) states the following:

> I don't like to see 'inflated' résumés that try to project experience that isn't real. I would rather see a statement of a sincere willingness to work, learn and grow. I look for the candidate that lists time on the "Trash Pick-Up" Committee vs. how many companies they have run. I prefer to see hands-on experience in our field if possible—even in a volunteer capacity—that says they understand the realities of our industry. And I believe that one of the most important skills you can have is the ability to write effectively and persuasively. Communication is critical—both verbal and written. Technology familiarity is almost expected today; multiple languages are valuable, but not yet critical to all events; and education is only as good as the student receiving it. I am more influenced by "who" taught them than where they went to school or what classes they took. "Who" tells me the value of what they learned. For that reason, references are also very important.

Sherry Student

sherry@sherrystudent.com (123) 456–7890

SUMMARY

- Dean's list student in Special Events Management
- Student Advisor to University president
- ISES student representative to the Greater County Chapter

More Résumé Recommendations

How many pages or how long should the résumé be? Many people in the industry feel everything should be on one page. Of course, one page would be nice if it contained all the necessary information. Résumés are easier to read on two pages since the one-page résumé is jammed full of information, and a small font makes it very hard to read. However, if a student just graduating from college has a three-page résumé, there is far too much information and it should be edited.

The recommended font is one that has no serif. Decorate the résumé with your experience and qualifications, not with a fancy font. Stick with Arial or Helvetica fonts. They are recommended because they provide a clean, sharp, and professional business look for your résumé. Also, they are available in almost any word-processing software. You want to avoid fonts such as Calibri, for example—a nice clean font, but one that might not open on all computers. Avoid fancy fonts that make it hard to read. It is best to keep it simple and easy to read.

Be sure to save your Word documents in .doc rather than .docx to ensure that all Word users can open your documents. Students tend to upgrade computers and programs more often than companies.

Font size should be 11 to 12 points, but no smaller than 10 point. If information such as your contact information is too small to read, the hiring manager may be unable or unwilling to make the effort to search for other ways to contact you.

List in chronological order:

- List work experience with the most recent first, and then work your way back. Over time, you will begin to drop off those jobs you had in high school and college. This allows the interviewer to see where the candidate is at this point and the experience that led up to the current role.
- *Note*: If the candidate is still in school or has very little experience, it is best to place "Education" above "Experience," as it shows the interviewer what the candidate has been doing most recently.

Grades on résumés should be included with fresh graduates:

- Information on grades and college honors are very relevant as a recent graduate and to show the level of commitment you had in school. After you are well into your career, you can eliminate the grades but retain information concerning honors. As you gain more experience, you will be measured by how successful you are in your performance on the job.

Put your name on page two:

- Place your name on page two at the top of the second page, as we read from top to bottom. Of course, there is still the debate regarding the need for a second page.

Number your pages:

- The goal of the person writing the résumé is to make it easy for the reader and if your résumé requires more pages it is suggested that it be: page 2 of 4, page 3 of 4 and page 4 of 4. It is easy to get pages out of order.

Send in a full-size envelope:

- When a résumé is sent in a standard envelope, the fold is always in a bad spot. A full-size upgraded envelope with a typed label and returned address should be used. The manila envelopes do not make the same positive impression as a matching color or white envelope. The advantage is that your documents look better when being read without the fold.

Always send a cover letter when mailing:

- This is a rule that should never be broken, as the letter can provide the hiring manager with information well beyond what is on the résumé.
- Andrea Michaels, president of Extraordinary Events, says, "Clear communication with no improper grammar, spelling mistakes, punctuation mistakes, and so on. That means they care about detail." Share clear, concise communication without bragging. Andrea says, "If they compliment former employers and acknowledge what they have learned from them, I also see respect and gratitude. And humility is important."

Include all your contact numbers:

- You can make it easy for the hiring manager to call or e-mail by providing all your contact information. Sometimes hiring managers get that urge to call a candidate because of something in their packet or because you might be an ideal person for an upcoming position. It happens all the time, so you should be sure to include all contact information.

Proofread the document:

- Some hiring managers will disregard a candidate if there are spelling mistakes. Use spell check, but better yet, have someone proofread all your materials. It is all about first impressions.

Using numbers and italics:

- Write out numerals up to "ten" and then use numerals from "11" on. It is suggested that italics not be used on your résumé, as that can "confuse" scanners and some e-mail attachments.

Using templates:

- Computer templates work fine if you are looking for a job in the fast-food industry, but not if you are seeking a position as a professional in an industry. The templates have very small contact information that is very difficult to read, and in some cases the header actually drops off the computer screen. If you should use a computer template, e-mail the résumé to yourself to see if the document reads as it was written, as well as to someone with a smart phone (Blackberry or iPhone) to see how easy it is to read on their device.

Avoid using abbreviations:

- Abbreviations should be avoided, and professional and technical information used when relevant. To simplify dates, the month and year are acceptable, with your most recent position being listed as 10/2009 to present.

Provide information on skills and achievements:

- Using the correct action verb as well as special events language is very important and requires that you review current and past duties and responsibilities. The goal is to show that you get positive results from your efforts. Quantify and qualify using statistics, percentages, and numbers:
  - "Responsible for . . . group of 20 volunteers coordinating with 900 guests."
  - "Increased . . . revenue by 33% in coffee sales by including a cookie."
  - "Supervised . . . tech crew of nine persons setting up lighting for New Year's Eve Party."
  - "Developed . . . the exhibit hall plan for 100 vendors, including all power requirements."
  - "Analyzed . . . annual chair rental budget of $5,000."

Rob Murphy, chief marketing officer of MC2, observes the following:

I look for people who have proven experience in getting things done in an environment where there are few, if any, set rules. I gravitate towards folks who can improvise under pressure and never look as if they were challenged. This means I look for résumés that are not every day, standard 9-5 jobs. I respect service industry experience like waiting tables, tending bar, working a customer service hotline, military experience, road crews for bands or theater production. All these require working with many people and getting jobs done.

Frank Supovitz, senior vice president of events for the National Football League (NFL), observes:

Special Events is a very broad and diverse industry. What employers want to see on a résumé is experience that is relevant to their business. As a sports event organizer, I like to see exposure to events that are similar in philosophy, if not scale and scope. Experience comes in many shapes and sizes. For an entry level position, volunteering to work on events at one's college, for a not-for-profit group that runs marathons or tournaments, even Boy Scout camping events, gives me a sense that someone has been involved with programs that require attention to detail, project management, and time management. Another great place to get that experience is to intern for a sports organization on game nights. This is especially valuable when going for jobs that are just above entry-level. Finally, membership in an events industry organization like ISES, is a great asset on a résumé.

Avoid using personal pronouns:

- Avoid using "I, my, and me" on a résumé. Instead of "I chaired my Student Parliament," write, "Chaired Student Parliament of Queen Margaret University."
- Another word to only use carefully is "all," such as "Supervise all employees" or "all invoices are my responsibility."

Do not include pictures and other personal information on résumés:

- There are a great many laws protecting candidates from discrimination, and the taking of photos is one of those rules the interviewer must follow. Questions about a candidate's race, religion, quality of health, marital status, or number of children are not permitted. By including that information on a résumé, you might indicate that you are unaware of these laws, which reflects poorly on your level of job experience. Because photos reveal this private demographic information, they should generally only be included when requested.

Protect your Social Security number:

- Never place your social security number on a résumé that will be freely passed around. This information should only be given upon request in a secure document.

Use special paper:

- Hiring managers receive lots of written materials, and most of it comes on standard 20-pound white paper. Taking the time to get an upgraded or thicker paper will have the feel of higher quality than most other documents the hiring manager is receiving. All of your materials should represent you in a positive manner.
- Many times the résumé is shared with other members of the team. Paper should be plain. The best way to check the results is to make a copy. That will show what your résumé will look like when copied or faxed. Some high-quality paper with watermarks looks wonderful, but if copied, it might look like you spilt coffee on it.

Provide references:

- As already stated, it is recommended that references be placed on a separate sheet and not included on the first page of a résumé. Include the contact information of your reference and your relationship. Inform your references of who, when, and what you are making application so they are prepared to help you if they are contacted. It is best to do this verbally, as well as sending a written message by e-mail or regular mail.

As candidates venture into the special events industry, they will find that many employers prefer people with experience and might take someone just because they have more experience than you. However, you have an advantage as you are still in the process of learning and growing and have not developed bad habits. The secret is to sell your potential by being a willing learner with an open mind to take on new things.

Knowing that most hiring managers only scan your documents, you must make sure your information is formatted in such a way that it is very easy for them to get the needed information they are seeking. Take your résumé to your mentor and ask that he or she tell you what stands out as your greatest strength and what are those things that you could make clearer. The résumé is a living document, as it represents you and the constant change taking place in your life. Over time, you will discover other really unique things to place on your résumé that truly represent you.

Cover Letters

The cover letter ranks up there with having to answer the interview question, "Tell me about yourself." To suggest that it is a simple formula that you can get out of this book or download online is false. If it were easy, there would not be so many poorly written cover letters. I would estimate that only about 20 percent of the letters I received at Disney were right on target. The greatest tendency was candidates repeating what was on the résumé and asking what kind of job openings were available. The really short letters just informed me that they were sending me their résumé, which was pretty obvious.

There should be three to four paragraphs in a formal letter format. The header should not be the same as your résumé, but should look like personalized stationery, with your name and contact information at the top of the page. We read from top to bottom, and it is helpful to the readers if they know who the letter is from without looking at the bottom first. So often, the letters start with "My name is . . ." and it is generally on the page as well as at the bottom for signature. The other phrase often used is "I am writing this letter . . ." which of course is also very obvious. It is very hard to come up with those commanding "first words" to get the attention of the reader. Let us break down the letter into three parts: the introduction/connection, the agenda, and the call to action.

The ideal way to launch your relationship with the hiring manager is to demonstrate that you know something about the organization. This is where your research really comes into play. It should have the tone of what you do for the company, not what the company should do for you.

First Paragraph Example

Dear Hiring Manager

It was exciting to learn that Exceptional Events was responsible for the annual Fourth of July Spectacular. Audience members were moved emotionally by the performing artist and I was intrigued by each element that your team blended together seamlessly. Event coordinator, Carrie Professional, was most gracious and allowed me to stand near enough to see fireworks preparations. Congratulations, and thank you for what was an amazing and memorable event.

Note that there was limited use of "I" and "me" in this first paragraph. It could be longer and include more information, but the goal is to demonstrate that you have knowledge of the organization. So often, letters are written with phrases like, "I am graduating and I am looking for an internship. I got very good grades and I am a very hard worker. I will be home most afternoons so you can call me."

Your agenda is more about you and what you are seeking from the company. This is the part of the letter that focuses on you.

Example of paragraph two—the agenda

This spring I will be completing my undergraduate degree in Hospitality Management and seeking an internship. Carrie recommended contacting you to arrange an informational interview to learn more about the various opportunities with Exceptional Events. With classes only on Tuesdays and Thursdays for the remainder of the semester, concluding the first week of May, I am available to meet at a convenient time for you.

When asking for an appointment, ask only for a half hour because most everyone can find 30 minutes to speak to a candidate. It is a welcome break from all the other duties they generally have during their day. The meeting with a key leader in the special events industry is only a small part of the process of establishing yourself in the business. At each step in your journey of learning, you will have more to share, but you will also have a better understanding of the various topics that could come up in your meeting.

Example of third paragraph—next step

Early next week I will call your office to make arrangements for a half-hour meeting if your schedule permits. Carrie invited me to tour your facility once our meeting time has been arranged. Thank you, and I look forward to speaking to you very soon.

Sincerely,

Sally Student or Adam Aspiring Professional

"The future belongs to those who believe in the beauty of their dreams."

Eleanor Roosevelt,
Former United States First Lady (1884–1962)

You are helping the hiring manager to help you. Your effort of providing the necessary information will determine if it is the right fit for both the company and you. The hiring manager will see the level of investment you have made to learn about their organization and they will be far more likely to hire someone that has a shared passion for the types of events they produce and a passion for the industry.

Career Connections

 ### Action Steps

- Prepare your résumé and a cover letter for a real or imagined job using the events companies researched in the last chapter.
- Tailor each résumé to fit the company and apply for a position you feel you would be best qualified for.
- Write a cover letter to the appropriate person in the company.
- Present the résumé and cover letter to a mentor and ask him or her to proofread it and give feedback.
- Select stationery and full-sized envelopes and create an address label for each sample résumé and letter.
- Make a list and contact those who you wish to be your personal references. Be direct, asking for honest feedback on how they would describe you to a possible employer.
- Review the materials with a teacher, mentor, or industry professional for recommendations.

Practice Activity

Break the class or group into teams of three or four, and based on the letters and résumés, create a list of types of questions that could be expected from the information in these two documents. Create a master list of questions to be reviewed by the class or group to determine the best and most positive way in which to answer the questions.

 ## Tool Kit

Enelow, Wendy S., and Louise Kursmark (2000). *Cover Letter Magic: Trade Secrets of Professional Résumé Writers.* St. Paul, MN: JIST Publishing.

Yate, Martin (2008). *Knock 'em Dead Cover Letters.* Cincinnati, OH: Adams Media.

 ## Web Connection

Create a free account at MPI's Career Connections, available at http://www.mpiweb.org/Marketplace/Careers.aspx.

Once you have an account, look at some of the jobs offered. Find one that interests you and write a résumé tailored to that job. See if you can find the website of the hiring company.

CHAPTER 8

Effective Interviewing

Do a rehearsal interview with a mentor. Afterward, analyze your performance.

When Does the Interview Begin?

This is a very important question, and the answer is that is has already begun, as your reputation precedes you. Your work ethic in school or on the job become key factors, because the interviewer could know someone that knows you and the manner in which you handle responsibility, which could becomes a factor in the selection process. You also reveal what you know and what your standards are in the job interview. Often it is not just what you say but what you do not say that gives the indication of your knowledge, skill level, and experience. Although you may not know when, where, or who will be at the interview for your dream job, you must begin the interview process now by taking charge of your future, making sure you are well prepared to show that you will be an excellent worker.

It is never too late to reposition yourself in a positive direction, knowing that in the long-term it is in your best interest. Be the best student or employee you can be by starting immediately to show others—as well as proving to yourself—that you have what it takes to be successful. You cannot change the past, but you can learn from it, evaluate your past practices, and ask yourself how you can do better. Gradual change is not enough, and might not even be noticed: you must make a stand, committing yourself to becoming the successful person you want to be.

People are like stained-glass windows. They sparkle and shine when the sun is out, but when the darkness sets in; their true beauty is revealed only if there is a light from within.
Elizabeth Kubler-Ross (1926–2004)

Over the years, I have had students make the transformation from trying to keep up with assignments to challenging me to take them to a higher level. I have also been impressed with entry-level managers taking on assignments as if they were vice-presidents of the organization. New standards of excellence are well within your control and are very achievable. In special events, it is said that you are only as good as your last event, and so goes it with what you are currently doing. Your mission should be to rise to a higher level and challenge yourself to set a new personal standard that will precede you in an interview. You will be judged by what you do more than who you are or what you want to be.

> ### Gene-Gem
> Don't let things happen—make them happen!

> ### Gene-Gem
> Cream rises to the top!

In your preparation, you must look at how your skills and knowledge will bring value to the company. Some candidates seeking positions set their sights on a level that may be higher than they are ready for, or that may not be available. They feel that if they hold out, the hiring manager will recognize their special talent and hire them at their desired level. People in the industry will tell you that getting your foot in the door is the first and often the hardest step. Once in the door, show the organization how you can be a great contributor, and then move up the company ladder. If you are repositioning yourself, often you must take a step back in order to take many steps forward in the direction you want to go. You can get to the level you want to be, but expect to invest time and effort, showing at each step that you are ready to take on responsibility when it is given to you.

Dealing with the Past

By investing in learning and training, you are setting yourself up for success. The knowledge and willingness to learn that you are able to offer is what the employer is going to buy. From time to time, you will see that people get hired and are not the right fit, which is bad for both the employee and the employer. This could happen to you, but do not let setback keep you from moving forward. The team dynamic interaction plays an important role in the success of a new team member. You might look good on paper and do very well in the interview; however, there are times in which things do not work out and it is in the interest of the group to move on. In your next job interview, it is very appropriate to share that it was not the right fit, but that you learned a great deal from the experience. Do not blame anyone or say negative things about the company. Most everyone has an experience where things didn't work out but they put it behind them and moved forward, appreciative of having the opportunity to learn from the experience. The interviewer might use words like "fired" or "terminated," and you might reply with the word "left" or "separated" from the company, taking responsibility for your actions but not blaming anyone or anything.

For those repositioning themselves in the industry, perhaps your experience will help you adjust more easily to the needs of the new team, even giving you the opportunity to showcase your leadership. Sometimes it seems no amount of effort can overcome a wrong fit, but they do happen. The dynamics of the team, the expectations of your leader, your own ability to adjust in a new environment can be a factor that can affect your level of success. No matter how this

> **Gene-Gem**
>
> Another word for succession planning is grooming!

turns out, there is much to be learned from both successful and unsuccessful experiences, and in the end, it is best not to make excuses or get defensive about this matter. Be open, honest, and up front about what happened.

The Interview and Your Bridge

In your interview, you might be asked to share your long-term goal, and in most cases, the interviewer/hiring manager should be able to see and understand how you could reach your aspirations. However, if you have a lofty goal or one that seems disconnected to the immediate mission of finding employment in the special events industry, it could be a distraction. Start by stating how this first step will set you off in the right direction of your goal, revealing the master plan. Make sure that it is logical, demonstrating that you have researched how you are going to get from where you are to where you want to be. All things being equal, the hiring manager will select someone to invest in and who will give the greatest level of return to the company.

Example: "My long-term goals are to be involved with large-scale corporate events, but I know it is necessary to get a solid understanding of all the components that go into making the events successful. That is why I am seeking this production assistant position with your company, as it will give me a chance to work with people that are well known and respected in the industry."

If a company is looking for short-term employees and you make it known that you are seeking a long-term goal beyond what might be offered, there might be an interest in having you fill in for a short time or work on a project that has an end date.

Example: "Long-term, I would like very much to be involved with corporate events but for now I am seeking opportunities to gain experience. Weddings are very complex and require a tremendous amount of planning and attention to detail, so these skills will be very transferable, particularly dealing with changes and adjustments during the course of the event."

The interview is that opportunity for you to share what you have done in the past that brought you to where you are today, which demonstrates that you are a viable candidate for the position. The hiring manager is the buyer, and you are the seller, and you are in the interview selling yourself, your skills, and your talent. The mission is to share how you

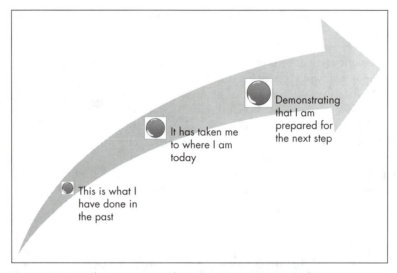

Figure 8.1 A Job Interview is About Your Past, Present and Future

will bring value to the organization, supporting the goals of the company at the direction of your leader.

Phone Interview Preparation

Many companies start with phone interviews to save time and to screen candidates before meeting them face to face. In preparing for your phone interview, review all the job posting information and the research materials you have gathered on the company, as well as having all the materials you shared with the target company in front of you so that you are looking at the same materials as the interviewer/hiring manager. At the top of the page, remind yourself to put a smile in your voice and be just as energized as you would be in a person-to-person interview. Use the same recommended technique for answering questions, being careful to speak clearly and with purpose. Using the following list, set up a spreadsheet in a format that is easy to adjust, and as you learn more about the company or discover issues that might be more relevant, make the necessary changes.

Steps for Planning Your Interview

- Collect as much information on the organization as possible. You will find a great deal on its Web site, and also on the individuals associated with the company. Read carefully the information on the special events those individuals have produced, or for which they were part of the production team.

- Read the job description carefully and write down the duties and responsibilities.
- List the experiences or training you have had that relate to those duties and responsibilities.
- With each item where you have experience, add what challenges you had accomplishing the task.
- Add how you dealt with the challenges.
- Add what you learned from the experience, and what you are most proud of.
- Should the question relate to an issue in which you do not have experience but you have knowledge, share your understanding of the issue, but do not make up an answer.

Be prepared for the following prompts:

1. Tell me about a time in which you were most effective at:
   - Leading a team
   - Solving a complex problem
   - Dealing a someone who did not agree with you
   - Completing a project or assignment that fell behind schedule
   - Overcoming setbacks on a project
   - Dealing with a coworker
   - Dealing with a client/customer
2. Tell me about your background and why you feel you are suited for this position.
3. Tell me why you are interested in being part of the special events industry.

Here are ten suggestions for answering these questions:

1. Paraphrase the question in your response to show that you understand. For example: "A time I was most effective was when . . ."
2. Think of the list you have made and the comparison between your experience, your training, and the job requirements. Since you have taken the time to think about that before the question, you are in a much better position to provide an answer.
3. When possible, give an example that closely demonstrates your experience or training.
4. Present the challenges that you faced. Remember that companies hire problem solvers.
5. Share how you overcame the problem or handled it responsibility.
6. Let the interviewer know what type of results you achieved.
7. What you learned from the experience is also very helpful in defining your values and what you are proud of with your example.
8. If things did not go as well as you might have liked, that can also be a very good example to share.

9. When finished, you can wrap it up by paraphrasing the question: "That was a time when I was most effective at. . . ."

10. Say no more, so the hiring manager knows that you have completed the answer.

EXAMPLE INTERVIEW ANSWER

Interviewer: Tell me a time in which you were particularly effective at painting a house.

Candidate:

Step 1: Paraphrasing the question: "A time in which I was effective at painting a house was . . ."

Step 2: (Use this moment to think of your list created as part of the preinterview planning.)Select and share an example: "I began painting houses as side-line, an opportunity to gain business experience providing quality service to a client.

Step 3: I received an invitation to bid on the home of a city official based on a past client's recommendation. My bid was not the lowest, but the client was very clear on wanting quality work. I was awarded the bid, but in the contract there was a five-day period in which the job had to be completed."

Step 4: Share the problem or challenge you faced in accomplishing the assignment: "As start date for the project got closer, the weather forecasted a hurricane possibly coming our way.

Step 5: Share how you overcame the problems: "I contacted the other painters in the area that did similar work, some of whom were my competition, and asked if they would work with me to accomplish the job in a much shorter time. I put together the team, knowing we needed painters who were very good at trim work and the others that could work quickly but do quality work on the walls. On the evening before starting the project, our team met to review the plan, and for me to get suggestions on ensuring the best result in the shortest amount of time. We all learned something from each other that night. Early the next morning, the team arrived before sunrise to lay out drop cloths and get the materials ready. As the sun came up, painting started; however, I made sure everyone had what they needed to do the job, and that we were being consistent with the application of the paint, then I joined painting walls.

At lunch time I was planning to take the crew to the local sub sandwich shop, but the owner said they had lunch planned for us. They served the best fried chicken I have ever eaten. The owners provided refreshments like iced tea and water to the crew. We completed the job in two days, and on the morning of the third day, we cleaned up and checked to see if we had missed anything."

Step 6: Share the results: "The owners were so happy that they gave us a bonus." (This is where most candidates would end, but if you add what you learned, it gives you the opportunity to tie things together.)

Step 7: What you learned: "As the crew and I reflected on how well we worked together, it became obvious that we could be much more successful if we worked together. I was a good up-front person who enjoys dealing with the clients and planning the project, while the other members of the team are very skilled at their craft and love what they do, so over time we all did so much better."

This is for bonus points: "By the way, that hurricane that was headed our way blew out to sea and there was no property damage for anyone."

Step 8: If things did not work out it would still provide an example and what you learned from the experience.

Step 9: Make it clear that you have completed your answer and by closing the loop with "And that was a time in which I was effective at painting a house."

Step 10: Another method of ending your answer is by saying nothing more.

Although the example is a bit long, it demonstrates the process. The interviewer learns a number of things about you beyond hearing that you know how to paint a house. You shared your commitment to customer relations and quality service. The interviewer also learned the reason you were considered for the project was a reference from a satisfied customer. In your leadership role you reached out and developed partnerships with others in your field because it was best for the client. That you were going to take your crew to lunch tells the interviewer that you look after your people but because of your exceptional relationship skills with the client, they provided lunch for your team. You also demonstrated strategic thinking in showing that everyone did better working as a team, plus you have shown good character in being happy that no one had property damage as a result of the hurricane blowing out to sea.

Your spreadsheet would look something like Figure 8.2 with the example of painting a house.

Talking About Yourself

Candidates often shared that any questions in which they had to talk about themselves were the hardest to answer. You are not alone, and should understand that in our society, it is considered rude to talk about yourself, and from your earliest childhood you have been trained not to be rude. One system to overcome this is to write a brief autobiography and then make bullet points to outline your journey. There is no need to start with "I was born at a young age and grew so that my feet always reached the ground." Go back to the fundamentals of what the interview is really all about: "This is what I have done in the past to bring me to this point, which demonstrates that my training and experience make me suitable for the position that I am seeking."

This simple approach must be delivered with energy, enthusiasm, and passion. The interviewer is looking for the "burn," and the interview is the spark to light the fire of success.

Those interviewing you will see that, when speaking about things you love, your energy level goes up, your excitement about sharing your experience becomes more intense, and you become more animated. Many candidates are very businesslike in their manner

Duties and Responsibilities	Example	Challenge	Overcoming Challenge	Results	What I Learned	Why I Am Proud
Painting a house	Small business doing quality work—Customer service	Five-day window, but dealing with a hurricane	Partnered with others—maintaining quality	Done ahead of schedule—formed new partnerships	Better results as a team	Team more successful and no property damage

Figure 8.2 Spreadsheet on Overcoming a Challenge

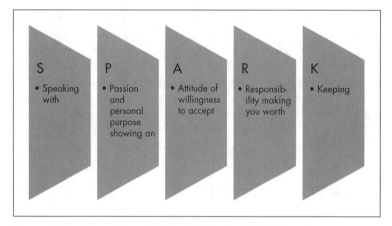

Figure 8.3 Gene Columbus Special Events BURN Model

of answering questions, as if a police officer were questioning them about an accident. Hiding behind cold facts does not let the interviewer get to know you or how you might fit into the team. Think back to a time when you were a lot younger and someone asked you what you wanted to be when you grew up. You may not be anywhere close to that type of position, but there was something that attracted you to that role. Be enthusiastic.

My personal example: When I was about five or six years old, I was walking down the street with my mother and suddenly there was a loud noise and a bell ringing. A very big door opened up and we stood back far enough to be out of the way, but I could see inside the building. There was a big red truck and men were sliding down poles and quickly putting on big boots, a big heavy raincoat, and then firemen's helmets. They jumped on the truck as it pulled out of the building and one of the firemen waved at me. I turned to my mom and said, "When I grow up, that's what I want to be!" The fact is, I had no interest in going off to fight a fire, but I loved the orchestrated way everything was choreographed, with everyone knowing what they were suppose to do. It was exciting, well-planned, and everyone around was completely captivated.

Of course, I might never use that in an interview, but it helped me as I moved forward in my journey of learning. Perhaps you should think back and write your story:

- "When I was ten years old I thought I'd like to be . . .
- but at thirteen I learned . . .
- then at sixteen I discovered . . .
- and at twenty-one I was on my way to being . . .
- now at this point in my life I look back thinking that I have always wanted to Sfollow my dream, and that dream is . . ."

Show your passion and the steps you have taken or are taking to pursue your dreams.

You know your story better than anyone and can tell it better than anyone. Rehearse what you will say so that you are not trying to come up with what to say when you are under the pressure of the interview. It does not need to be long—it should be no more than a minute to a minute and a half. That is why the bullet points are so helpful.

> **Gene-Gem**
>
> You get about 10 to 12 minutes of quality time in the half-hour interview to demonstrate that you are the right person for the job—don't spend most of that time sharing how much your dog loves you!

Establish a Theme

Over time you will learn that you can develop a theme for your interview, which becomes an anchor so that you do not go too far off your course. Research the organization for its mission and you will find that it is about helping others. I have yet to see a company mission that is: "To have people pay a lot of money to make my company successful with a minimum of effort while they love everything we do."

Themes can be as simple as:

- "Always doing what is best for the client," particularly if you are seeking a customer-service role.
- "Always providing the finest in quality," if you are seeking a more creative role.
- "It's all about the team," for leadership roles.
- "It is all about the plan," if event planning is part of the responsibility.

As you look at the job requirements, you will see key areas of responsibility, and that will provide you with various topics to use for your theme. As you answer that first question, you can include your theme. That theme is most helpful for answering the typical last question, which is, "Do you have any questions?" Your questions can relate to your theme.

The other popular final questions might be, "Is there anything else you would like to share?" This gives you the opportunity to close the loop on the theme that you began with in your first answers.

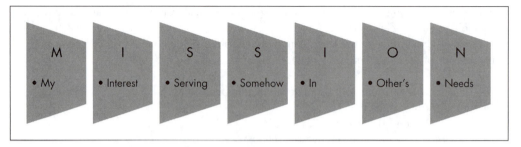

Figure 8.4 Gene Columbus Special Events MISSION Model

Here is one example of a final statement: "My current plan is to finish my degree and begin the next phase of my education, which is applying what I have learned in a professional environment. Our discussion has confirmed the overwhelming need to develop a strong plan and implement the plan. As a person who loves details, this role is very exciting, and one in which I could learn and expand my skills as a planner."

What the Interviewer Looks For

There are a number of things that interviewers look for in a candidate, and I will share my top ten:

1. Responsibility—If candidates do not demonstrate that they are willing and able to be responsible for their actions, then it is likely they will not be successful at duties assigned to them.
2. Accountability—Being accountable for your actions is part of responsibility, and often "fixing blame rather than fixing problems" is like a cancer in a team. If you are wrong, admit it and learn from it.
3. Holding others accountable—This is key in leadership, and too often it is thought to be confrontational; many people have difficulty dealing with confrontation. However, if expectations have been established, then accountability is more of a checking-in on progress.
4. Honesty—Nothing has a longer life than a lie. Spinning things so that you look good could backfire, and if you are not being honest and the word gets out, no one will trust you.
5. Truth—Use care on how you dispense the truth. Sometime the truth hurts, and telling someone they are "fat" may be true, but it is often unkind and hurtful.
6. Humor—An important factor, but humor should never be at the expense of anyone, including you.
7. Trust—It can be measured in an interview by how you characterize your peers, former employees, teachers, and so on. Trust is earned, but inexperienced candidates are usually trusted until they give reasons for not trusting them.

8. Communication—It's most of what you are doing in your interview, and if you have a good plan and have done your research, you will be in the best position to communicate in a positive manner.

9. Partnering—This is so important for being a member of a team. "I'd rather do it myself to make sure it is done correctly," sends bad signals that you believe that everyone must prove to you that they are up to your standards.

10. Courage—This is a key ingredient, as you must have the courage to say and do what is right.

What the Professionals Ask

In preparation for this book, I contacted a number of special events professionals, asking them what they looked for in a candidate and what type of response they expected to certain questions.

- Josh McCall, chairman and CEO of Jack Morton Worldwide, looks for "People Skills . . . Great attention to detail . . . A passion for creativity and a vision to see a concept through to execution . . . A high degree of empathy and an ability to understand how to create an emotional connection with different audiences." He says, "Our founder, Jack Morton, always told me that you should never be afraid to ask for people's help in business and in life."

- Andrea Michaels, president of Extraordinary Events, shared a list of questions she asks all candidates:
  1. What do you know about my company?
  2. Who do you think our competitors are?
  3. What experience have you had?
  4. What did you like most about your last position?
  5. What did you like least about your last position?
  6. What is your greatest skill/asset?
  7. What do you least like doing?
  8. What's the best event you've ever seen, and why?
  9. What do you do to educate yourself?
  10. If you were a movie, which movie would you be?

- Frank Supovitz, senior vice president of events for the National Football League (NFL) asks these questions: Tell me about a tough spot you were in and how you dealt with it. When every detail is important, how would you prioritize issues that need solving? What do you imagine your career will be like in 5 years? In 10?

- Michael Goldman, senior executive producer for ProActive, Inc. and Freeman Creative Group, has these questions for the candidates. Are you Mac and PC fluent? Which do you prefer, and why? Are you equally able to deal with a nervous client and an angry teamster? Do you agree that sleep is overrated?

- Gabriel Ornelas, director of Ragsdale Center at St Edward's University feels these questions help him better understand the candidate: How do you deal with last-minute changes and stress? Why do you want to do this specific job? What does this job represent to you? If you don't get this position, what is your next step? Why us?

- Greg Bell, talent relations director for Walt Disney Parks and Resorts, provided this comprehensive list:
  1. Tell me a little bit about yourself, specifically relating to your special events background. Looking for: 90 seconds or less, a short career path, influences, and passion.
  2. Tell me about your last project or a recent project and the scope and scale of that event, as well as your responsibilities. Looking for: project scope and scale with hopes that this will provide topics to explore further in the interview.
  3. Tell me about a difficult client and what those issues were. Looking for: challenge identification, problem solving.
  4. What is your process for building and leading your special events team? Looking for: team building and leadership skills, including building and maintaining agenda items and deadlines.
  5. What is the most successful event you have worked on, and what made it successful? Looking for: passion, scope, and communication.
  6. What is more important in a project: budget, timeline, or client wishes, and why? This is a trick question, and one that separates the professionals from the experienced. A professional knows that all three of these elements are crucial. A person with limited experience will try and figure out what might be important to the person asking the question and will probably choose budget, as that, by itself, is a lower-level consideration with short-term results.
  7. What have we not spoken about that is important for me to know? Looking for: items that the candidate thinks are important for me to know and that I did not ask.
- Tammy Bowman, executive producer with Automotive Marketing Consultants Inc., shared this information: "I want to know about the types of events they have done as well as their responsibilities for those events. For example, if they were a production coordinator and had to wrangle travel and schedules and pay the bills, which tells me that this person is detailed, organized and good at multitasking. If those tasks frustrated them, then they may be a person that works hard but needs to have a more focused task. I can also tell what they like, don't like, and if they are a team player or not. I will explain the available roles, the project and the tasks at hand."
- Rob Murphy, chief marketing officer with MC2, covered a number of types of positions, saying, "It really depends on the job function. With designers, I need to know about how they approach a challenge and the thinking that they apply to it. Their process and skill levels are most important. Project managers need top organizational skills. Account managers need a 'politically correct' nature as they need to make everyone happy on both sides. Field people need tenacity and strong leadership skills. I would base my questions on uncovering these strengths."

- Richard Aaron CMP, CSEP, president of BizBash Media, asks these questions: "How would your prioritize these certain tasks (I offer up a list of several) presented in your day if you had to? How do you relax, and what are your favorite non-work activities?"
- Steven Wood Schmader, CFEE, president and CEO of International Festivals & Events Association (IFEA), has this list of questions: "Tell me why you chose to apply for our job? What did you see in us? What do you think you can gain from working here? What do you think you can bring to the job? What makes you qualified for the position being offered? Tell me about your experience. Share with me some of your best and worst jobs and job responsibilities, and what made them good or bad. What did you learn from those experiences? What are your long-term career goals?"
- Carolyn S. Baragona, owner/vice president of *Event Solutions* magazine and trade-show, has a flexible approach: "After discussion of our goals, I want to know what the other person's vision for the event is. Then . . . how much will it cost?"

As your read what these successful special events professionals have to say about the interview, you will see that they want to know about you, your experience, and what you can do to help make their organization more successful. The questions are about you, but it really comes down to what you do and how you do it.

Career Connections

 Action Steps

- Write a bio, bullet-point it, and practice with a mentor or team member to answer the question "Tell me about yourself," in 60 to 90 seconds. Focus on what you do more than who you are.
- Make a list of steps you feel you will have to take over the next five years to achieve the goals you set for yourself in the timeline. Share this information in 30 to 60 seconds with your mentor or team member.
- Develop answers to the questions "Tell me a time in which you were effective at . . ." earlier in this chapter. Practice giving the answers to your mentor or team member.
- Practice turning a negative question into a positive answer.
  - *Tell me about your weaknesses.*
    We all have areas of development, and mine is the need for more experience contrasting with my desire to learn.
  - *Tell me about a time in which you failed to meet a deadline.*
    Deadlines are a key part of the special events industry, and I have to say I have been lucky enough to work with a remarkable team who have always made our deadlines.

○ *Tell me about what you would like to avoid in your job.*
Since my goal is to learn as much as possible, I would rather not avoid anything, as I am sure there is much to learn from every experience.
○ *Tell me about a time in which you disagreed with the person in charge.*
I would not characterize it as a disagreement because I learned a great deal from a person in charge. She was wonderful, and as much as I wanted to help she said it was easier to do it herself. Rather than learn by doing, I learned by watching.
○ *Tell me about a time in which your ethics were challenged.*
There was a situation where someone was doing something that she knew was wrong and her excuse was that "everybody does it!" My reply was that we are not everybody, we are somebody—somebody that always does the right thing.

 ## Practice Activity

Choose five questions from those quoted from professionals. Now plan an answer to each question according to the question-answering strategy outlined in this chapter. Ask your mentor or a friend to pretend to interview you with your five questions, and answer them as professionally as you would in an interview.

 ## Tool Kit

Gottesman, Deb (1999). *The Interview Rehearsal Book.* New York: The Berkley Publishing Group.
Powers, Paul (2005). *Winning Job Interviews.* New Jersey: The Career Press.

 ## Web Connection

Career One Stop, a Web site promoted by the U.S. Department of Labor, offers some tips on interviews here: http://www.careeronestop.org/ResumesInterviews.

CHAPTER 9

Interview Etiquette

We know how the hiring manager reads our résumé, so it is time for us to create our résumé.

The word *etiquette* refers to the manners as required by society that are often not written, but which everyone is expected to follow. You may have certain rules of the road in your interactions and communications with others, both in your private and professional life, and you may be considered rude if you do not follow these manners. In this chapter, we explore a number of ways in which you can enhance your image with proper written communications, being appropriately dressed, and displaying manners in a business meal, with some great advice from industry professionals.

Fundamentals of Résumé Writing

In an earlier chapter you learned how the hiring manager reads your résumé as well as a format in which to create that document. The following bullets summarize some basic guidelines that will help you to create your résumé:

- Your résumé establishes the first impression with the potential employer, and its purpose is to get you an interview.
- Your résumé must be easy to read, as the hiring manager will only spend a very short amount of time looking over your document.
- Your résumé advertises your skills and what you can do for the company.
- Make your résumé chronological, with the most recent work experience listed first.
- If you are in school, or recently completed your education, place that information above experience, as it is the most recent activity.
- If you lack, or have limited experience, begin now to get involved with activities that provide an exposure to the field and provide items for your résumé.

- If you have experience, it should be highlighted with the name of the company, title of the position and level of responsibilities you had, plus measurable achievements or accomplishments.
- You should include any certifications that you may have or are in the process of obtaining.
- Include any professional affiliations such as ISES or MPI.
- Place references on a separate sheet to be given upon request, but do not include their names and contact information on your résumé.
- Do not include any information regarding salary expectations or history of the wages you have earned.
- Exclude issues related to ethnic background, marital status, national origin, or sexual orientation.
- Include your contact information, including cell phone number, as well as your e-mail address to make it easy to contact you.
- Use good judgment in providing your home address. If you are a college student, consider providing your "permanent address" as the home of your family. Students can also acquire a post office box (P.O. box) at the college or university.
- Establish a professional e-mail address if you do not already have one. You might establish a dedicated e-mail address to place on your résumé and cover letter. Check with your e-mail provider for a free account from companies like yahoo .com or gmail.com.
- Résumés do not use complete sentences but rather phases. Use precise verbs like "directed," "organized," or "developed."
- Send your résumé to a smart phone—which is what some hiring managers use to read their messages—including attachments, to see how your résumé looks in that format.

Recommended verbs related to communications:

Arrange	Developed	Informed	Unified
Addressed	Designed	Led	Persuaded
Authored	Drafted	Motivated	Presented
Assisted	Edited	Monitored	Publicized
Composed	Explained	Negotiated	Published
Conferred	Formulated	Navigated	Sustained
Corresponded	Focused	Originated	Wrote
Clarified			

- When sharing information about your contribution to your former employer, it should relate to the positive impact you had with the company: Increase in sales or profitability, creation of new business, productivity, better communications, higher standards of service, development of new skills, and so on.
- List extracurricular activities you have been involved with during your time in school, including clubs and community projects.

- Provide any experience with international studies (including when, where, how long, and what you did), including Peace Corps or missionary work.
- Foreign language skills are very marketable but be clear about your level of fluency. Note whether you have "moderate" skills, if you can read the language, and if you are fluent or conversational. Also, indicate if you are bilingual.
- Include computer skills and your level of proficiency such as knowledgeable, familiar, proficient, or highly proficient.
- If you have served in the military, provide the branch, your highest rank, when you served decorations or awards and any special training you received that might apply to the position you are seeking.
- In the special events industry there is a need to do presentations, so if you have experience speaking or doing presentations in front of a group, include that information.
- Many résumés use "work experience" as a category. It is recommended that you drop the four-letter word "work" and just use "experience."
- Think about keywords rather than buzzwords when writing and speaking about your long-term goals in the industry.

Accountability	Honesty	Quality service
Benchmarking	Integrity	Sales initiatives
Communications	Leadership	Strategic thinking
Consensus	Long-range planning	Team development
Creativity	Multitasking	Value added
Decision making	Problem solving	

- Do not use abbreviations unless they are certifications, such as PhD, MFA, MBA, CMP, CFEE, or CSEP.
- Make a list of your references with your relationship to them, such as teacher, coworker, former employer, family friend, and so on. Proved their contact information, making sure they are informed of possible calls. You should let your references know to which company and position you have applied, to prepare them to speak about you in a positive manner.
- Many hiring managers hire a person with a good attitude before hiring someone just because they have experience, which means potential is a key criterion in the selection process.
- Experienced hiring managers look not just at what you have done but also what you are capable of doing in the future.
- Qualities hiring managers look for are enthusiasm, energy, optimism, persistence, resilience, empathy, and persuasiveness. With preparation you will have the confidence to demonstrate these qualities.
- Have your mentor check your materials carefully.
- Share with your mentor the check list you have created for yourself in preparing your résumé and cover letter.

"A good résumé reflects the level of the person's experience, gives specific facts and numbers and shows how the candidate's experience can benefit the employer."
— *Beverley Kagan, Certified Professional Résumé Writer (CPRW)*

Monster.com has more than job postings on its Web site; they also include many resources to assist you in the interview process. Explore the resources available at this Web site.

CareerBuilder.com is another Web site that has much to offer in the way of jobs and advice on your job search. They offer great tips on customizing your documents for a particular position and company.

A job search on CareerBuilder.com came up with the following position:

Special Events Manager

Coordinates and arranges for meetings and special events of various sizes. Plans logistics and negotiates contract(s) for conferences, and/or events, with respect to budgets, speakers, entertainment, transportation, facilities, technology, equipment, logistical requirements, printing, food and beverage, and other related issues. Serves as liaison between contractors, organizers, and management with regards to all facets of the programs and events. Negotiates terms, executes, and administers multiple contracts with facilities vendors for service, in accordance with budget constraints and company policies and procedures. Designs and prepares various marketing materials, to include brochures and flyers, for meetings and conferences.

This is typical of the type of position description you will find. You are armed with information regarding what the employer is seeking in the candidate, but in the case of CareerBuilder.com you may not know the name of the organization that posted the position. Read the posting carefully and ask yourself if you have experience or knowledge in that area. CareerBuilder.com might be serving to screen candidates; should you meet the basic requirements, you could move forward. If you do not have that in your background, it is worthwhile for you to look closely at what most organizations are looking for and begin to get the necessary training. Should there be information in the job posting regarding the company, research, and learn all you can before submitting your tailored résumé, going to that company for the posted position.

Once you have written a well-thought-out résumé that has been reviewed by your mentor, create a list of words from your résumé that might trigger questions. Ask yourself why you are using a particular word, and determine if you are using the best words.

When your mentor or advisor has reviewed your résumé, request a mock interview so that you can practice answering questions. This will be very helpful, giving the opportunity to share your answers with another person and hearing yourself say the words. Review with your mentor the process recommended in this book for answering questions so that they can provide feedback. Generally, the first few times you use this process, the answers will be long. Your mentor will help you by letting you know when you are providing too much information.

Types of Interviews

In interviewing, one size does not fit all. There are various ways in which hiring managers conduct interviews.

- The direct interview is very structured in a one-on-one meeting, generally in an office where the interviewer asks questions and you provide answers. The goal is to determine if you have the necessary training, skills, and experience to fill the special events role. This is what to expect in most job interviews.
- Meet-and-greet style interviews are far more relaxed, with conversation and discussion on issues related to the position. Although it is relaxed, you need to be prepared to provide examples of your experience and skills. This is a good time for sharing your stories on personal experiences and a great way to showcase your personality in a positive manner. The interviewer/hiring manager wants to see you with your guard down and how you interact with others. Once the interviewer/hiring manager has won you over they will see how well you listen, your communications skills, and your openness as well as if you continue to project a positive attitude.
- Role-play interviews are challenging, as they are knowledge-based situations where often there is not a right or wrong answer. This technique reveals much about your instincts with problem solving and is difficult to prepare for. It is best to stay true to yourself, your mission, the company, and the best interests of all concerned. Set your priorities based on the position description, which often describes the client, the quality of what you are to provide to the client, your fellow team members, and the business results.
- Telephone interviews are often used to screen the candidate before moving forward. Since phone interviews are very popular, remember to remove distractions and have all the materials you submitted available so that you are looking at the same documents the interviewer is reading. Do not chew gum and have music playing in the background. Speak normally, but slow down, as the interviewer/hiring manager will not see you and your body language, so put a smile in your voice. If you are not able to appropriately speak on the phone because of where you are, request that you call them back or to give you a few minutes to get to a more suitable location.

- Job fair interviews are often very quick and you will be required to get right to the point of selling yourself. Often, there are many candidates seeking the same position, so you must make a positive impression in a short amount of time. Much depends on first impressions, and therefore you must be very organized, well groomed, and prepared to sum up what you do in a matter of minutes. This is where your elevator speech really pays off, and a well-written résumé gets attention. Also, portfolios are often an asset in this setting but expect only a quick look with few questions. As they are looking, provide a short overview of what they are looking at. It is best if you practice in advance.

- Panel interviews have more than three interviewers asking questions. It is best for you to answer the question to the person asking the question, making sure to include all members of the panel by looking at them, to ensure they are being included. Normally, you will be asked the same questions as all the other candidates, and it is an ideal situation to use the recommended process suggested in Chapter 8.

- In all interview situations, you should sit up straight, not lean back in the chair, and never fold your arms as if to protect yourself, but rather place them in your lap or on the table. Hold your head up and make eye contact, in addition to smiling. A candidate once told me that she put her watch on the other wrist because it was a different feeling and a constant reminder to be physically aware of how she was presenting herself. Most of all, try to relax while still being energized.

- A technical interview is very skills-focused, where your answers to questions require specific details related to the position. Make sure you understand the questions

---

Ten sample questions you may be asked during your job interview:

1. Tell me about your current job or position.

2. If I were to call some of the people you have worked with, what would they say about you?

3. What would you say is your strongest attribute?

4. How would you see yourself applying that attribute to this position?

5. What in your opinion makes a good employee?

6. How do you work under pressure?

7. Tell me about an accomplishment that you are most proud?

8. What kinds of things excite you about your job?

9. What do you consider to be most important to you in your job?

10. If you leave your current position today, how will you be most remembered?

Figure 9.1 Top Ten Interview Questions

and ask for clarification if necessary, but follow the same step-by-step answer as outlined in Chapter 8.

Figure 9.1 lists the top ten interview questions. There are other types of questions that relate to past job performance, and you may be asked to answer one or more of the prompts in Figure 9.2 as well.

Illegal Questions

All interview questions must be job/experience related and not about:

- Race
- National origin
- Family
- Non–job-related issues

Tell me about a time when you were effective at:

1. Dealing with a difficult situation with a co-worker.

2. Working under pressure.

3. Persuading team members to do things your way.

4. Dealing with having made a mistake.

5. Dealing with a situation of being unable to complete a project on time.

6. Being creative in solving problems.

7. Adjusting to a difficult situation.

8. Anticipating potential problems and developing an effective strategy.

9. Dealing with a report that was well received.

10. Tolerating an opinion that was different from yours.

11. Dealing with disappointment in your behavior.

12. Dealing with a demanding customer.

13. Having made a bad decision.

14. Having to make an unpopular decision.

15. Dealing with peers that said negative things about you and your work?

Figure 9.2   Fifteen Job Performance Prompts

If you are faced with these types of questions, your options are as follows:

- Ask how that information relates to the position.
- Ask a question rather than answering, or give an answer that does not include private information.
- Answer the legitimate question and ignore the illegal or improper questions.
- Answer the question, giving away your right to privacy.
- Refuse to answer, telling the interviewer you think the question is improper.

In Chapter 8 we reviewed how to answer questions that focus on your experience with problem solving. There are other informational questions in which you should provide a timeline or a simple straightforward answer. You might be asked if you are from this area. If the answer is yes, you might add something that relates to the area. If it is no, then you might follow up with where you are from and how long you have been in this area.

You might be questioned about your training, and once again this is the opportunity to present positive information about the faculty and program that you appreciate for guiding you in this exciting world of special events. Always praise your teachers, but use care regarding your school as the best, as the hiring manager might have attended a rival school. Likewise, use care in rooting for your favorite sports team in the interview, as you might be dealing with a fan from another team.

Questions You Might Ask

Often you will be asked if you have any questions as the interview wraps up, and if there are no questions, it is best to just say that you feel the hiring manager provided all the needed information concerning the position. However, Figure 9.3 lists some questions you might ask.

Some people suggest that you ask the hiring manager how they got their start with the company. This is a judgment call, and you need to look for the signal if the interview is finished. Pushing forward with that question might appear that you are not respecting the other person's schedule. However, it is a great question if the hiring manager seems open to continuing the conversation. The interviewer might give you a quick overview of his or her history with the company, which could provide the opportunity for you to ask for advice regarding your job search.

Leave on Good Terms

No matter what happens in the interview, thank the hiring manager for the time he or she spent with you. Smile, giving him or her a firm handshake, and use eye contact as you say

---

Ten Key Questions You Could Ask During the Interview

1. What are the specific duties required?

2. Where does this position fit in the organization?

3. Who supervises the person in this position?

4. How would I be evaluated?

5. What is a normal work week like?

6. What direction is your organization going in the future?

7. What are some major challenges here?

8. How could I help with these challenges?

9. Is there additional information I can provide you?

10. When will you be making the selection for this position?

Figure 9.3   Ten Key Questions to Ask During the Interview

---

1. Eager to learn

2. Outgoing and alert

3. Friendly and poised

4. Ambitious but eager to learn and grow

5. Articulate

6. Attentive

7. Good-humored

8. Sincere

9. Motivated

10. Honest

Figure 9.4   Ten Final Impressions

thank you. This is the final opportunity to show your professionalism. Figure 9.4 lists the ten final impressions of yourself that you should leave with the hiring manager.

This is achieved by making eye contact, listening carefully, answering questions in a positive manner, smiling, showing enthusiasm, speaking carefully, being honest, and being respectful to everything and everyone you talk about in your interview. If you don't know something, do not fake it. The hiring manager knows the answer and just wants to see if you also know the answer.

Dressing Successfully

It is better to be overdressed than underdressed at an interview. Dressing in business attire for an interview is always safest, even if the interviewer/hiring manager is dressed casual. Women should wear what is comfortable in a business setting. Suits, dresses, or slacks or skirts with a blouse are most common. Care should be taken in wearing too much make-up or perfume. Short skirts and low-cut blouses should be avoided. Select conservative earrings. Select shoes that match your outfit and are appropriate in a working setting.

Men should wear a business suit or a blazer with nice slacks. A tie should be simple, without loud-colored patterns and a dress shirt should be pressed and tucked into your pants. Denim jeans and sneakers with a sports jacket might be a good look for going out on a date but not for job interviewing. You should wear leather dress shoes that are shined, with socks in the appropriate color, not athletic white socks. Wear only mild cologne, make sure your fingernails are clean and clipped and your hair combed.

Some organizations may like a more casual appearance for their staff, as it is part of their brand. Always play by the rules of the company you are making application for employment. However, when in doubt, dress for success. If you are not sure, ask the person making the appointment for your interview what is appropriate. Be prepared to have a second outfit to wear if you are invited for a call-back interview.

Being clean and well-groomed is important in making a good first impression, including brushing your teeth and using a breath mint. Never chew gum in an interview. You will be nervous, so be sure to address the issue of body odor. Present yourself the way you would present yourself to the clients, because that is how hiring managers will evaluate you. Many people have tattoos, but you should consider how you will display them in the job interview. Piercing beyond earrings should be avoided (see Appendix 9 for a checklist on dressing.).

Dining and Interviewing

Many people like to take candidates to a meal as a way of learning how they behave in a social setting. Keep everything simple, with your primary objective being the interview and not eating. Figure 9.5 lists some key tips for improving your dining and interviewing abilities.

Sharing a meal is a positive experience, and your mission is to enhance your image as a candidate. Enjoy the chance to share information about your skills and experience more than enjoying a good meal.

1. Gender is always an issue in that a gentleman is always a gentleman and a lady is always a lady when interacting and dining.

2. This is a business meeting and not a date.

3. Gentlemen may hold the door, and allow the lady to enter first.

4. Gentlemen always wait until the lady takes her seat.

5. Napkins go on the lap after seating.

6. Take the lead from the host as to conversation or reviewing the menu.

7. If conversation begins and the wait staff comes to take the orders, wait until everyone has ordered to answer or finish an answer.

8. Gentlemen let the lady order first.

9. Male or female candidates unsure of what to order should ask for recommendations from the host.

10. Do not order alcohol unless the host insists, but drink very little so that you are not in any way impaired.

11. Elbows never go on the table.

12. Your drink is on your right side and your salad and bread plate is on your left.

13. Silverware use is always from the outside in—use the outside fork and knife for your salad. Hold the fork or spoon much the same way you hold a pencil. Cut with the knife rather than the side of the fork.

14. When finished place both on the plate at 4:50 (if the plate were a clock).

15. Never stack the plates or bowls together.

16. With bread and butter, take butter and place it on your bread dish, break off a piece of bread and butter only that part of the bread.

17. Never pick up the plate and hand it to the server, as there is a chance you could spill on yourself or others at the table.

18. Drinks like iced tea can build up condensation and drip.

19. Cut your meal into small, bite-sized pieces to make chewing and digestion easier.

20. Chew your food (with mouth closed) before answering.

21. Put the fork or spoon down when speaking and do not wave them to make a point.

Figure 9.5 Twenty-Six Tips for Dining While Interviewing

22. Use your napkin to wipe your lips but not your nose.

23. The napkin stays in your lap until the completion of the meal. Note: When dining in countries other than North America the napkin may not be placed in the lap. Watch the host for examples of how to use the napkin.

24. Should you leave the table, the napkin is placed on the chair, not the table.

25. Answer questions from the wait staff with "Yes, please," or "No, thank you."

26. Etiquette varies from culture to culture and country to country. Watch the host for cues on how to fit in comfortably, and do your homework about the local culture before the meal.

Figure 9.5 (Continued)

What Do Professionals Ask in Interviews?

I asked some of the leading professionals of the special events industry to share with me the questions they ask candidates during interviews. The following is a sample of the responses.

Andrea Michaels, president of Extraordinary Events, says that when she is interviewing, "I want them to acknowledge exactly what they know and don't know, what they want to learn, and not just brag. I want to see how they think 'on the spot,' what kind of creativity they exhibit. I don't want to be flattered. My first question is always 'what do you know about my company,' and if I get a blank stare, they haven't done their homework and they are history. I also don't ever want to hear 'I think it sounds like so much fun.'" Michaels goes on to say that the best advice she received about the event industry is to "Hire the best people money can buy." It would be your task to demonstrate your knowledge without bragging or using flattery to hide what you do not know. Michaels is very clear that it is important for her to understand what you do not know as well as what you do know. She also stresses the importance of researching her company before interviewing for them.

Alisa Schwartz, freelance event manager and former student who recently joined the job market, states that "Presentation of yourself, your paperwork and your communication, including e-mail, is imperative. A sloppy dresser or misspellings in an e-mail say that you don't care enough about yourself, so the next logical thought would be why you would care enough about a job." In both cases there is an underlying theme of paying attention to details and exceeding expectations.

Schwartz goes on to say, "Come up with a comparison from what you have done to the job you are applying for. For example, say you've had a job at a coffee shop—were you managing other people and their schedules, were you dealing with money, did you always show up on time and have no reprimands? Now compare this to an event. Leadership, organization, and responsibility are not things you can teach, so if you can manage a team of people, take orders and then implement solutions, be reliable and on time, you have the basics for event management. Special events aren't only the Grammy Awards or Apple's annual meeting. Special events can also be weddings, business lunches, birthday parties, the Super Bowl half-time show, fashion shows, and bar mitzvahs." Schwartz goes on to offer this recommendation: "Thank everyone you meet with a thank you note, and don't be afraid to follow up with an e-mail every so often just to keep in their mind. Use the people around you, such as your classmates and teachers as possible connections. Never burn bridges—this is a small industry. Ask for what you want; the worst someone can say is no."

Arnold Guanco, manager of special projects for the Philippine Basketball Association, says, "In my experience, I started with small community events and went to the very high-level international meetings and international sporting events. Honestly, education is one of the least things that employers stare at in a résumé. A lot of the players in the industry don't have any formal education in events to start with. You have to show them what you have done first before other things get noticed. Being tech savvy is another big thing. You don't only manage events these days, you need to know how to produce good print collateral, good presentation, or maintain a Web site." When it comes to the interviews, Guanco says, "I want to hear something interesting they did beyond what is expected of him or her. I am more interested in the right attitude. You can teach somebody to do things effectively and efficiently but you can't change a bad attitude. It's all about values at home and the people around you." Guanco says that it comes down to attitude: "With the right attitude, you can impress upon employers that you can do the impossible, and have commitment and grace under pressure."

Charlotte J. DeWitt, CFEE, president of International Events, Ltd. considers "past experience, how they handled stressful or crisis situations; creative ideas; the ability to 'pinch hit' rather than be a prima donna; the ability to work and make decisions independently. Attitude to peers as well as to the general public and enthusiasm" are what DeWitt looks for in candidates.

It goes beyond just what you say in the interview. David Peters, president of Event Mall, says, "The types of questions I ask are about their expectations and experience. We role-play in the interview to hear how the individual handles challenges and we review their history. We also test IQ, check their background, and we do Myers-Briggs." Peters states that his company follows a process with all candidates. "The truth is, we check up on the candidates before moving forward, and once they are on-board, there is no faking it past week four."

Being completely honest is extremely important to the company, and embellishing your résumé or your level of responsibility may be detrimental to your chances of getting hired. Once hired, if you do not deliver what you claimed was within your level of ability, it will cause a negative reaction from the company. Furthermore, avoid starting your reply with, "To be perfectly honest. . . . " Your interviewer expects that you will always be perfectly honest.

Frank Supovitz, senior vice-president of events with the National Football League (NFL), says, "I want to hear about applicable experience. I see a lot of résumés from real estate agents, bank tellers, and a host of others looking for a new career. What have you done that demonstrates the same competencies and capabilities I'm looking for—customer service, logistics, negotiating skills, and perhaps as importantly, dedication without regard to the time on the clock." Supovitz says, "Special events is not a career. It's a lifestyle."

Greg Bell, talent relations director for Walt Disney Parks and Resorts, has a lot of firsthand experience interviewing candidates, and he says, "The most important response a candidate can give to an interview question is a proven example of the topic being discussed. For instance, when I have asked candidates to give me an example of when something went awry with the timeline of a project and how you resolved it, first of all, I want to hear a compelling illustration of problem-solving, and second, it should be relevant to the subject matter. The response does not need to be completely about the special events industry, but it does need to be undeniable in dealing with timeline issues. Keep in mind that real-life experiences are examples of integrity." Bell emphasizes that "a real-life experience is always the best response to an interview question. Hypothetical responses are poor choices for a candidate and ill advised." He adds these words of encouragement: "An interview is something to be excited about, not nervous about and speaking from knowledge is an integral aspect of a productive exchange."

Gregory L. DeShields, senior director of corporate relations at Temple University's School of Tourism and Hospitality Management, says, "I believe employers are seeking a diversity of industry experience (meetings and events) and a track record of success producing events with compatible client affiliations." DeShields stresses that you must be able to answer questions such as "What clients have you worked with in the past? What was your most successful event production, and why? Where do you see the future of you career?" DeShields emphasizes "Due to today's economic climate, several event professionals are probably rethinking their career direction; I believe the special events industry is extremely promising, however, it is important to allow flexibility regarding how to achieve career success."

John J. Daly Jr. CSEP, president of John Daly Inc., reminds you to "be flexible, have a 'can do' attitude and live by good honest ethics to both clients and suppliers." Among other things, Daly "looks at length of time on jobs prior" and says; "Remember what your service and education is worth in dollars."

Josh McCall, chairman and CEO with Jack Morton Worldwide, includes these four interview questions:

1. Tell me about an experience in your life that you are most proud of and why.
2. Who has had the greatest influence on your life so far?
3. Why do you think you can be successful in our agency?
4. What do you know about our agency?

McCall wants to know how candidates' experiences are relevant to his agency and why they consider themselves a good candidates for us to consider. McCall also encourages you to "follow your passion, as this is an industry that you need to work very hard at, and therefore, you must be passionate about what you do, so you can enjoy it."

Laura Schwartz, former White House director of events under the Clinton administration, wants to know "How they can diversely apply things that worked in prior events they have done (either as the producer or an assistant to the producer) to the task at hand, and creating new and different approaches that will effectively communicate the message the client is looking for. Schwartz says, "I also want to hear about their working relationships with vendors and locations that may be of use to the particular event. What is their practical experience in the field?" She emphasizes to "always have some questions—be prepared to be engaged!"

Richard Aaron CMP, CSEP, president of Bizbash Media, wants to know "that they can multitask during the day and handle shifting priorities. Events jump expectations all the time. How flexible or rigid is a candidate?" Aaron also points out the need for candidates to "have excellent technology skills in tools such as excel or registration systems." Aaron recommends that you "keep investing in the education process and expanding knowledge through many industry certifications or classes at Universities or conferences. Get started blogging or writing in an area of expertise you can clearly own. Develop a speaking platform on that arena. It takes more than 20 years to realize that, so get started early."

Rob Murphy, chief marketing officer with MC^2, wants to know "that you are independent, self-motivated and passionate about doing something that is new and different. We need to find out if you are motivated by working on changing projects as opposed to having a repetitive, predictable job." He points out that "you are only as good as your last show . . . make absolutely certain it is a good one." Murphy stresses that "this industry either captivates you or you run away screaming. If you have a passion for this work, make sure your superiors know it. This is not an industry for quiet types. Assert your ideas and deliver on them. Your ideas can be as good as anyone's—so let them be known. The people who last in this world are usually consistent, reliable, industrious, creative, and brave. I have seen more bravery in this business than in other marketing services I have worked in. I have heard numerous times from clients and suppliers alike, 'He or she really screwed up—but at least he/she tried.' When you work with no rule book other than 'it needs to happen now,' bravery is an important quality."

Steven Wood Schmader, CFEE, president and CEO with International Festivals and Events Association (IFEA), says, "I want to know what they have been doing (even if it is unrelated to our field), why they are leaving their present job, and I watch out for people who have a résumé of short stays in previous jobs. That is an immediate red flag. I prefer to see and hear of a purposeful background with each step leading to a larger goal."

Tammy Bowman, executive producer of Automotive Marketing Consultants Inc., says, "I talk to them about past projects, and I will ask them about their favorite project. Once I learn which project stood out to them the most, I ask them what about that project made it their favorite. This is when you see what they really get 'jazzed' about." Bowman points out that it is necessary to "Respect the skills of your team members and always be open to providing guidance and opportunities to those that have a real passion for the world of production and events. In the end, it is not brain surgery. It is just entertainment!"

Often in my interviews I would point out that this is your interview and the chance to share how your background has prepared you for a position with our organization. I look for those opportunities to ask questions when I see candidates getting excited about information they are sharing. This builds their excitement and confidence, which, in turn, provides me with a better understanding of their talents and skills.

Career Connections

 ## Action Steps:

- Create a first-draft résumé and share it with mentors for their reaction.
- Review the ten interview questions listed earlier in this chapter and write how you would answer each question, providing positive information.
- Write answers to the 15 performance-based questions, turning each negative question into a positive answer.

 ## Practice Activities

- Select friends or classmates to have a business lunch with you, practicing each step and coaching one another on areas that need improvement. Dress as you would for interviewing and get feedback on your appearance.
- Ask your mentor to join you for breakfast or lunch, requesting the mentor ask questions in a mock interview—but this time, you will be providing your answers while having a meal.
- Break down your résumé into words or phrases on a list for your mentor and place, next to those words or phrases, why it is on your résumé as well as an example of a time when you demonstrated that quality or action.

 ## Tool Kit

Axtell, Roger (1993). *Do's and Taboos Around the World*. New York: John Wiley & Sons, Inc.

Gross, Kim Johnson, and Stone, Jeff (2002). *Dress Smart Women—Wardrobes That Win in the New Workplace*. New York: Warner Books, Inc.

Molloy, John T. (1988). *Dress for Success*. New York: Warner Books.

 ## Web Connection

www.careerowlresources.ca
  http://jobsearch.about.com/od/interviewsnetworking/a/dressforsuccess.htm

PART FOUR

Power Tools

CHAPTER 10

After the Interview

When the interview is over, you are not done. Practice writing thank-you notes to managers for interviews. These little decencies will set you apart from the crowd, moving you toward your dream job.

Expressing Appreciation for the Interview

Writing thank-you notes is not only polite but in the case of a job interview, it gives you, as a candidate, one more opportunity to share information about yourself, express your interest in the position, and extend the positive impression you made with the interviewer/hiring manager. Saying thank-you demonstrates that you are a considerate person who appreciates the efforts of others.

Your thank-you letter or note should be sent immediately after the meeting, demonstrating that you go the extra mile in building relationships. It confirms that you are thoughtful and will treat clients, vendors, and coworkers in an appreciative manner. Take care of your targeted employer the same way you would deal with the people and organization doing business with your potential employer. Just as you would be expected to follow up with a client, vendor, or supplier with whom you are seeking to develop or maintain a business relationship, you should do the same for your potential employer.

A well-written thank-you letter or note can move your interview evaluation off center and land you the job. It is just as important as the cover letter, as it closes the loop on the actual interview process. The cover letter and the thank-you letter are the bookends to your actual interview.

Care must be taken in not being aggressive or overly confident with what you write in the thank-you letter. This can be a big turn-off to your future employers. Telling them that you believe you are the best candidate and would be perfect for the position is perhaps too much. Do not compare yourself to others, but focus on being appreciative for the time invested with you in the interview process and your strong interest in the position.

Your thank-you letter could be the biggest difference between you and the other candidates, as many candidates do not put in that much effort after the actual job interview. You would be surprised at how many candidates do not send thank-you letters. Distinguish yourself as someone who goes above and beyond in every aspect of a professional relationship.

Format for the Thank-You Letter

Keep your letter to one page and fairly brief (see Figure 10.1). Your goal is to express appreciation to those involved in the interview process. Like the cover letter, it should be only three or four paragraphs long. The focus is to thank the person while reminding him or her who you are and when you met, as well as mentioning others that were involved with your interview.

Provide supporting information in the second paragraph concerning your skills, covering areas you might not have had the opportunity to share in the interview that would be of interest and relevant to their company. You can also clarify any issues that came up in which you did not readily have the information to give during the interview.

Finally, wrap up with words of appreciation and how you are looking forward to hearing from them. Include your contact information, making it very easy to reach you.

Format for the Thank-You Letter Where You Are Not Being Considered

If you were told during the interview that you were not being considered for the position, your thank-you letter focus should be to keep the door open for future opportunities. Your brief thank-you letter should not try to change their minds but to present you in a professional

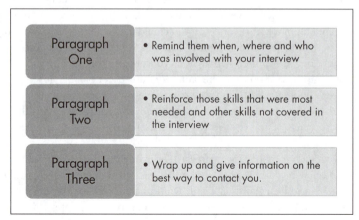

Figure 10.1 Paragraph Breakdown of a Thank-You Letter

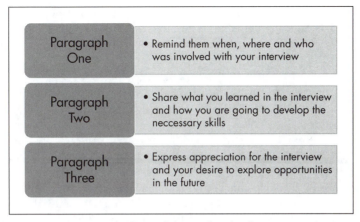

Paragraph One	• Remind them when, where and who was involved with your interview
Paragraph Two	• Share what you learned in the interview and how you are going to develop the neccessary skills
Paragraph Three	• Express appreciation for the interview and your desire to explore opportunities in the future

Figure 10.2   Paragraph Breakdown of a Thank-You Letter When not Being Considered

manner. This is a way of demonstrating that you are polite and can deal with rejection in a professional manner. Again, keep it to three paragraphs.

Your focus should be on thanking them and reminding them of when and with whom you met. Do not make excuses or remind them of anything negative in your interview. Share that you learned something in the interview, showing respect for the organization and service they provide, as well as your appreciation for their honesty. If they pointed out areas for development and you have a positive approach in addressing these issues, then it is appropriate to share that information. Close by saying that once you gain more experience, you would like to discuss opportunities, but this should be very soft sell. You have nothing to lose, and possibly much to gain with this effort, as it could turn things around for you in the future.

Many times in the past I received calls from associates in the industry looking for personnel, and I would refer candidates who were not the right fit for our team but could be of value to other companies. Generally, it was because the candidate tried hard and showed professionalism. Since the special events industry has a strong focus on networking, calling on each other for assistance, it is wise for you to make good impressions with everyone, because you never know when or where they might be able to help you.

The Value of the Interview Recap

Remembering all the details of your interview can be a challenge for the interviewer/hiring manager, since typically they interview many candidates, taking notes while engaging in the discussion. On the other hand, you will remember most of the details, and it is recommended that you write a recap of what questions were asked and how you answered. This is for your personal use and will be very valuable in planning your next job interviews. If there is an item on your résumé that catches the interviewer's attention, it is very possible that other interviewers will have similar questions. Information in your cover letter or résumé that raises questions in a negative manner needs to be looked at carefully and adjusted if appropriate. It is best to consider not only what you have written but how you wrote the information. Your personal recap will remind you of what interviewers seem to target with your documents, and will be of great assistance in understanding what is working as well as what might not be working.

I made it a practice of having the candidates write a recap of the interview to be returned the next day. The purpose was to see how accurately they recounted our meeting, as well as to evaluate their written communications. I looked at how timely the materials were sent, how complete they were and if it was well written. Often, this made the difference if the candidate would move to the next step in the interview process. This is a technique that is becoming more popular, so you should be prepared to recount your conversation, sharing the highlights of your interview. You would be doing the same thing for your prospective employer by providing a thank-you letter or note, which serves as an example of your written communication skills as well as your follow-up and attention to detail. Unless requested, the normal thank-you letter is not a detailed recap of everything that was discussed but an expression of appreciation for the time granted to you to share your story with the interviewer/hiring manager.

Staff members involved with the interview process often share formally typed thank-you letters with other members of their team. It is recommended that you send individual letters to each person, including the names of everyone who took part in your interview. It serves as a reminder of who from the company were involved in your interview process. The information can be basically the same, but it is suggested that you find a way to personalize each letter. Many candidates write one generic letter and then address the same letter to each person. If you wish to stand out, include something unique on each letter that helps to connect you to the individuals. There are a number of ways to accomplish this, such as thanking the person for the following:

- Putting you at ease
- Complementing your résumé
- Asking a question that displayed your skills
- Answering questions about the organization
- Showing you around the offices
- Suggesting a particular book are magazine to read
- Suggesting people you should call
- Suggesting events you should try to attend

There are many ways to connect to each person you met in your interview process, and the thank-you letter or note should serve as a way of making you memorable.

The Personal Handwritten Card

A handwritten note can be very personable and memorable. If your handwriting is hard to read, then it is recommended that you type a thank-you letter on the same stationery

---

THANK YOU!

Dear Kerry,

The time we had together on Monday was most informative and helpful, and I appreciate the time you took telling me about Amazing Events. It was inspiring to hear the story of your career journey and your commitment to give back. I am honored that you shared you experiences, good and bad, with me. You are truly making a difference in the lives of many people, and I am very thankful to be one of those people.

Sincerely,
Sally Student

Figure 10.3   Sample Handwritten Thank-You Card

you used to write your cover letter. Many printers can print on cards, and by using a font such as Brush Script or Lucida Handwriting, it gives your note a look of being handwritten (see Figure 10.3).

A well written, easy-to-read, simple thank-you card is very nice, and people react in a positive manner, regarding it as being very professional. Not hearing from you might give the impression that you don't care are not really interested in the position.

■ Address Something That Did Not Go Well in the Interview

Should you have an interview in which there is a question about something with which you were not familiar and were unable to provide an appropriate answer, your thank-you letter can demonstrate how you researched and found the correct answers. I was very impressed with a candidate to whom I had asked a technical question that she did not know. She was uncomfortable, not having an answer, and promised to find the information. The next morning on my desk was a hand-delivered envelope with her thank-you letter, which included a detailed description of what she was unable to answer in the interview. Her effort led to a second interview, where I shared how impressed I was at the effort she had gone to with her follow-up. She may have told us that she pays attention to details and follows up on all issues, but in this case she showed us that she was a person who goes above and beyond.

Ongoing Updates

Often, you will hear from organizations that there are currently no openings but your information will be kept on file. It is recommended that your letter of thanks be sent informing them that, as you gain new experience you will be sending an updated résumé as a reminder of your on-going interest in their company. The timeline of sending updates depends on when you get opportunities and are able to update your résumé, but it is best to send reminders every three to four months (see Figure 10.4).

Gloria Graduate

1234 Home Address
Phone: (123) 456-7890

My City, State 09876-4321
E-mail: ggraduate@mail.com

Irene Interviewer
Manager of Production
Amazing Events
P.O. Box 1234
Big City, State 12345-6789

Wednesday, May 13, 2010

Dear Ms. Interviewer:

It was wonderful spending time with you on Tuesday discussing the various opportunities available with Amazing Events. It was informative and exciting to learn about your past award-winning events and what you have planned next season. I was impressed with your commitment to training and cross training for your staff and one can see why your team works so well together.

Having recently completed my undergraduate degree in special events management, I am exploring opportunities where I can contribute as well as continue to learn. Our program at State University was very well rounded and included opportunities to work with event companies investing in students. Of course, I feel honored to have been selected last year to work with Amazing Events on the annual Mayor's Ball benefiting the children at the Downtown Elementary School. I learned a great deal from that experience and set a goal of being part of your organization because of your commitment to the community.

I was enraptured with hearing the plans for this year's Mayor's Ball and should you need volunteers, please count me in. Since last year's event I have focused on a number of areas that we only touched lightly on in the interview. Let me itemize them for you:

Computer graphics has always be an interest and I have spend the past two semesters in intermediate and advanced classes. My minor in art fits very well into my long-term goal of focusing theme parties and décor.

Production management was a requirement in our program, and these classes expanded my knowledge and understanding of budgets. I have come to really enjoy the business side of events. I have become very proficient at Microsoft Excel.

Figure 10.4 Sample Follow-Up Letter

This past year I was elected senior class president and made many friends and contacts. We have a very strong bond and I have learned a great deal about the challenges of leadership. There were a number of issues on campus this past year but my work with the administration, faculty, and staff has proven to be very successful.

In the time we were together, I could see that I share the same values of Amazing Events and would be honored to be a member of your team. The pride taken in staff members and your gracious hospitality in showing me the offices and warehouse left quite an impression. If you treat a candidate this way, I can see why so many of your clients come back again and again.

Thank you, again, for your interest and the very informative meeting. I look forward to the next step in the process.

Sincerely,
Gloria Graduate

Figure 10.4   (*Continued*)

Internet Communications

Many companies keep electronic files of candidates, and thank-you notes are not easy to send via the Internet. If you have information that you want in your electronic file, you will have to send it electronically. It should be a PDF file so that the reader sees it as you wrote it. Candidate file folders are easy to maintain, and as new materials are sent, the interviewer/hiring manager can simply save the information in your folder. Most interviewer/hiring managers will not take the time to scan your letter for your file. If you have been requested to apply via the Internet, send your thank-you letter the same way. However, it is recommended that you also send a hand written thank-you note in regular mail.

References

As part of the follow-up to your interview, references will be requested. Most often, there is a request for three or more people who know you and can speak about your work ethics, interpersonal skills, reliability, and honesty (see Figure 10.5).

Of course, there are many more questions that could be asked, but you should choose your references carefully, making sure they know you and your abilities.

You should ask the people you are considering as a reference if they are comfortable with your request. You might not be able to tell them the actual questions that will be asked, but you want to be sure that you will have someone who will be honest as well as

The types of questions your references will be asked are:

- How long have you known this person?
- What is your relationship to the person?
- How well do you know this person?
- Can you speak knowledgeably about this person as an employee?
- Does this person make good decisions?
- How would you rate their ability to communicate?
- How would you rate their honesty?
- How did this person relate to peers?
- How well does this person respond to those in charge?
- How well does this person follow directions?
- What are this person's strong points?
- What are the weak points of this person?
- How would you rate his or her ability with responsibility?
- If you were an employer, would you hire this person?
- Would you rehire this person?
- Are there any issues that we should be concerned about regarding this person?

Figure 10.5   Typical Questions Asked of a Reference

supportive of you. Do not assume, just because you ask a person to be a reference, that he or she will only give glowing information about you. Most people will be honest when called, so it would be in your best interest to share as much information about the company and the position you are seeking with the people on the reference list. In addition, your reference should have information concerning your personal development. Review the list of questions above with your references and see if they are comfortable answering the questions or if they need more information from you.

Questions Concerning Salary/Wages

Never discuss salary or wages until an offer is being made, aside from answering the question about salary range in the interview process. This question of salary in the interview is often difficult to answer because you do not want to sell yourself short nor put yourself out of being considered because your expectations are too high. It is best to answer with a nonanswer that you expect the company to pay in a fair and competitive manner and feel certain that, when the time comes, there will be a more detailed discussion on the total employment package. Should the job posting include the salary range, then you should tell the interviewer that you are comfortable with the posted range. If you are not comfortable with the posted range, the employer might be turned off if you go through the interview and then say that you expect to be paid at a higher rate than posted.

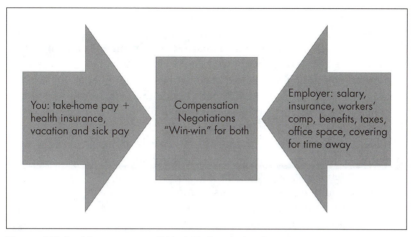

Figure 10.6 Negotiating a "Win-Win" with the Company

Salary is only a part of the cost of an employee, as there are also benefits that companies must provide. The option of health insurance is one of the most popular extra benefits individuals look for from their employer. Most employees pay a portion of these costs, but there often is a large contribution from the employer. What are not options to the employer are vacations, personal days, workers' compensation, unemployment insurance, social security benefits, and sick pay. There are additional costs, particularly if your position requires someone to fill in if an employee is absent. The cost of employee benefits ranges anywhere from 30 to 60 percent above the gross salary you receive in your paycheck. In salary negotiations you may be thinking about your take-home pay after taxes, while the employer may be thinking about the total cost of you as an employee.

Salary/Wages Negotiations

It is always exciting to get a job offer, but there are a few things you need to think about before accepting the position. The compensation package is very important, and you will need to know what is included beyond the salary/wages that are being offered. You should look at the total value of the offer, not just the paycheck. Best to take time to review the offer and not accept until you fully understand your conditions of employment. Here are some details of which you should have a clear understanding:

- What are your duties and responsibilities?
- To whom you will report?
- What are the hours and working conditions?
- How will you receive your training, and will there be ongoing training?
- Is there an employee policy manual that you can review?

- Are there performance appraisals, and how often?
- Are you on a weekly salary or an hourly wage?
- Is there an annual review, including salary/wage adjustment based on performance?
- What is the expected number of work hours each week?
- Is there compensation for hours exceeding the base number of 40 hours?
- If you exceed the number of hours per week, is there an overtime payment?
- Are their health benefits, and does the employee contribute?
- Is there dental, optical, and life insurance available?
- Is there a 401(k) or other retirement plan?
- Are there reimbursements of all or part of relocation expenses?
- What are the long-term growth opportunities?
- Is there education/training reimbursement?
- What are the vacation and sick day policies?
- Is there a "personal day" policy?

Job Description	Job Expectation
Procuring all research materials	Not only find the materials but make it easily ready to be placed in presentational format.
Coordinating presentation materials	Once selected, they need to be artistically formatted for PowerPoint or printed presentation, making changes at the direction of the creative team.
Scheduling and coordinating rehearsals	Schedule the location, communicate with all parties as to where to go, ensure that the location is clean and has all the necessary sound equipment, changing rooms, tables and chairs and refreshments.
Maintaining timelines	Know where everyone is at every moment and that key members know where they are to be. Communicate a weekly and daily schedule.
Preparation of authorizations and purchases	With the authorizations, preparer needs to have the budget information to ensure the purchase is within the plan. Handle mailing and track when each is sent.
Produces a complete production book	Maintain an ongoing master list of everything that happens with the production, including who, how much, where, and when, as well as why things happened. The main source of where the project is at any moment of the process.
Completes any and all show production tasks	This is anything from getting coffee to hosting the children of the client—no list would ever be complete.

Figure 10.7 Understand the Duties and Job Expectations

In your discussion, you should request not only the job description but what the expectations are for the role you would be assuming. The short list of duties can have a great deal more detail involved in it, as seen in Figure 10.7.

Negotiation is the effort to reach an agreement through discussion and compromise. Once you have a good understanding of what is expected of you as an employee, you are in a better position to know if the offer is reasonable. Your strategy should be not to talk about the amount of money until you understand the total package. In fact, money is uncomfortable for most people to talk about, as it is rude to discuss your salary or how much others are paid. Many companies insist on confidentiality as it relates to your compensation. In some cases, a company will post a salary range, but that is rare. Hourly wages are far more open and information is more available because of the minimum wage requirements. Getting information on pay can be very challenging, as companies pay different amounts for the same roles, depending on experience. It is very much a supply and demand principle, and the smaller the number of well-trained, highly qualified individuals, the greater the demand. Organizations will pay for skilled people. Your mission on your journey of learning is to develop skills that will bring value to the organization.

Many of the conditions of employment are not negotiable, such as issues related to the policy manual. Normally, work conditions are the same for all employees from the entry-level to the senior management. However, there might be an option for selection of various benefits. Employee benefits are generally based on a percentage of the salary or the salary range. Some companies have benefit options, giving flexibility with the employment compensation package. For example, you may not need childcare but would like a more complete dental insurance plan. Some companies can shift the dollars in your benefits to accommodate this type of request.

Most employers expect some level of negotiation, and it is far better if you let the employer be the one to mention money first. Look at the total package and not just what you will take home in your paycheck. You need to be realistic with your salary, and it is wise to figure out what the absolute lowest salary is that you could accept. When thinking about future salary, your current salary/wages are a good place to start, and then consider the value you will bring to the company, not on what you want or need. It is not a good strategy to point out all your expenses, as they are not relevant to the hiring manager in this process. It is unlikely that you would be paid more because you have more debt, and it is unlikely that you would be paid more than the people already doing the same job. Your goal is to be paid fairly.

You bring your qualifications, training, experience, and skills, and the hiring manager brings the money to buy your skills. Fair market value is always the question, and it depends on which side of the negotiating table you are sitting. If the offer is low, be professional and ask if there is flexibility, and what would it take to get the rate to a higher level. Be a good listener and think carefully about what you have to say. Above all, keep it friendly, as this will be a person you will be working for and you will want to get off on the right foot. Never push the hiring manager into

> **Gene-Gem**
>
> It's a day work for a day's pay. For those that only do enough to get by, they should only expect enough to get by.

saying, "Take it or leave it," as there might still be an interest in hiring you, but concerns about how easy it would be to deal with you.

If you do not get the amount you were hoping for, you can ask for a six-month review, and based on your performance, that consideration be given to open the discussion on salary. This sends a strong signal that you are intending to work very hard and be successful. Finally, you might ask if there could be a signing bonus to help you in your transition into the new position. Normally, there is a budget to hire a person into the position, and if there are dollars available for a signing bonus, it is a very good compromise.

Overall, exercise self-control and separate emotion from the process. Some people find it helpful to speak in third person: "If the employee is paid on a weekly salary, what are the hours he or she is expected to work?" The focus is on creating a win-win situation for both you and the employer.

Employers are also willing to pay for top talent, as that is one of the most important factors in advancing their business. Your effort prior to the interview process of gaining the necessary skills will pay off when the time comes for establishing your salary. The demanding language courses, the business classes, sciences, theater courses, volunteering, and leadership efforts added to your passion for the special events industry will place you in a desirable position for the employer that is willing to pay appropriately for your services.

Words of Wisdom from the Professionals

Tammy Bowman, executive producer of Automotive Marketing Consultants, points out that "Employers are looking for people that are excited, eager, flexible and great team members." Bowman also says, "In special events, you have to be able to think on your feet and make decisions quickly. Willingness to accept change and adapt is important as well." In your relationship with the person you hope will be your boss, you must think on your feet and show him or her that you want to create a win-win situation in establishing your conditions of employment. Bowman reminds us that in special events, "it is important to be someone that provides solutions and not just challenges. I will take a great attitude any day over someone with lots of experience and a bad attitude." Attitude is very much the key in every aspect of the interview, including the negotiations.

Steven Wood Schmader, CFEE, president and CEO with International Festivals and Events Association, reminds us, "Good is the enemy of great, and relationships are more valuable than money." This advice should be considered carefully as you enter salary discussions. These discussions establish the solid foundation of your relationship with someone you will be working for.

Rob Murphy, chief marketing officer with MC2, says, "Most employees come from an acquaintance, as people in the industry know rather instinctively who is a likely fit. We have a saying in our business—that if you survive the first year, you're in it for life." As you interview, the people in the industry will be sharing information about how well you did in your interview, so it is best to always put your best foot forward.

Josh McCall, chairman and CEO of Jack Morton Worldwide, emphasizes that "education is critical in all fields of endeavor. A good education is of greater value than experience." McCall said, "Networking is the best way to find a job in the special events industry." He recommends that you "begin with the leading players in the different areas of the industry that you can identify in an Internet search or through trade publications and industry rankings. Then, write a good letter, or e-mail to the CEO of the agency telling him/her why you are passionate about joining their firm. Follow up with persistence until you get a meeting with someone in the firm that you can impress in an interview that you are well prepared for. Too many people are not well-prepared for interviews."

Greg Bell, talent relations director, Walt Disney Parks and Resorts, says, "When hiring an entry-level employee, it is important to understand entry-level responsibilities. The most sought-after attributes for this level of position would be organization, reliability, timeliness, ability to work with little direction, and of course flexibility. All that being said . . . the old adage of having 'two ears and one mouth' is a good rule of thumb for entry level employees. Entry-level employees are not usually the decision makers on elements of the project but will be exposed to project meetings where vast amounts of details are exchanged."

Bell adds, "In the special events industry, networking may be the single most important aspect of employment. The important thing to remember here is that there is always a 'give and a get' when networking. Too often, networking is confused with 'getting the next job.' Networking is about what an individual brings to the table and how that can help not only the client, but also the other members of the network society." Bell says, "This may mean taking on a job with a financially low return on investment, but the exposure or credibility of this opportunity may be something that money can't buy. It may also mean that at times, you will be known for sending work on to someone else when you are already booked and even though you could not take on the job, you are seen as part of the solution and . . . who knows, this may trigger a whole new entrepreneurial outlet for starting a referral company. The important thing here is to always try to be part of the solution—big or small. It is an investment with exponential gains."

Frank Supovitz, senior vice-president of events with the National Football League, emphasizes, "Remember that you meet the same people over and over again. Engender respect as a professional among your colleagues and don't hold grudges. You will meet the same people at different stages in your career and at different stages in their career. You'd be surprised to learn how many people I interview for jobs or consider as contractors to whom I once delivered interoffice mail. I'll bet there were people delivering my mail ten years ago to whom I'll be responsible as a coworker, supervisor, or client in ten years." Supovitz points out in this business, "You are never as good as the praise or as bad as the criticism."

David Peters, president of Event Mall, states, "The attributes I believe employers look for in hiring entry-level special events workers is a willingness to put in the hours. They have to be technologically savvy, hard working, and self-starters. It takes years of experience to learn about the industry, but in the classroom the students get exposed to a great deal of information. However, classroom knowledge has no value without experience." Peters also states, "Employers are looking at résumés for individuals in this area with a solid knowledge base. Tech is big now and experience matters. References are very important and they will be checked."

Next Step

Often, the next step in the process between educational training and being part of the work force is an internship. Internships are considered by most to be a transition, and are often viewed as a continuing or extended learning opportunity. Most internships require that the employers provide information on performance, and interns are graded on their performance. This experience takes you out of the classroom, seminar, or other training environment to where you are involved with events under the watchful eyes of professionals. You are still thought of in many ways as a student but must perform like a professional.

Expanding Your Skills

You will learn quickly that there are many things that can and do go wrong with a special event and, working with an events professional as an intern, you will gain a great understanding of how to deal with challenges. This is the chance to use your training and apply it to real special events. However, you will have the members of the team of experts to advise and guide you along the way.

Gene-Gem

We are all meant to rise to a certain level in life—the more training you have, the quicker you will get there!

Your experience as an intern serves as the foundation for your interviews, positioning you as someone who understands and has experienced the process. You will speak intelligently about the topic from firsthand experience working on events. Your portfolio and journal will include samples of your work and photos of the event. You will have practice telling the story as you showcase your portfolio. Your presentation will be filled with energy and excitement about all your great special events opportunities.

Portfolio

In preparing your portfolio, break it down into projects so that you can easily move materials, depending on who you will be meeting. Break down corporate events, exhibits, weddings, themed parties, government events, sporting events, and so on. Move the most appropriate materials to the front of the portfolio to ensure that you can showcase that material. Label the page with the name of the event, where it took place, the client, the producing company, and your role with the event. In addition, label each picture so that if you are requested to leave your materials overnight for a senior member of the staff, the information is clear with or without you presenting.

Practice telling the story of what is in your book. The pictures, drawings, and art materials tell one side of the story, but you need to tell the story quickly so you can show as much as they want to see. Take only a few moments for each page unless the interviewer/hiring manager wishes to ask questions or takes an interest in a particular item. The portfolio can be a great sales tool, but if poorly presented, it will slow the pace of your interview. You want to keep the energy and excitement up for the entire interview process. Practice presenting your portfolio as if there will be no questions, and then practice as if there are questions on every item.

Keeping You and Training You

After a company has invested in your training as an intern, often there is a desire to keep you as a return on investment. Internships are an important part of many companies' hiring processes, and are sometimes viewed as an extended interview. From your vantage point as an intern, you will see many opportunities to explore various aspects of the company, as well as the industry. Often, the intern is used in the capacity of being an assistant, and since interns are there to learn the business, generally they are given more detailed instructions on what to do and how to perform their duties.

As an intern, being responsible is one of the most important qualities you bring to an organization. The team must know that they can count on you and not have to search for you or double-check your work. The most responsible interns I worked with at Disney were always focused on meeting deadlines, and they continuously checked and double-checked every detail. They went above and beyond to make sure they had all the materials necessary for their assignments.

> ### Gene-Gem
>
> The best feedback on how well you have done as an intern is measured by how strongly the company wants to keep you!

By exceeding expectations, you will get positive reactions from the special events team. Being on time and ready to work, with a willing spirit, will bring long-term positive results for all concerned.

Patience and perseverance have a magical effect before which difficulties disappear and obstacles vanish.

John Quincy Adams (6th president of the United States, 1767–1848)

The investment of time and effort before launching your career will pay off in the long run. Continue to learn in this ever-changing industry, with the goal of always exceeding expectations in every aspect with which you are involved. The special events industry is in the business of making memories, and it might be a worthwhile exercise to project where you will be in the future. Look back on your life and career and ask what you want to remember and how you want to be remembered. Start now on that pathway, knowing you have much to do, many new friends to make, and a lot of great memories to create.

Career Connections

 ## Action Steps

1. Draft three thank-you letters to serve as basic templates, using your mock interview with your mentor as the experience. Write thank-you letters after:
   - You have received positive reinforcement regarding your interview and prospects for the position.
   - You have been told that you would not be considered for the position.
   - You are unsure of the interview outcome.
2. List your expenses, establishing the absolute lowest salary you can live on.
3. Create a list of possible references:
   - Compose a letter or e-mail message requesting the desired reference's help and support.
   - If the person agrees to be a reference, discuss how the reference would characterize you to a possible employer.
4. If you are a student, check with the Career Center for information concerning salary ranges in your special events area of focus.

 ## Tool Kit

Chapman, Jack (2000). *Negotiating Your Salary*. Wilmette, IL: Jack Chapman.

Dawson, Roger (2006). *Secrets of Power Salary Negotiating*. New Jersey: The Career Press.

Enelow, Wendy S., and Kursmark, Louise M. (2007). *Cover Letter Magic*. Indianapolis: JIST Publishing, Inc.

 ## Web Connection

Salary calculator from CareerBuilders.com, www.cbsalary.com
United States Institute for Theatre Technology (USITT) www.usitt.org
South Eastern Theatre Conference (SETC) www.setc.org

CHAPTER 11

Credentials: A College Degree, Professional Certification, and/or Internships?

Reaching Your Goal

The ultimate goal of education/training is to apply your skills learned in the world of special events or related fields. Your knowledge and understanding of the components of creating and managing special events is what you learned in your training program, but it will ultimately be your work in the industry that will bring your long-term success. Your mission is to be well prepared, and there are various routes you can take to reach your desired destination in the special events industry. You can attend a college or university, master the craft by receiving a certification, or finding an employer who will provide you with on-the-job training. Which direction you take will largely depend on factors related to where you are in life. The common denominator is that you will need a level of knowledge for employers to be willing to hire you, and in most cases it will not matter how you gained the knowledge or experience, but how you can apply it to bring value to the hiring company.

I have had many discussions with many individuals, including high school students, college graduates, interns, high-level managers, and senior executives about career aspirations. It always comes down to the same question: "What should I do?" Throughout your career you will continuously want to know what will take you in the best direction for your career. I learned that most people gravitate toward those things they most enjoy and avoid having to deal with things that they don't like. In the workplace, people tend do things they like often because they are good at it. However, it is essential to have a solid base of understanding for all aspects of special events to ensure your long-term success.

Gene-Gem

Make sure you really know what you are wishing for because you might get it.

Gene-Gem

It is important to know where you are in order to know where you are going.

No matter where you are in your career, it is important to evaluate how you can reach that dream job of doing something you love. It requires an investment of time, and, often, money. As you make this wise investment for your future, you need to consider carefully the results you hope to achieve. If you are well into your career, wishing to advance and gain more creditability in the industry, you should consider certification. Most certification programs bring creditability to individuals, as you are required to meet the standards of the industry. Those standards are demanding, because if they were not, anyone could receive certification. Having a certification in the hospitality industry is the mark of someone who has proven knowledge and understanding of the standards of his or her line of business. Education and certification are not exclusive of one another, so consider making certification part of your commitment to life-long learning. A full list of professional event certifications is presented in Chapter 5.

Certification versus College

Certification, by definition, confirms by a formal review, education, or assessment that a person understands and is competent to complete a job or task. Although similar, certification is different from a licensure in a legal definition, but both are required to demonstrate a level of knowledge and ability. In the events industry, certification confirms an individual as a professional who has been embraced by peers and an established organization as having demonstrated the necessary skills and knowledge required in the discipline.

Far more common are individuals achieving college degrees in hospitality management and tourism. This degree confirms that the individual met or surpassed the academic requirements established by the college or university and has a fundamental understanding of various aspects of the industry. Upon completion of the college degree, the individual has knowledge without experience, and generally begins his or her career as an intern or in an entry-level position.

College graduates earn more income in their chosen careers over the span of their work life than those without the benefit of a college education. Also, college-educated individuals can expect to have a better quality of life for themselves and their families.

With the increasing cost of higher education, many ask, "Is college meant for everyone?" Certainly, the high cost of tuition and the possible accumulation of debt in student loans makes this question harder to answer. Even with scholarships, there are still basic living costs, and, for many families, particularly in the lowest income brackets, the challenges seem to be insurmountable. However, considering the life-long benefit to the individuals and their families, the investment might be well worth the challenge.

If college is not an option for you but your passion for the industry is strong, you need to knock on more doors and be willing to start at whatever level someone is willing to give you. No doubt you will have to work very hard to prove yourself, but your mission is on-the-job training. Immerse yourself in every aspect of the business, and when the time is right, explore professional certification.

Dr. Joe Goldblatt, CSEP, shared this explanation of the differences between certifications and a college/university degree:

> *Professional certifications first appeared at the beginning of the twentieth century in the USA to provide credentials for individuals in certain professions such as accounting, medicine and others. A certification is an award granted by a professional society or association to an individual based upon the individual achieving a certain degree of professional experience, education and successfully passing an examination or assessment. A college / university degree is generally granted by an accredited college or university for having successfully completed a course of study that, in the United States, would include general studies such as the sciences, English and other subjects as well as a major in special events. . . . The main difference between a professional certification and an academic degree is the requirement for recertification. Professional certifications require recertification every three to five years. Recertification is based on evidence of continuing education in the field.*

If you are seeking a degree program at a college/university, here are Dr. Goldblatt's top five recommendations in selecting a program that is right for you:

1. Find a program that includes both traditional academics and practicing professionals as part of the faculty.
2. Find a program that requires the production of a real event prior to graduation.
3. Find a program that has an advisory board composed of industry professionals.
4. Find a program that has strong industry connections with professional associations such as ISES, MPI, PCMA, IFEA, and others.
5. Find a program that includes curriculum that is aligned with industry standards.

Also, consider a program that also offers class credit toward certification in your area of interest. This will provide you with access to industry professionals, which could lead to internships or entry-level positions. It is often said that it is not what you know but who you know that gets you that first job. Let me add that who you know might get you in the door, but it will be what you know that will keep you inside the door.

In selecting an educational program, it is recommended you attend a program with other students who are highly motivated and committed to their field of study. Students learn a great deal from their classmates, particularly if there are opportunities to work on projects. Look beyond the classrooms to where you will be sharing time with classmates working on projects as a contributor, learning teamwork by experience.

Examples of University Programs

With over 300 college and university programs available, the following is a small sample of what is being offered. A full list of educational programs on special events appears in Appendix 2.

The Value of Education

On the one hand, having been an adjunct professor for many years, I see advantages in having a college degree. On the other hand, having been in the special events industry for even more years, I also see the advantages of experience, and of certifications. No matter which direction you take, there are rewards for your effort. Over the span of your profes-

The George Washington University

The Department of Hospitality and Tourism Management, including the International Institute of Tourism Studies, offer graduate, undergraduate, and certificate programs in tourism destination management, sports management, events management, and hospitality management. Located in Washington, D.C., which is the home to many leading international tourism organizations, associations, meetings and events firms, sports teams, and hotel companies, the GWU program provides students with many opportunities for networking, internships, and entry-level jobs. It offers these degrees: master of tourism administration (on-campus or distance learning); bachelor of business administration (with a concentration in sports and events management or hospitality management); a five-year BBA/BTA program; and event

The George Washington University (Continued)

and tourism professional education (certificate) programs.

The Event Management Certificate Program, first developed by Dr. Goldblatt in 1994, is for students interested in the theoretical and practical aspects of event and meeting management, including research, design, planning, coordination, and evaluation of events and meetings of various types and sizes. Students study best practices in promotion, organization, and risk management. Emphasis is on the management competencies required for a successful career as an events and meeting professional.

(*Source*: www.gwutourism.org)

Tourism Studies

- Introduction—tourism and hospitality management
- Sports and event management
- International hotel management
- Administration—tourist and hospitality management
- Tourist development
- Tourist marketing
- Sports marketing
- Tourism research
- Rick management for events and meetings
- Event management
- Contract and negotiation for meetings and events
- Advanced topical studies—hotel sales
- Issues in sports governance
- Designation development through hosting sports and events
- Relationship management in hospitality
- Advanced topical studies

University of Nevada Las Vegas

Being in the middle of Las Vegas, a prime tourist destination, provides the UNLV students with many opportunities to see and experience hospitality firsthand. The Harrah Hotel College offers degrees in:

- Food and beverage management
- Hotel management
- Recreation and sport management
- Tourism and convention management

University of Nevada Las Vegas (*Continued*)

The Tourism and Convention Administration Department of Harrah Hotel College offers a major in meetings and events management with a bachelor of science in hotel administration, as well as a bachelor of science with a major in recreation. Students can focus in areas such as meetings and expositions, entertainment and event management, tourism administration, and therapeutic recreation. Other courses include hospitality accounting and finance, hospitality management, and cruise ship management. Also available is a major in Recreation, with a concentration in the Professional Golf Management program, certified by the PGA.

Visit its Web site at: www.unlv.edu.

(*Source*: www.unlv.edu)

University of Central Florida—Rosen School of Hospitality Management

The Rosen College of Hospitality Management provides a comprehensive educational experience that prepares students for management opportunities by offering a bachelor of science in hospitality management, restaurant and food service management, and a certificate program in event management.

The Rosen School, as it is often called, is located in what they call the largest learning laboratory in the world for hospitality and tourism, Orlando, Florida. The Central Florida area hosts more than 40 million visitors annually, with more than 120,000 hotel rooms, 4,000 restaurants and 75 theme parks and attractions. The Rosen School campus boasts of having one of the most up-to-date facilities available for students training for hospitality management and tourism. The area provides a great many advantages because of the scale and scope of the tourism industry in central Florida. Tourist-focused businesses provide part-time jobs or internships to students, where they learn firsthand about their area of study. As an example, a student interested in fine dining might have the opportunity to intern at a wine shop, learning about wines from around the world. These are very valuable experiences, and are outstanding on your résumé.

Visit its Web site at www.hospitality.ucf.edu.

(*Source*: www.hospitality.ucf.edu)

Leeds Metropolitan University

For many years, Leeds Metropolitan University has led the United Kingdom as an outstanding program for event management. Leeds Metropolitan University provides students with unique opportunities to participate in festivals that celebrate arts, sports, and business. There are opportunities to learn both in the classroom and by actually taking part in the festivals.

Visit its Web site at www.lmu.ac.uk.

(*Source*: www.lmu.ac.uk)

Johnson & Wales University

This Hospitality College provides training in the expanding global hospitality industry from hotels, resorts, and spas to careers in adventure and ecotourism, sports and event management, as well as entrepreneurial ventures. Its programs are developed with industry input, combining classroom study with hands-on learning, while using industry-standard software. With industry-experienced faculty, students work on real projects and discover networking opportunities.

Bachelor of Science Degrees:

- Baking and pastry arts and food service management*
- Culinary arts and food service management*
- Hotel and lodging management
- International hotel and tourism management
- Restaurant, food and beverage management
- Sports/entertainment/event management
- Travel, tourism, and hospitality management

The Alan Shawn Feinstein Graduate School offers a master of business administration degree in hospitality with a concentration in event leadership. This concentration was developed in 2001 by Dr. Joe Goldblatt, and was the first MBA degree with a concentration in event leadership.

Certificate Program:

- *Travel Agent Certificate*

Non-Degree Program:

- "Undeclared" (a two-year program that tracks into the Hospitality College's bachelor's degree)

Visit its Web site at www.jwu.edu.

(*Source*: www.jwu.edu)

*Offered jointly through the Hospitality College and the College of Culinary Arts

Queen Margaret University

This degree in event management offers you an understanding of the nature of the product itself; an understanding of the political, economic, and social context, within which the production and consumption of these products and services take place; an understanding of the management and organization involved in the provision and consumption of the hospitality and tourism products and services; and a range of specialist applications and skills, such as law and understanding of the research process. In addition, you will have the opportunity to participate in the workplace through a period of industrial placement.

QMU provides an excellent example of the progression of learning in a university.

Year One:

- Introduction to events
- Cultural management and events tourism
- Markets and customers
- Foundations of management
- An elective choice

Year Two:

- Events project management
- Principles and practices of events management
- Supervised work experience/work-based learning
- Managing resources
- People in organizations
- An elective choice

Year Three:

- Recreating the city: events, image, and regeneration

- The risk society: events policy and law
- Strategic management
- Business consultancy
- An elective choice

Year Four:

- Strategic directions: consumption and culture
- Entertainment and the experience economy
- Development and issues in global events
- Business excellence
- The future of management

Strategic management
Dissertation

Structure:

This is a three- or four-year modular course over two semesters per year.

Placement:

On completion of Year Two, you may undertake a 16-week paid placement in industry. This invaluable work experience can take place either in the United Kingdom or overseas. Single-semester study exchange agreements exist with universities in the United States, France, Germany, and Spain.

In addition to the undergraduate program, Queen Margaret University will offer the world's first executive master's degree in international planned events (MPE), commencing in Autumn 2010. This program will be offered by distance learning, using teleconferencing from personal computers and three one-week residencies in major event cities such as Edinburgh.

Queen Margaret University (*Continued*)

The University is located in Edinburgh, Scotland, home of the Edinburgh Festival Fringe, the world's largest performing arts festival. There are many opportunities for students to view, learn, participate, and experience a wide range of activities in the hospitality and tourism industry.

Visit its Web site at www.qmu.ac.uk.

(*Source*: www.qmu.ac.uk)

sional career, you will reap more benefits sooner if you have the necessary skills, and you get those skills by investing in your personal development.

The better prepared you are to enter the industry, the better the chances are for you to land a great position. Your first position can be a foundation or cornerstone, upon which you can build, with success after success. With each success comes confidence, in your eyes and the eyes of others. More opportunities become available, and you will reach a point where you will be able to be selective as to what you want to do, as well as what you have time to do. Doing what you love creates fulfillment, and that will increase

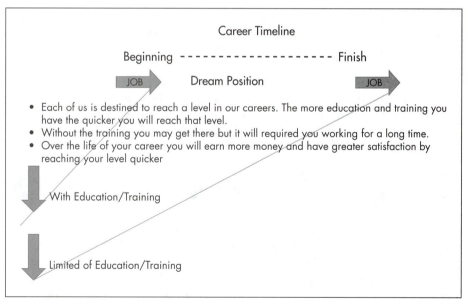

Figure 11.1   The More Education You Have, the Sooner You Will Reach the Level Where You are Meant To Be

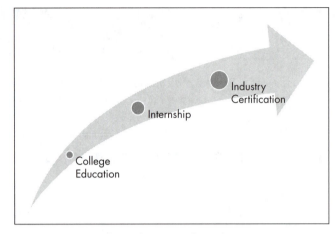

Figure 11.2 Traditional Steps in the Industry

your energy and excitement about what you are doing, while taking everything you do to a new level. Your reputation for success will put you in demand, and you will pick what you most want to do. It is all built on your training and knowledge, as well as having faith in yourself.

When you come to the end of all the light you know, and it's time to step into the darkness of the unknown, faith is knowing that one of two things shall happen: Either you will be given something solid to stand on or you will be taught to fly.

Edward Teller (1908–2003)

These are traditional steps into the special events industry: attending a college or university, being accepted as an intern or with an entry-level position, and/or receiving a certification.

Internships

Internships are continuations of training, or an even more intense training program in which a person transitions from the formal setting of the classroom to the work site, learning to apply their skills (see Figure 11.3). Many employers understand the value of bringing individuals into their organization to assist with projects, but also to get a sense of their abilities in a work environment. For the intern, it is an opportunity to see and experience what happens in a real-world situation.

In your transition from the classroom to the workplace, you will still be part of the learning process. Just as in the classroom, there are assignments for which you are evaluated and graded. As an intern, you will be given assignments and you will be evaluated as to how well you perform duties and work with the team. You must always do your best, as there is always someone watching and evaluating. Your teachers, your boss, and your clients all expect you to do your best work every time.

If you are in career redirection, your internship is the chance to enjoy the experience of being on a special events team, proving to yourself as well as others why you should be part of the industry. You have the advantage of an established work ethic, and are leaving a comfort zone to pursue a new direction. For some professionals redirecting their careers, a new supervisor may be younger and in many ways less experienced, but coming to terms with that issue is very important. Become an asset for your supervisor and assist in a very positive manner. Each of you will learn from the other.

The internship is an exciting and wonderful part of the educational process. Expect to get a lot of guidance and exposure to the process of how events come together. You are entering an industry that generates hundreds of billions of dollars each year, with tens of thousands of events being done every day around the world. There are thousands of small and large companies that provide employment for thousands of people, so the odds are very good that there is a place waiting for you. Even in times of recession, people get married, have birthdays, celebrate anniversaries, go to concerts, support community efforts, have holiday parties, have fundraisers, retire, and so on. Like all businesses, there are ups and downs, but special events will never go away, even in the worst of times.

In your preparations for launching your career, understand what is so eloquently explained by Dr. Joe Goldblatt in his book *Special Events: Twenty-first Century Global Event Management,* when he details the five critical stages of all events: research, design, planning, coordination, and evaluation. These all fall into the management framework of administration, coordination, marketing and legal, ethical, and risk management. By the time you are applying for your internship, you should have a good grasp of this template and use it in planning your internship interview.

- *Research:* Find special events companies that do the types of events you would be most interested in exploring, such as sports, weddings, corporate, social, nonprofit fundraisers, and so on. Make a list, and then prioritize which organizations you are

---

Paid Interns

- Establishes "a day's work for a day's pay"
- Capitalizes on the desire to get the most value possible from the investment

*Unpaid Interns**

- An opportunity to observe and learn
- Used as volunteers

---

* Note: Never use an unpaid intern to replace a paid employee.

Figure 11.3 Internships

going to target. However, keep an open mind to try something you might not have considered.

- *Design:* Your résumé and cover letter are only part of the plan. Create a portfolio of projects you have done in and out of school. All your materials need to be first class, as you want to represent yourself the way you will represent the targeted organization. Each company should have materials that focus on the company, which you should access from its Web site.
- *Planning:* Just as you plan an event, develop a plan for how you are going to connect to the targeted company. The more detailed your plan, the better prepared you are to take advantage of opportunities with that company. Since you would not do an event without a plan, you should not do an interview without a plan.
- *Coordination:* Attention to detail is your key to success, from the paper you select for the hard copy of your letter and résumé to the shoes you wear. Coordination on each detail leading up to and executing the interview has to be well thought out and implemented.
- *Evaluation:* Often this is overlooked, but it is a critical part of the process. If you get the internship or position, it is very appropriate to request feedback on your interview, as well as requesting that you get ongoing performance reviews. This prevents you from being surprised when, at the end of the internship, you are told you are not the right fit and you find out that you innocently did something early on in your internship that was never addressed.

> ### Gene-Gem
>
> Use care when asking for feedback on what you don't do very well because people will accommodate you by pointing out things you are not good at—and that's how they will remember you!

There are some degree programs that require an internship as part of the requirement, but even if it is not required, it is highly recommended. There are both short-term and long-term advantages with internships, but the most important advantage is that it gives you firsthand experience. Seeing all the component parts and how they interrelate will connect what was learned in the classroom to what is done in the field. It is exciting to see a live event executed, where everything must be done in a certain order and adjustments are made as challenges arise. You learn by seeing how each member of the team works as a member of the unit.

Most colleges and universities require the intern to have the following:

- A contract between the company and the intern
- An evaluation during and after the internship
- A number of hours to be worked over a set number of weeks
- An internship done in the area of the student's field of study
- A recommended "grade" for the intern
- A report on areas of learning

The hardest part of being an intern is finding and getting the position. There seems to be many more candidates than positions, so it is critical that you prepare yourself and have a solid plan on how you are going to approach the process of finding and securing the much-coveted positions. Go back to the basics of "opportunity versus preparedness" and make a renewed commitment to prepare as much as possible so that you find yourself with more than one option.

Interviewing for an internship is fundamentally the same as for any other position. The key is to learn all you can so that you can bring value in the special events industry. The organization that hires you as an intern will mold, shape, train, and hopefully keep you. Get started with an organization that you admire, and once you land the internship, make the most of your time by bringing value to them and their clients—this could lead to a full-time position.

> ### Gene-Gem
>
> If an opportunity presents itself to you and you are not prepared, it is a missed opportunity. But the act of preparation can create the opportunity.

Certainly, the internship is the chance to see if it is a good fit for both you and the company, but even if you are unsure whether you want a long-term relationship with a company, always do your very best to preserve and perpetuate your reputation. If you gain proprietary information about a company that provided an opportunity, never share this private information, as it always gets back one way or another, which will be negative to your reputation. You will find that paths cross many times in this industry, and you never know when you might be working together or will need the other person as a resource in some way. People will respect you more if you show that you can be trusted.

Internships are an important part of this process. In the interview for the continuation with the company, you as a candidate are able to give great examples of what you have learned and areas you are seeking to develop. From the vantage point of the intern, there are many opportunities to explore various aspects of the industry. Often, the intern is used in the capacity of a production assistant, with duties involving the company's process of creating and implementing events. Since the intern is not expected to already know the business, generally he or she is given more detailed instructions and guidelines. Internships are a continuation of your training, and the transition from academic training to on-the-job training.

> ### Gene-Gem
>
> Set a personal standard that you will never compromise; as the demands of the industry become greater, so much so your ethical standards.

Most organizations have job descriptions, position descriptions, or job outlines, and it is very important get them and read them carefully (see Figure 11.4). There could be additional material available, but understanding your responsibilities is the key to success.

Responsibilities will be adjusted to suit the needs of the company or task being assigned. This is good information, as it gives you a roadmap to prepare for answering the questions. Generally speaking, the interviewer or hiring manager will ask questions related to what is on the job outline/description. If you break it down and want to show that you have the potential to do this role, start making a list of each duty and what experience

Production Intern

- Responsible for procuring all research materials for the Production Team.
- Accountable for gathering and coordinating presentation materials, including PowerPoint.
- Responsible for scheduling and coordinating rehearsals, vendors, and technicians, suppliers, and talent and maintaining timelines, schedules, meetings, and status reports.
- Supports the production team in the research and preparation for authorizations and purchase orders.
- Produces a complete production book and provides pertinent information for all aspects of the event.
- Completes any and all production tasks as requested by the production team.

Figure 11.4 Sample Job Description

or knowledge you have with each item. You will be amazed at how much material you have or areas of focus to learn about that aspect of the position.

As an intern, you generally will not be expected to have much in the way of experience, but they will expect you to have knowledge on the process. If you have a target company and your ultimate goal is to work for it full-time, you need to invest a good deal of time before and during your internship. The successful intern learns all he or she can about how to do the job. It is exciting when it all comes together and you celebrate your successes, but part of the fun is getting there, doing the research, challenging yourself to do more and doing it better. Remember that today's special events are the foundation for what you will build on tomorrow. How can you improve on what was done, what emerging trend can you take advantage of that will captivate and delight your audiences, and how can you contribute to those trends? Always continue to learn more about your industry and continue with an organization doing something for which you have a real passion.

One of most important qualities necessary to be successful as an intern or an entry-level employee is responsibility. You are evaluated on everything, so it is recommended that you go above and beyond in the performance of your duties. Be ready to take action at the assigned time. One young man told me that he was no good for anything until he had his first cup of coffee. My question was why he waited until he got to work to have his first cup of coffee. Think of the impression he made by saying he was not able to do his job until he was ready—not when the company wanted and needed him. Bring value to the company by being on time and ready to work, with a willing spirit that will result in long-term positive results for all concerned.

The interns I have worked with brought a special energy and excitement to the workplace. Enthusiasm can be contagious in an organization. Your fresh eyes looking at how things are done and asking questions make us wonder why we never asked that question, which can be very helpful in finding new and better ways of doing things.

New interns seem to raise the excitement level for our staff, as it gives us opportunities to look back and remember why we wanted to be a part of this wonderful industry. We can tell our interns how we started, reflecting on all the people that helped us along the way, and knowing that it is our turn to help someone else. That is part of a grand tradition in the special events industry. As you receive help getting your start in the events industry, the day will come when you will be expected to pass it on and help others get their start.

Career Connections

 ## Action Steps

- Visit the Web site of each of the certifications listed in Chapter 5, considering when in your career you may be ready to apply for certification.
- Look at the Web sites of the colleges and universities mentioned in this chapter and review the types of training programs being offered.

 ## Practice Activity

Survey industry professionals who have earned an industry certification and ask them the following questions:

1. What is the value of your certification?
2. How easy/difficult was the examination?
3. How long did it take you to complete the process?
4. What was the hardest part of the certification process?
5. Have you seen a change in your career since receiving the certification?
6. If you had to choose between a certification and a college degree, which would you select?
7. Did you have an internship-type experience in your career?
8. What advice would you give for someone seeking that type of opportunity?

Go to the Web site of each of the certification programs, reading all the requirements, and map out for yourself a master plan on how and when you will earn your certification.

Select five organizations that you are going to target for internship, learning all you can about them:

1. Do they have a formal internship program?
2. If so, how long is the program?
3. Is it paid or unpaid?
4. Does the program include training and exposure to various areas in the company?
5. When is their interview process and what does it consist of?

Tool Kit

Oldman, Mark, and Hamadeh, Samer (2004). *The Internship Bible*. New York: Princeton Review, L.L.C.

Wise, Carolyn C. (2009). *The Vault Guide to Top Internships*. Vault, Inc.

 Web Connection

Quintessential Careers, www.quintcareers.com.

   This is an excellent general Web site that has much to offer in the way of suggestions on your quest for an internship:

- What you need to know
- Help finding internships
- Internship tips
- Making the most of the internship
- Turning an internship into a job

There is much to explore on this site, including recommendations on general cover letters. There are good tips, even if they are not focused on the hospitality industry.

APPENDICES

APPENDIX 1

Recommended Reading

There are a variety of publications that focus on the special events and related industries, and these are where you will find the latest information on emerging trends in the industry. Successful industry leaders often submit articles that can give you greater insight into the process. Whether a student, intern, or certified professional, by reading about how industry experts deal with challenges, you learn a great deal. Information is now available in books, magazines and newspapers, but let us begin with that most popular and emerging resource, the Internet. The Internet can often provide incorrect, unchecked information, so make sure that you only read reliable sources, and fact-check all Internet information.

The following is a list of recommended Internet resources.

Recommended Web Sites

- The Center for Association Leadership (www.asaecenter.org)
- Association Meetings (www.meetingsnet.com/associationmeetings)
- Association News Magazine (www.associationnews.com)
- Association Trends Job Board (jobs.associationtrends.com)
- BizBash Media (www.bizbash.com)
- Business Traveller (www.businesstraveller.com)
- Canadian Meetings Professional, Inc. (www.canadianmeetings.com)
- *Convene* magazine (www.pcma.org/Convene.html)
- *Corporate and Incentive Travel* magazine (www.themeetingmagazines.com/index/cit)
- Corporate Meetings & Incentives (www.meetingsnet.com/corporatemeetings incentives)

- *Event Solutions* (www.event-solutions.com)
- *Event Source* (www.eventsource.net)
- Exhibit City News (www.exhibitcitynews.com)
- *Exhibitor* magazine (www.exhibitoronline.com)
- *EXPO* magazine (www.expoweb.com)
- Hospitality Upgrade (www.hospitalityupgrade.com)
- Hotel World Network (www.hotelworldnetwork.com)
- Hotel F&B (www.hotelfandb.com)
- International Association of Assembly Managers, Inc. (IAAM) (www.iaam.org)
- Financial & Insurance Meetings (meetingsnet.com/financialinsurancemeetings)
- International Festivals and Events Association (www.ifea.com)
- *Lodging* magazine (www.lodgingmagazine.com)
- Hospitality Sales and Marketing Association International (http://www.hsmai.org)
- Medical Meetings (www.meetingsnet.com/medicalmeetings)
- MeetingsNet (www.meetingsnet.com)
- Meeting Professionals International (www.mpiweb.org)
- Meetings & Conventions (www.mcmag.com)
- Meetings Media·(www.meetingsmedia.com)
- *Mid-Atlantic Events* magazine (www.eventsmagazine.com)
- Meetings Industry Soapbox (www.misoapbox.com)
- Small Market Meetings (www.smallmarketmeetings.com)
- Smart Meetings (www.smartmeetings.com)
- *Special Events* magazine (www.specialevents.com)
- *SportsTravel* magazine (www.sportstravelmagazine.com)
- Tradeshow Blues (www.tradeshowblues.com)
- Tradeshow Week (www.tradeshowweek.com)
- Western Association of Convention and Visitor Bureaus (www.wacvb.com)

Recommended Books

I highly recommend that you start with Dr. Joe Goldblatt's book *Special Events: A New Generation and the Next Frontier*. You will find a wealth of information, including an even greater list of reading recommendations. Dr. Goldblatt wisely recommends reading one book a week, in addition to news articles and other sources of information. I encourage you to read various books on careers in events. The following is a master list of recommended books, many of which are listed throughout the book as Career Connections.

Special Events Career Building Books

Axtell, Roger (1993). *Do's and Taboos Around the World*. New York: John Wiley & Sons, Inc.

Blaustein, Arthur I. (2003). *Making a Difference: America's Guide to Volunteering and Community Service*. San Francisco, CA: John Wiley & Sons, Inc.

Bolles, Richard N. (2009). *The Job-Hunter's Survival Guide.* Random House.

Chapman, Jack. (2000). *Negotiating Your Salary.* Wilmette, IL: Jack Chapman.

Cohen, Norman H. PhD (1999). *The Mentee's Guide to Mentoring.* HRD Press.

Dawson, Roger (2006). *Secrets of Power Salary Negotiating.* New Jersey: The Career Press.

Enelow, Wendy S., & Kursmark, Louise M. (2007). *Cover Letter Magic.* St. Paul, MN: JIST Publishing, Inc.

Enelow, Wendy S., and Kursmark, Louse. (2000). *Cover Letter Magic: Trade Secrets of Professional Resume Writers.* St. Paul, MN: JIST Publishing, Inc.

Friedmann, Susan (2003). *Meeting & Event Planning for Dummies.* For Dummies.

Goldblatt, Joe (2001). Th*e International Dictionary of Event Management.* Hoboken, NJ: John Wiley & Sons.

Goldblatt, Joe and Kathleen S. Nelson (2001). *The International Dictionary of Event Management.* Hoboken, NJ: John Wiley & Sons.

Gottesman, Deb (1999). *The Interview Rehearsal Book.* New York: The Berkley Publishing Group.

Gross, Kim Johnson & Stone, Jeff (2002). *Dress Smart Women Wardrobes That Win in the New Workplace.* New York: Warner Books, Inc.

Levit, Alexandra (2008). *How'd You Score That Gig?: A Guide to the Coolest Jobs—and How to Get Them.* New York: Ballantine Books.

Lore, Nicholas (2008). *Now What? The Young Person's Guide to Choosing the Perfect Career.* New York: Fireside.

Lore, Nicholas (1998). *The Pathfinder: How to Choose or Change Your Career for a Lifetime of Satisfaction and Success.* New York: Simon & Schuster.

Maxwell, John C. (2008). *Mentoring 101.* Nashville: Thomas Nelson.

Mangelsdorf, Martha E. (2009). *Strategies for Successful Career Change.* New York: Random House Ten Speed Press.

Molloy, John T. (1988). *Dress for Success.* New York: Warner Books

Monroe, James, and Robert Kates. (2005). *Art of the Event.* Hoboken, NJ: John Wiley & Sons.

Myers, Ford R. (2009). *Get the Job You Want, Even When No One's Hiring.* New York: Random House Ten Speed Press.

Powers, Paul (2005). *Winning Job Interviews.* New Jersey: The Career Press.

Roane, Susan (2007). *How to Work a Room: Your Essential Guide to Savvy Socializing.* Collins Living.

Rosenberg, Bob, and Lampard, Guy (2005). *Giving From The Heart A Guide To Volunteering.* Lincoln, Nebraska: iUniverse.

Schawbel, Dan (2009). *Me 2.0: Build a Powerful Brand to Achieve Career Success.* New York: Kaplan, Inc.

Silvers, Julia Rutherford (2003). *Professional Event Coordination.* Hoboken, NJ: John Wiley & Sons.

Supovitz, Frank, and Joe Goldblatt (2004). *The Sports Event Management and Marketing Playbook.* Hoboken, NJ: John Wiley & Sons.

Sonder, Mark (2003). *Event Entertainment and Production.* Hoboken, NJ: John Wiley & Sons.

Wellington, Sheila, and Betty Spence (2001). *Be Your Own Mentor: Strategies from Top Women on the Secrets of Success*. New York: Random House.

Yate, Martin (2008). *Knock 'em Dead Cover Letters*. Cincinnati, OH: Adams Media.

Zichy, Shoya, and Bidou, Ann (2007). *Career Match: Connecting Who You Are with What You'll Love to Do*. New York: AMACOM.

Travel and Tourism Industry Books

Baum, Tom, and Mudambi, Ram (1999). *Economic and Management Methods for Tourism and Hospitality Research*. New York: John Wiley & Sons.

Cater, Erlet (ed.), and Lowman, Gwen (ed.). (1994). *Ecotourism: A Sustainable Option?* New York: John Wiley & Sons.

Coltman, Michael (1989). *Introduction to Travel and Tourism: An International Approach*. New York: John Wiley & Sons.

Conlin, Michael V. (ed.), and Baum, Tom (ed.). (1995). *Island Tourism: Management Principles and Practice*. New York: John Wiley & Sons.

Giulianotti, Richard (ed.), and Robertson, Roland (2007). *Globalization and Sport*. Hoboken, NJ: John Wiley & Sons.

Guerrie, Yvonne (1999). *Organizational Behaviour in Hotels and Restaurants: An International Perspective*. New York: John Wiley & Sons.

Harrison, Lynn C. (ed.), and Husbands, Winston (ed.). (1996). *Practicing Responsible Tourism: International Case Studies in Tourism Planning, Policy, and Development*. New York: John Wiley & Sons.

Heath, Ernie, and Wall, Geoffrey (1992). *Marketing Tourism Destinations: A Strategic Planning Approach*. New York: John Wiley & Sons.

Lunderg, Donald E., and Lunderg, Carolyn B. (1993). *International Travel and Tourism*, 2nd ed. New York: John Wiley & Sons.

McCabe, Vivienne, and Poole, Barry (2002). *The Business and Management of Conventions*. Hoboken, NJ: John Wiley & Sons.

Plog, Stanley (1991). *Leisure Travel: Making it a Growth Market.., Again!* New York: John Wiley & Sons.

Pond, Kathleen Lingle (1992). *The Professional Guide: Dynamics of Tour Guiding*. New York: John Wiley & Sons.

Poynter, James (1993). *How to Research and Write a Thesis in Hospitality and Tourism: A Step-By-Step Guide for College Students*. New York: John Wiley & Sons.

Price, Martin F. (1997). *People and Tourism in Fragile Environments*. New York: John Wiley & Sons.

Shaw, Gareth, and Williams, Allan M. (2002). *Critical Issues in Tourism: A Geographical Perspective*, 2nd ed. Hoboken, NJ: John Wiley-Blackwell.

Weaver, David (2007). *Ecotourism*, 2nd Edition Hoboken, NJ: John Wiley & Sons

APPENDIX 2

Schools of Hospitality Management

There are many options for training in special events. In Chapter 11, only a few were highlighted as examples of the types of training available. Events are interconnected with many different aspects of the industry; therefore, it is worthwhile to have a broad understanding of as many elements as possible in the hospitality industry. Visit Web sites to see the wide variety of training available, and read course descriptions. You will see that disciplines intersect, overlap, and partner in the industry.

Note: Institutions of higher education regularly change their programs. Please contact the individual institution for further information about their current offerings.

Schools of the Hospitality Industry

- Academie Internationale de Management (AIM)—Hotel Management—Paris, France—www.academy.fr
- Alexandria Technical College—Hotel and Restaurant Management Program—Alexandria, MN—www.alextech.edu/hotelrestaurant
- Arkansas Tech University—Hospitality Administration—Russellville, AR—www.atu.edu
- Art Institutes Int'l Minnesota—Culinary Arts and Hospitality Management—Minneapolis, MN www.artinstitutes.edu/minneapolis
- Asheville-Buncombe Technical Comm. College—Dept. of Hospitality Education—Asheville, NC—www.asheville.cc.nc.us/bh/hospitality/Default.asp

*Source: Convention Industry Council website: www.conventionindustry.org

175

- Auburn University—Hotel and Restaurant Management Program—Auburn, AL—www.humsci.auburn.edu/hrmt
- Blue Mountains International Hotel Management School—Leura, Australia— www.hotelschool.com.au
- Borough of Manhattan Community College—New York—www.bmcc.cuny.edu
- Boston University—School of Hospitality Administration—Boston, MA—www .bu.edu/hospitality/
- Canadian Tourism College—College of Tourism and Hospitality Management— Vancouver, BC—www.tourismcollege.com
- Cecil B. Day School of Hospitality Administration—Georgia State University— Atlanta—http://robinson.gsu.edu/hospitality/index.htm
- Champlain College—Hospitality Industry Management Program—Burlington, VT—www.champlain.edu/majors/hospitality
- Chemeketa Community College—Hospitality Systems Management Program— Salem, OR—www.hsm.org or www.chemeketa.edu
- College of Charleston—Hospitality and Tourism Management—Charleston, SC—www.htmt.cofc.edu/
- Columbus State Community College—Hospitality Management—Columbus, OH—www.cscc.edu/hospitality
- Conrad N. Hilton College of Hotel and Restaurant Management Program— Houston, TX—www.hrm.uh.edu/
- Cornell University—School of Hotel Administration—Ithaca, NY—www.hotelschool .cornell.edu
- Culinary Institute of America (CIA)—Hyde Park, NY—www.ciachef.edu
- Culinary School of the Rockies—Professional Culinary Arts Programs—Boulder, CO—www.culinaryschoolrockies.com
- Dakota County Technical College—Meeting and Event Management—Rosemount, MN—www.dctc.mnscu.edu
- Dedman School of Hospitality at Florida State University—Tallahassee—www .cob.fsu.edu/dsh
- Delaware State University—Hospitality and Tourism Management—Dover—www .desu.edu
- Douglas College—Hotel and Restaurant Management Diploma Program— Coquitlam, BC—www.douglas.bc.ca
- East Carolina University—Department of Hospitality Management—Greenville, NC—www.ecu.edu/che/hmgt
- Eastern Michigan University—Hotel and Restaurant Management—Ypsilanti— www.emich.edu/sts/hrm/
- Emirates Academy of Hospitality Management—Dubai—www.jumeirah.com/en/ Jumeirah-Group/The-Emirates-Academy/
- ESHOTEL—Ecole Supérieure de Gestion Hôtelière et de Tourisme—Paris/Lille, France—www.eshotel.fr
- Fairleigh Dickinson University—International School of Hospitality and Tourism Management—Teaneck, NJ—www.fdu.edu/

- Florida Atlantic University (FAU)—Hospitality Management—Boca Raton—business .fau.edu/hospitality
- Florida Gulf Coast University—Resort and Hospitality Management (RHM)—Fort Myers—cps.fgcu.edu/resort
- Florida International University—School of Hospitality and Tourism Mgmt—Biscayne Bay Campus, N. Miami—hospitality.fiu.edu
- Frederick Community College—Culinary Arts and Hospitality Institute—Frederick, MD—www.frederick.edu/courses_and_programs/hospitality.aspx
- George Washington University—Department of Tourism and Hospitality Management—Washington, DC—business.gwu.edu/tourism
- Griffith University—School of Tourism and Hotel Management—Queensland, Australia—www.griffith.edu.au/business/tourism
- Highline Community College—Hotel and Tourism Management—Des Moines, WA—www.flightline.highline.edu/hotelhospitality/
- Hong Kong Polytechnic University's School of Hotel and Tourism Management (HTM)—www.polyu.edu.hk
- Hotel School—Sydney, Australia—http://hotelschool.scu.edu.au
- Humber College—School of Hospitality, Recreation and Tourism—Toronto, CN—http://hospitality.humber.ca/
- IMI International Hotel Management Institute—Switzerland—www.imi-luzern .com/
- Imperial Hotel Management College—Hotel Management School—Vancouver, BC—www.ihmc.ca/s/Home.asp
- Indiana University–Purdue University (IPFW)—Hospitality and Tourism Management—Fort Wayne—www.ipfw.edu
- International College of Management—Sydney, Australia—www.icms.edu.au/
- Iowa Lakes Community College—Travel And Tourism Management—Emmetsburg—www.ilcc.cc.ia.us
- Indiana University—School of Physical Education and Tourism Management—Indianapolis—www.iupui.edu/~indyhper/
- J. Sargeant Reynolds Community College—Culinary Arts, Tourism and Hospitality—Richmond, VA—www.jsr.vccs.edu
- Johnson and Wales University—Hospitality College—Charlotte, NC—www.jwu .edu/charlotte
- Johnson and Wales University—Hospitality College—Denver, CO—www.jwu .edu/denver
- Johnson and Wales University—Hospitality College—North Miami, FL—www.jwu .edu/northmiami
- Johnson and Wales University—Hospitality College—Providence, RI www.jwu .edu/providence
- Kemmons Wilson School of Hospitality and Resort Management—University of Memphis—Memphis, TN—memphis.edu/hospitality
- Kendall College—Hospitality and Restaurant Management—Chicago, IL—www .kendall.edu

- Leeds Metropolitan University, U.K. Centre for Events Management, Leeds, England—www.lmu.ac.uk
- Lester E. Kabacoff School of Hotel, Restaurant and Tourism Admin.—University of New Orleans, LA—http://business.uno.edu/hrt/
- Lexington College—Hospitality Management—Chicago, IL—www.lexingtoncollege.edu
- Lincoln University—Hotel and Institutional Management—Lincoln (Canterbury) New Zealand—www.lincoln.ac.nz
- Lynn University—College of Hospitality Management—Boca Raton, FL—www.lynn.edu/academics/colleges/hospitality-management
- Mercyhurst College—Hotel, Restaurant and Institutional Management Dept. (HRIM)—Erie, PA—www.mercyhurst.edu
- Miami Dade College—Hospitality Management Program—Miami, FL—www.mdc.edu/wolfson/academic/Hospitality/index.asp
- Michigan State University—The School of Hospitality Business—East Lansing—www.bus.msu.edu/shb
- MiraCosta College—Hospitality, Restaurant, Travel and Tourism Programs—Oceanside, CA—www.miracosta.edu/hospitality
- Montclair State University—Recreation and Leisure Studies—Upper Montclair, NJ—www.montclair.edu/HPPERLS/Courses/PERLDescriptions.html
- New England Culinary Institute (NECI)—Hospitality Education Programs—Montpelier, VT—www.neci.edu
- New York University—The Preston Robert Tisch Center for Hospitality, Tourism, and Sports Management—New York—www.scps.nyu.edu/areas-of-study/tisch
- Niagara University—College of Hospitality And Tourism Management—Niagara Falls, NY—www.niagara.edu/hospitality
- Normandale Community College—Tourism and Hospitality Management—Bloomington, MN—www.normandale.edu
- North Carolina Central University—Hospitality and Tourism Program—Durham—www.nccu.edu
- Northeastern State University—Hospitality and Tourism Management—Tahlequah, OK—arapaho.nsuok.edu/~mdm
- Northern Alberta Institute of Technology (NAIT)—Hospitality Management—Alberta, CN—www.nait.ca
- Northern Arizona University—School of Hotel and Restaurant Management—Flagstaff—www.nau.edu/hrm
- Northwestern Business College—Chicago, IL—www.northwesterncollege.edu/
- Oklahoma State University—School of Hotel and Restaurant Administration—Stillwater—osu.okstate.edu
- Penn State—School of Hotel, Restaurant, and Recreation Management—University Park—www.hrrm.psu.edu
- Professional Development Institute of Tourism (PDIT)—Parksville, BC—www.pdit.ca

- Purdue University—Department of Hospitality and Tourism Management—West Lafayette, IN—www.cfs.purdue.edu/htm
- Queen Margaret University—School of Business, Enterprise and Management, Tourism, Hospitality and Events,—Edinburgh, Scotland www.qmu.ac.uk
- Red Deer College—Hospitality and Tourism Program—Red Deer, Alberta, CN—www.rdc.ab.ca
- Richland College—Travel, Exposition and Meeting Management Program—Dallas, TX—www.rlc.dcccd.edu
- Robert Morris University—Hospitality And Tourism Programs—Pittsburgh, PA—www.rmu.edu
- Rochester Institute of Technology—School of Hospitality and Service Management—Rochester, NY—www.rit.edu/cast/hsm
- Roosevelt University—Steinfeld School of Hospitality and Tourism Management—Chicago, IL—www.roosevelt.edu/
- Rosen College of Hospitality Management—University of Central Florida—Orlando—www.hospitality.ucf.edu
- San Diego State University, Hospitality and Tourism Management Program—San Diego, CA—htm.sdsu.edu.
- Schiller International University—Hotel Management University—Engelberg, Switzerland—www.schiller.edu
- Seneca College—School of Tourism—Markham, Ontario Canada—www.senecac.on.ca
- Seton Hill University—Bachelor of Science in Hospitality and Tourism—Greensburg, PA—www.setonhill.edu
- Sinclair Community College—Hospitality Programs (Culinary/Travel/Tourism)—Dayton, OH—www.sinclair.edu
- Southern Cross University—New South Wales, Australia—www.scu.edu.au
- Southern Illinois University Carbondale—Hospitality and Tourism—Carbondale, IL—www.siu.edu
- St. Cloud State University—Travel and Tourism Program—St. Cloud, MN—www.stcloudstate.edu
- Sullivan County Community College—Division of Business and Culinary—Loch Sheldrake, NY—www.sullivan.suny.edu
- Sullivan University—National Center for Hospitality Studies—Louisville, KY—www.sullivan.edu
- SUNY College of Agriculture/Tech.—Culinary Arts, Hospitality and Tourism—Cobleskill, NY—www.cobleskill.edu
- SUNY College of Technology At Delhi—Hospitality Programs (including Food and Beverage)—Delhi, NY—www.delhi.edu
- Temple University—School of Tourism and Hospitality Management (STHM)—Philadelphia, PA—www.temple.edu
- Texas Tech University—Restaurant, Hotel and Institutional Management—Lubbock—www.ttu.edu

- University of Arkansas, Fayetteville—Hospitality and Restaurant Management—Fayetteville—http://www.uark.edu/home/
- University of Calgary—World Tourism Education and Research Centre—Calgary, Alberta, CN—http://www.ucalgary.ca
- University of Central Florida, Rosen School of Hospitality—Orlando—www.hospitality.ucf.edu
- University of Colorado at Boulder—Tourism Management Program—Boulder—www.colorado.edu
- University of Delaware—Hotel, Restaurant and Institutional Management—Newark—www.udel.edu
- University of Denver—School of Hotel, Restaurant and Tourism Management—Denver—www.du.edu
- University of Guelph—School of Hospitality and Tourism Management—Guelph, Ontario—www.uoguelph.ca
- University of Hawaii-Manoa—School of Travel Industry Management—Honolulu—www.uhm.hawaii.edu
- University of Massachusetts—Department of Hospitality and Tourism Management—Amherst—www.umass.edu
- University of Missouri-Columbia—Hotel and Restaurant Management—Columbia—www.missouri.edu
- University of Nebraska at Kearney—Travel and Tourism Program—Kearney—www.unl.edu
- University of Nevada, Las Vegas—Harrah College Of Hotel Administration—Las Vegas—hotel.unlv.edu/departHotelMgt.html
- University of New Brunswick—Bachelor of Applied Management In Hospitality/Tourism—New Brunswick, Canada—www.unb.ca
- University of New Hampshire—Department of Hospitality Management—Durham—www.unh.edu
- University of New Mexico—Travel and Tourism Management—Albuquerque—www.unm.edu
- University of North Texas—Hospitality Management—Denton—www.unt.edu
- University of San Francisco—Hospitality Management Program—San Francisco, CA—www.usfca.edu
- University of South Carolina—School of Hotel, Restaurant and Tourism Management—Columbia—www.sc.edu
- University of South Florida/Sarasota-Manatee—B/S in Hospitality Management—Sarasota—www.sarasota.usf.edu
- University of Tennessee—Consumer and Industry Services Management—Knoxville—www.utk.edu
- University of Wisconsin-Stout—Hotel, Restaurant and Tourism Management—Menomonie—www.uwstout.edu
- Virginia State University—Hospitality Management Program—Petersburg—www.vsu.edu
- Virginia Tech—Hospitality And Tourism Management—Blacksburg—www.vt.edu

- Washburne Culinary Institute—Culinary Arts Careers—Chicago, IL—www .kennedyking.ccc.edu/washburne
- Washington State University—School of Hospitality Business Management—Pullman—www.wsu.edu
- Western Culinary Institute—Hospitality/Restaurant Management, Pâtisserie and Baking—Portland, OR—www.chefs.edu/portland
- Widener University—School of Hospitality Management—Chester, PA—www .widener.edu
- William Rainey Harper College—Hospitality Management—Palatine, IL—www .harpercollege.edu

APPENDIX 3

Professional Organizations

Networking is an essential part of being a successful special events professional. As you explore the following organizations, you will learn that they are a great resource in finding experts on a wide range of areas. Even if you are not specializing in that aspect of the industry, it is very important that you are aware of how these professional organizations support the needs of their clients.

- Association of Collegiate Conference and Events Directors-International (ACCED-I), www.acced-i.org
- Association Management Companies (AMC) Institute, www.amcinstitute.org
- Alliance of Meeting Management Consultants (AMMC), www.ammc.org
- American Hotel and Lodging Association (AH&LA), www.ahla.com
- American Society of Association Executives and the Center (ASAE and The Center), www.asaecenter.org
- Association for Convention Operations Management (ACOM), www.acomonline.org
- Association of Destination Management Executives (ADME), www.adme.org
- Council of Engineering and Scientific Society Executives (CESSE), www.cesse.org
- Center for Exhibition Industry Research (CEIR), www.ceir.org
- Exhibit Designers and Producers Association (EDPA), www.edpa.com
- Exhibition Services and Contractors Association (ESCA), www.esca.org
- Financial and Insurance Conference Planners (FICP)—formerly ICPA, www.ficpnet.com
- Green Meetings Industry Council (GMIC), www.greenmeetings.info
- Healthcare Convention and Exhibitors Association (HCEA), www.hcea.org
- Hospitality Sales and Marketing Association International (HSMAI), www.hsmai.org
- International Association of Assembly Managers (IAAM), www.iaam.org

*Courtesy of Convention Industry Council: www.conventionindustry.org

- International Association of Conference Centers (IACC), www.iacconline.org
- International Association for Exhibitions and Events (IAEE)—formerly IAEM, www.iaee.com
- International Association of Professional Congress Organizers (IAPCO), www.iapco.org
- International Association of Speakers Bureaus (IASB), www.iasbweb.org
- International Congress and Convention Association (ICCA), www.iccaworld.com
- International Special Events Society (ISES), www.ises.com
- Meeting Professionals International (MPI), www.mpiweb.org
- National Association of Catering Executives (NACE), www.nace.net
- National Business Travel Association (NBTA), www2.nbta.org
- National Coalition of Black Meeting Planners (NCBMP), www.ncbmp.com
- National Speakers Association (NSA), www.nsaspeaker.org
- Professional Convention Management Association (PCMA), www.pcma.org
- Religious Conference Management Association (RCMA), www.rcmaweb.org
- Society of Government Meeting Professionals (SGMP), www.sgmp.org
- Society of Incentive and Travel Executives (SITE), www.siteglobal.com
- Trade Show Exhibitors Association (TSEA), www.tsea.org
- U.S. Travel Association (U.S. Travel), www.tia.org

Professional and Trade Associations

- Academy of Hospitality Industry Attorneys (AHIA), www.ahiattorneys.org
- American Association of Airport Executives (AAAE), www.aaae.org
- American Society of Travel Agents (ASTA), www.asta.org
- Association of Corporate Travel Executives (ACTE), www.acte.org
- Association of Retail Travel Agents (ARTA), www.artaonline.com
- Corporate Event Marketing Association (CEMA), www.cemaonline.com
- Exhibitor Appointed Contractor Association (EACA), www.eaca.com
- Hospitality, Financial and Technology Professionals (HFTP), www.hftp.org
- International Airline Passengers Association (IAPA), www.iapa.com
- International Air Transport Association (IATA), www.iata.org
- The International Association of Hispanic Meeting Professionals (IAHMP), www.iahmp.org
- Pacific Asia Travel Association (PACTA), www.pata.org
- Society for Collegiate Travel Management (SCTM), www.fbs.usc.edu
- Society of Independent Show Organizers (SISO), www.siso.org
- World Tourism and Travel Council (WTTC), www.wttc.org
- The International Association of Speakers Bureaus (IASB), www.iasbweb.org

*Courtesy of Convention Industry Council: www.conventionindustry.org

Travel Safety

- U.S. Department of Homeland Security, www.dhs.gov
- Travel Industry Association, www.tia.org
- Transportation Security Administration's (TSA), Travel Guide for the Flying Public www.tsa.gov

Sample Résumés

Earlier in the book, you saw samples of résumés with an objective, which is highly recommended when sending your materials to a large organization. However, for smaller companies, where your cover letter will be forwarded on with your résumés, you should consider including a Summary of Qualifications.

Carlos Santiago   carlossantiago@cmail.com   (123) 456–7890
Summary of Qualifications

Multilingual manager with seven years' experience supporting events groups nationally and internationally. Skilled problem solver, budget analyst, proficient with visa regulations and intercultural communications. Proven track record for bringing in events on time, on target, and on budget.

EXPERIENCE

- World Wide Events, Inc. New York 2003 to Present

Event Planner and Producer
- Lead creative team in strategies supporting the desires and brand of corporate clients
- Create and review creative treatment and budgets for client presentation
- Present and negotiate contract details
- Ensure total satisfaction of the client
- Train and lead operational team in various locations through Central and South America

Key Accomplishments
- Increased sales by 50 percent in three years and average 20 percent additional each of the past four years
- Established sales representatives in 12 market locations throughout South America

---

- Improved efficiency of day-to-day operations with new regular conference meetings
- Miami Tourist Connection. Miami Beach, Florida 2001 to 2003

Sales Manager
- Expanded the business connections in Greater Miami by tenfold
- Served as producer for the Miami Expo attended by more than 15,000 Latino promoters
- Developed markets for new destination for events companies in Spain, Mexico, and Puerto Rico
- City of Miami. Miami, Florida 2000 to 2001

Internship—Special Events Coordinator for annual Holiday Parade and Celebration
- Developed the parade float line-up, communicated to all participants, assisted in recruiting volunteers
- Provided detailed information to KMIA-TV for on-camera personalities

EDUCATION

- University of Miami, Hospitality Management (BS) 2000

PROFESSIONAL ASSOCIATIONS

- ISES, MPI, Latin American Events Council of Mexico (LAECM)
- Skills
- Fluent in Spanish and French, and proficient in Italian
- Strong music background, piano
- Volunteer
- South Street Elementary School—Classroom aid for English as a second language 1999 to present
- Boys and Girls Clubs—weekends and summer volunteer counselor 1999 to present
- If you are repositioning, highlight your past accomplishments in this manner:

Mary Professional

1234 Your Street Home phone: (123) 456–7890
Hometown, State 23456 Cell phone: (123) 567–8901
mprofessional@eventsspecials.com

PROFILE

Accomplished professional with corporate expertise in event productions, operations, profit and loss (P&L) analysis, and process improvements involving existing growth organizations and new start-up business. Consistently demonstrates strategic vision in executing business imperatives while maximizing return on investment (ROI). Track record of spearheading assignments that create operational improvements to drive productivity, reduce costs, and achieve outstanding customer satisfaction.

Core Competencies

- Strategic planning
- Client value analysis
- Process management
- Relationship management
- Event production and management
- Operations management
- Financial reporting and analysis
- Financial forecasting
- Project management

Summary of Qualifications

- Amazing Events Company 2003 to Present

Production Manager (2007 to Present)
- Planned and managed 200+ events per year leading team of 35+ creative and operational staff

Project Manager (2005 to 2007)
- Developed database for tracking events, equipment, and personnel, resulting in 22 percent improvement in overhead while improving sales closed rates by 14 percent

Business Manager (2003 to 2005)
- Updated financial tracking and reporting for all departments, including establishing spreadsheets for each department for maintaining budgets and forecasts
- Developed rate schedule for quick turn-around for sales department providing clients quotes

Education

- Northern Graduate School of Management, Master of Business Administration (MBA)2002
- Southern University, Hospitality Management 2000

Skills

- Proficient in Microsoft Office, Photoshop, Graphic Design programs and highly proficient in PowerPoint
- Basic stage lighting and audio design and operation—Calling cues
- Proposal, script, and speech writing
- Conversational Spanish (read but not write)

INTERESTS

- Reading, plays, musicals, concerts, festivals, fine arts

VOLUNTEERING

- American Heart Association Annual Fund Raiser—Event Coordinator
- Downtown Children's Hospital—Storytelling and Crafts
- Art in the Park—Event Development and Operation

As a variation on the menu style résumés, this is a popular format:

MARY B. SMITH   **PHONE:** (123) 456–7899

Special Event Manager
2468 Uptown St. Big Rock, VA 12345   E-mail: MBS@email.com

OBJECTIVE

Seeking a challenging opportunity in special events management utilizing training and experience to ensure seamless experiences for attendees while providing excellent business results

EXPERIENCE

- Big-time Theatre – New York, NY   (Summer 2009)
  - Prod. Stage Manager   Hot Shoes   Dom Director, Artist Director
  - Prod. Stage Manager   Bells   Dom Assistant, Director

- High Seas Cruise Line – Miami, FL   (2007 to 2009)
  - Prod. Stage Manager   Golden Show   Sweet Voice, Director
  - Prod. Stage Manager   Night Mare   Dee Manding, Director
  - Prod. Stage Manager   Nutty Nuts   Strong Vision, Director
  - Rehearsal Stage Mgr.   Love This Town   She A. Pro, Director
  - Rehearsal Stage Mgr.   Fly on the Wall   Albert Artist, Director

- Big Town Events – New York, NY   (2006 to 2007)
  - Event Coordinator   Opening Night at the Palace
  - Stage Manager/Event Coordinator   Empire State Ball
  - Assistant Project Manager   Time Square New Year's Eve Party

- Big Apple Events – New York, NY   (2004 to 2007)
  - Event Manager   Macy's Halloween Parade
  - Production Assistant   Governor's Ball

- On Your Feet Dance Company – New York, NY   (2003 to 2004)
  - Assistant Stage Manager   National Tour   H. B. Driver, PSM

- Theater—Theatre Company – Boston, MA   (2002 to 2003)
  - Stage Manager   Shows Go On   Dominic Director

- Billstown Film Festival – Orlando, FL   (2001 to 2002)
  - Assistant Event Manager   Goodness It's Cold   Leo Dark, Director
  - Assistant Event Manager   Once and Only Once   Leo Dark, Director

EDUCATION

- University of Atlantic   (1997 to 2001)
  - BA Special Events Management
  - Minor Theater with emphasis in Stage Management

SPECIAL SKILLS

- Proficient in Microsoft Word and Excel, Microsoft Internet Explorer, Microsoft Publisher
  - Basic Understanding of Programming—Running Light & Sound Boards
  - Basic Understanding of Spanish

VOLUNTEER ACTIVITIES

- Theatre for Children—Volunteer Stage Manager
- Have a Heart Annual Gala – Volunteer Event Manager

APPENDIX 5

Query Letters

Sample letters

Your cover letter checklist:

- ☐ Research the target company.
- ☐ Review with your mentors and other advisors, ensuring it is perfect.
- ☐ Send in Priority Mail envelope, as it gets attention. A low cost in relation to the high-value reaction.
- ☐ Address it to someone in the company.
- ☐ Write with your reader in mind.
- ☐ Do not restate what is on your résumé but share what is not on the résumé.
- ☐ Keep it to one page if possible.
- ☐ Share why you are seeking a position with the company.
- ☐ Keep it professional.

Example A
Terry Transition
1234 Main St.
Somewhere, CA, 98765
Phone: 123-456-7890
gracegraduate@cmail.com

May 1, 2010

Paula Producer, Event Producer
Wonderful Events Company
1000 Event Lane
Wherever, NY 12345

Dear Ms. Producer:

For the past three years, the Wonderful Events Company has been nominated and received numerous awards and continues to excite members of the industry with creativity and uniqueness. Having had the opportunity to speak to Carrie Coordinator about the detailed planning that went into your production of the Make the World a Better Place Gala, it became apparent that there are many ways to learn, grow, and contribute with WEC. Therefore, I am submitting my résumé for your review and consideration.

Having worked in Amazing Weddings for the past four years I have a strong commitment to customer service and detailed planning. My love and training in graphic art serves the company well, and has provided me with many opportunities to create materials for marketing promotions as well as one-of-a-kind logos using the names of the bride and groom. With the very strong visual approach taken by WEC on the Web site, the presentational materials, and in the events, I know there is much I could offer to expand what is now being done. There would be great opportunities for me to learn and grow in that process as well.

Please expect a telephone call next week to arrange a time that is convenient for us to meet and discuss current and future opportunities.

Thank you for your consideration.

Sincerely,
Terry Transition

Example B
Betty Beginning
1234 Main St.
Somewhere, CA, 98765
Phone: 123–456–7890
gracegraduate@cmail.com

May 1, 2010

Paula Producer, Event Producer
Wonderful Events Company
1000 Event Lane
Wherever, NY 12345

Dear Ms. Producer:

It was with great excitement that I learned that Wonderful Events Company is offering internships starting in the spring. For the past three years I have attended the Career Job Fair, where we had the opportunity to meet and say hello. You were so generous with your time, answering many questions and then speaking to as many students as possible. The internship with WEC would be the ideal next step in my development and long-term goals.

   With a background in theater, focusing on stage management, the production internship would be a perfect match for my past training in technical theater and stage management. Carrie Coordinator shared with us that special events were like doing theater in fast-motion. That is what most attracts me to the production department and where I can make the greatest contribution. The BFA training included:

- Scenic, lighting, audio and costume design
- Production management, including building budget spreadsheets
- Coordination of the front of house dealing directly with patrons to ensure excellent service
- Two semesters of being an assistant stage manager
- Two semesters of stage managing a main stage production
- A minimum of 16 weeks in an internship, which I am seeking with WEC

   Next week, expect a telephone call so we can arrange a time to meet and discuss the internship. Thank you for your consideration. I look forward to meeting you soon.

Sincerely,
Betty Beginning

Example C
Rene Renew
1234 Main St.
Somewhere, CA, 98765
Phone: 123–456–7890
gracegraduate@cmail.com

May 1, 2010

Paula Producer, Event Producer
Wonderful Events Company
1000 Event Lane
Wherever, NY 12345

Dear Ms. Producer:

At the recommendation of our mutual acquaintance, Nancy Network, it was suggested that I contact you concerning a job opportunity with Wonderful Events Company. I am well aware of your organization, as I attended the annual gala for Make the World a Better Place and was very excited at the possibility of discussing employment opportunities with such a well-respected company in the special events industry.

With a background in sales and customer relations, I was responsible for increasing revenues by more than 75 percent with our three divisions in my current position at All Types of Events. In the rental area, we bar-coded all equipment and devised a tracking system for all inventory, including a maintenance record. This valuable information provided our department with a "life expectancy" and reliability factor. As the leader in our photography service department, I led the team in the transition to digital, archiving all past materials. In addition, I had responsibility for maintaining and updating the company's Web site and introduced video playback as a feature.

All Types of Events will be relocating to Faroffland, Florida, and for family reasons, it is not possible for me to leave the area. With my strong background in computer programming and information services, I bring a unique talent to your events company. I would welcome the opportunity to meet and speak with you directly on how I might be of value to Wonderful Events. Thank you.

Sincerely,
Rene Renew

APPENDIX 6
Sample Thank-You Letters

Sample Thank-You Letter A
Betty Beginning
1234 Main St.
Somewhere, CA, 98765
Phone: 123–456–7890
gracegraduate@cmail.com

May 1, 2010

Paula Producer, Event Producer
Wonderful Events Company
1000 Event Lane
Wherever, NY 12345

Dear Ms. Producer:

Thank you again for the wonderful and insightful information about the Wonderful Events Company in our meeting yesterday. You clarified a number of areas of interest for me and I left feeling very positive about my experience. Carrie was particularly helpful in the pre-meeting, showing me the well-organized production offices. One can see why the staff is so motivated about doing their best work.

You suggested that I attend the next Event Professionals meeting next week, and it is now on my calendar. I look forward to seeing you there and taking you up on your offer to introduce me to other individuals in the business. I appreciate your willingness to assist in helping me find opportunities to get more experience so that WEC can consider me in the future.

Again, it was a pleasure meeting you and the other members of your staff, and I will continue to keep you updated as I gain more experience. I look forward to seeing you at the meetings next week.

Sincerely,
Betty Beginning

Sample Thank You Letter B
Terry Transition
1234 Main St.
Somewhere, CA, 98765
Phone: 123–456–7890
gracegraduate@cmail.com

May 1, 2010

Paula Producer, Event Producer
Wonderful Events Company
1000 Event Lane
Wherever, NY 12345

Dear Ms. Producer:

When asked about my interview with Wonderful Events, the first word out of my mouth was "amazing!" From the moment I walked in the office to driving out of the parking lot, everyone was very friendly and open, answering all my questions. I was particularly impressed with the design and development area, where your team is working on the opening of a new performing arts center. It will be nothing short of spectacular.

   Having spent the past few years focusing on Once in a Lifetime Weddings, I can see that much of what I have learned is transferable to WEC. The reputation of the company is very well known and respected. I appreciate your encouraging words for a possible position but understand that it is important that you complete the interview process, meeting all the candidates. Your comment that "you certainly could handle what we do very well" was a wonderful vote of confidence and is reassuring that I am heading in the right direction.

   I look forward to hearing from you in the next few weeks and should there be any other questions you might have, please call. This is a very interesting possibility and one in which I am very excited. Thank you.

Sincerely,
Terry Transition
Sample Thank-You Note A

From the desk of
Terry Transition

Dear Paula,

Yesterday was far beyond anything I could have expected. You and your staff were most gracious, and I appreciate the time spent with me. I now can see why your team is so energized under your leadership. Thank you for making all the arrangements, particularly lunch with Kerry Creative. I look forward to continuing the discussion regarding this position.

Best wishes,
Terry
Sample Thank-You Note B

From the desk of
Terry Transition

Dear Kerry,

Thank you for taking time to join Paula and me at Benny's Grill. The lunch was wonderful and the company even better. I loved the story about your client that wanted to arrive at the convention site by hang-glider, but at the rehearsal wanted you to fly in, so he could see the effect. I look forward to continuing the discussion regarding the position as WEC looks like a great company to work for, with staff members who are very talented at what they do.

Best wishes,
Terry

APPENDIX 7

Online Networking

Look for jobs at these sites, but plan to spend time reviewing the other materials offered on career and personal development. Once you have greater insight on the process at these large clearinghouses, you will have a better understanding and will be better prepared for going to the targeted company's site and applying for a job. As you explore opportunities online, remember that identity theft is the number-one fraud in the United States, and you should not include your social security number on your materials. In addition, send your materials when possible as a PDF file, so they cannot be altered. Protect your personal information and only provide information when you are sure that it is safe to do so.

Many professionals are now using LinkedIn and Facebook to communicate information regarding job opportunities. These sites help to connect those in need of a job, with companies in need of employees. This is not a replacement for one-on-one networking, but it is the emerging vehicle for staying in touch and connected. Once again, you must keep this very professional and remember that everything you write might show up where you may not expect it. Keep everything positive and never write anything negative about anyone or anything. At the old saying goes, "If you don't have something good to say, it is best to say nothing at all."

There is much to be explored on the Internet, and often it is hard to know where to start. To give you some idea of the many options available, start by going to about.com Job Search. There you will find links to connect you to various sites to help with your process:

1. Monster.com has been seen in commercials on the Super Bowl and it is super sized, as its name would imply. It is a massive site with information to help you with all phases of preparation and job searching.
2. Clearinghouse sites such as careerbuilder.com have valuable information and include statistics, résumé templates, cover letter suggestions, and much more. They also have links to a large number of employers, including companies that might have openings in your area of interest. Careerbuilder.com is a great start in looking for jobs online.

3. Job-hunt.org is not as large but is filled with great suggestions. It tends to target more senior-level positions. It has excellent advice on a number of issues, including using a commission-based recruiter, as they may "shop" your résumé around to employers and your résumé could end up as spam, which is not in your best interest. I found the seven steps they recommend in starting the job search to be very helpful and easy to understand.

4. Yahoo's hotjobs.com is one more source in your quest, to be well prepared for your job search. They have excellent information on whether or not to use a career objective on your résumé. Although the information is generic and simple enough to understand on how to create a résumé, it will be easy for the hiring manager to read and understand.

5. The *Wall Street Journal* offers the careerjournal.com, where I found interesting articles related to employment. The articles change, but there is always excellent information on issues such as starting fresh with an unpaid internship. There is information for recent graduates as well as information for those in career redirection.

6. The *New York Times* has a link that connects you to nytimes.com and Monster.com, which also has excellent articles on effective job search techniques. It keeps tabs on the latest books on the subject of interviewing and career development.

7. There is a fee for assisting with your resume on resumes.com but there is also a great deal of excellent free information to assist you in preparing your materials. The information is very clear and has format examples for your review. In addition, there is a great list of interview tips, which is a reminder of things to do before, during, and after your interview.

8. Mindtools.com should be on your favorites. Visit it often to continue expanding your understanding on how to be effective on the job, in school, and home, as well as how to deal with people in a positive manner. There is much to learn in each of the primary categories:
   ○ Leadership
   ○ Time management
   ○ Problem solving
   ○ Stress management
   ○ Decision making
   ○ Information skills
   ○ Project management
   ○ Communication skills
   ○ Practical creativity
   ○ Memory improvement

   This site deals more with your personal development, which is directly related to your ability to present yourself as a viable candidate.

9. Indeed.com provides a "one search—all jobs" function. At the time of compiling this list, there were a large number of positions listed. Many were in the nonprofit fundraising segment, but nonetheless, this is a great site to keep up with where to find the job opportunities.

10. The government is also a location to be explored. You will need to take three steps: first go to usa.gov, click on Jobs and then on government jobs.
11. At LinkUp.com, you will find free collected job postings from company Web sites. It lists numerous pages of special events opportunities, as it does a master search of Web sites.
12. SimplyHired.com means just that—type in the position, and a list of positions appears. There were a number of positions that had special events as part of the duties. This site also does a master search of companies and connects on the word recognition.
13. Craigslist.org offer job-hunt.org that is very direct and to the point. It offers great advice and lots of resource available particularly about making sure you are protected from people who might be using job postings to gain access to personal information.
14. VisualCV.com offers a very impressive online resume that is very slick and easy to read. It might be best for those redirecting their career than those starting out. It is well worth the time to check out the site and read some of the sample resumes.
15. Backstage Employment Network at www.plsnbookshelf.com lists jobs and positions in both theatrical and convention settings. Production companies that do both theater work and special events are using this site. Audiovisual (AV), sound, lighting, and costuming are listed, in addition to project management, stage managers, on-site managers, and much more.
16. Industry organizations such as ISES and MPI post job opportunities that focus on the special events industry; their Web sites should be visited regular.
17. LinkedIn.com, known for networking also offers a job search option. It is easy to get information by simply typing a keyword and a postal zip code and it provides a list of available jobs.

APPENDIX 8

Sample Questions

Here is a list of questions that you are most likely to be asked in your interview. There is no way of predict what you might be asked in an interview, but if you use these questions to develop answers, you will be better prepared to deal with the unexpected questions.

1. *Question*: Tell me about your current job or position.

   Answer: They will want to know about duties and responsibilities, not just the job title. This is providing historical information and is best given chronologically, as well as giving details on your duties.

   Example: "I have been in my current position for three years, having stated as an intern, and was given additional production responsibilities when I was given a full-time position. My current duties are mainly in event coordination, where I have a pre-event checklist that I review with the production depart-ment. Then on-site, I coordinate the event set-up, including the lighting, audio, staging, floral and greens. I make sure talent is taken care of as well as keeping the event on time. I get to work with the banquet staff, deal with any issues the client might have, and, of course, the strike of the event afterward. I am the first to arrive and the last to leave. It has been a great learning experience and a chance to meet many people."

2. *Question*: If we were to call the people you have worked for, what do you think they would say about you?

   Answer: This is a very popular question, and the wrong answer is that you don't know. Start now to find out so you can share what people have told you about your performance.

   Example: "Recently my supervisor and I had a discussion in my annual perfor-mance appraisal, and she shared that the management team most appreciates my positive attitude and willingness to do whatever is necessary to ensure the success of the team. She pointed out that when the team was faced with the challenge of the professional speaker being delayed in route for our event, I had my laptop and went online and booked another flight. I was at the airport to pick her up, and she was at the conference with plenty of time to prepare for speaking to our group."

3. *Question:* What do you think the people who worked around you would say about you?

   Answer: They are looking for you to talk about how you work well with others and understand the necessity of working together with other members of the team.

   Example: "Being a member of a remarkable team that encourages one another, I would say they would call me a cheerleader when things get tough because by motivating others, I motivate myself."

4. *Question:* What was the worst job you have ever had?

   Answer: Use care and never go down a negative street in an interview. It is acceptable to say that you cannot think of a really bad experience, as you have learned something from every experience.

   Example: "I cannot think of a worst job, as I believe that it is up to each of us to come to the workplace with an upbeat attitude. Yes, there have been times that were very challenging, such as we were on a deadline to set up an outdoor event and it was raining very hard and we knew that once the rain stopped, there would be very little time to set up. However, everyone pitched in and we made it. It was tense for a while, but I enjoyed seeing all the bosses jumping in helping us; it was a good opportunity to see leadership by example."

5. *Question:* What would you say is your strongest attribute, and how would you apply that to our position?

   Answer: This is not a time to apologize for having skills but to share them in a manner that is straightforward.

   Example: "Based on feedback from the past, I would say my strongest attribute would be my willingness to learn. How that would apply to your position is that learning is something I enjoy and most people consider me to be a quick study, so once I understand the process and the expected results, I would work hard to exceed your expectations."

6. *Question:* What makes a good employee?

   Answer: This is your opportunity to talk about responsibility for making the company successful.

   Example: "Good employees understand their responsibility to the overall success of the company. They are on time for work and focus on their duties while at work. They represent the company and always follow policies in dealing with coworkers, clients, vendors, and anyone in which they come in contact. Employees are ambassadors for the company."

7. *Question*: What are your weaknesses?

    Answer: Many times, this type of question is used to knock you off balance, and the interview gets to see how you deal with confrontation or challenging situation.

    Example: "We all have areas for development and there are a many areas in which I am seeking to gain experience. I was told by a wise man that I have not lived long enough to have a lot of experience. One of the reasons I am speaking to you about a position is to work and learn from the best."

8. *Question*: How well do you work under pressure?

    Answer: This is sometime a very difficult question to answer because most of us think we work really well under pressure. Best to share information on how you make sure that you are prepared and know your options.

    Example: "Knowing there could be challenges in the process of doing special events, planning is the cornerstone of how I prepare. Knowing my options is critical so that when there is pressure, I have considered in advance the various options."

9. *Question*: What accomplishment are you most proud of?

    Answer: Best examples are those that also give credit to others on the team and for a cause bigger than you.

    Example: "Last year I worked with a group of volunteers on a fundraiser supporting XYZ, and my role was to work with a group of children with special needs. It required more time than expected, but the event was very successful thanks to all our wonderful volunteers. Seeing the reactions of the attendees made the effort all worthwhile. We could all be very proud watching that group of children do a simple yet moving performance. I have to admit that I was as emotional as everyone else in the room."

10. *Question*: What kinds of things get you excited about your job?

    Answer: This helps the interview better understand what you like doing.

    Example: "What excites me most is when I get the approved proposal and have to transform that into a production plan with all the equipment and manpower. Once that is fully understood, then I get to work on the schedule and confirm all the elements. It's like assembling a jigsaw puzzle so that when it is all together, it's a beautiful picture."

11. *Question*: What two or three things are most important to you in your job?

Answer: The interview/hiring manager will be listening for what you will do for them more than what he or she has to do for you.

> *Example*: "What is most important to me is fully understanding the expectation of management, as well as to know how I am doing and what areas I need to work on in addition to what I am doing well. I also enjoy being part of a winning team."

12. *Question*: If you leave you current job today, what would you be remembered for?

Answer: They want to hear how you talk about your current role and the level of success you had in your position.

> *Example*: "Based on past feedback from my supervisor and peers, I would think they remember me most for my "can-do" attitude and willingness to jump in and help where needed. I also will be remembered as the person who remembered everyone's birthday with a card and cupcake.

QUESTIONS MEANT TO CHALLENGE AND PUT YOU UNDER PRESSURE:

1. *Question*: What would you like to avoid in your next job?

Answer: This can be turned into a positive, but keep on track with your career goals.

> Example: "If possible, I would like to work toward my long-term career goal of creating special events, and I will do everything so I fully understand the resources and the process. If I were to avoid something along the way, it might be that ultimately I would avoid what I want to do most."

2. *Question*: What can you tell me in five minutes that would persuade me that you should have the job?

Answer: It is unlikely the interview will take out a stop watch and actually time you, but this is your chance to share how your background and training match the position description.

> *Example*: "Based on my understanding of the position, you're looking for a person with skills in (list three or four), all in which I have a strong background. But looking beyond the skills, I bring with me a strong passion for special events and a determination to provide quality experiences for everyone concerned: the clients, coworkers, vendors, and anyone else I might be in contact with while performing my duties. I believe in strong relationships, positive interaction, making what we do the best it can possibly be while enjoying the chance to do something I love. My goal is to make your company

look good and contribute to the overall success in both the execution of events and profitability of the company."

3. *Question*: How competitive are you?

Answer: Do not be shy about the word competitive, as it is part of the industry. To stay competitive, a company needs to always be improving.

Example: "I must admit that like so many others, I like to be on a winning team. Competition is a very good thing as it continuously challenges you to be better. I feel I am competitive as a team member wanting to be the best we can be and always looking to set a new standard."

4. *Question*: What frustrated you in your last job?

Answer: Once again, you must use care in saying negative things about past employers, but turn it around into a positive.

Example: "I really cannot say it was frustrating on my last job, but there was a level of disappointment when we would work very hard on a proposal for a client and not get the contract. We certainly got our share, but our team members would pour their hearts and souls into a proposal that we knew would be really exciting to produce—and then not getting to follow through by actually doing the event was disappointing, but I understand that is part of the business."

5. *Question*: Have you ever been fired?

Answer: Tell the truth but do not blame anyone.

Example: "As a matter of fact, I was dismissed from a position. I must admit that I learned a lot from that experience, including being honest with others as well as myself about my level of understanding of the duties. I should have admitted that I didn't really understand how to do some of the duties of the job, and because I thought my boss would think me lacking experience, I didn't say anything. I made mistakes of not asking for help, but I promise I won't make that mistake again."

6. *Question*: What motivates you?

Answer: The interviewer is looking for loyalty and commitment to the organization. Focus on making the company successful and thereby making all those that are part of the company successful.

Example: "I am motivated by having challenging projects that continues to raise the standards that places demands on the creative process in developing new and exciting events. I am motivated by success and understand that we are only as good as our last event."

APPENDIX 9

The Interview Check List

In preparing your interview checklist and organizing your materials, think in terms of a three-ring binder with tabs for each category.

Résumé

☐ Create my résumé template to customize to the target company.
☐ Adjust my objective to the position they are seeking.
☐ Check terminology on my résumé ensuring it is the same as the job posting.
☐ Review carefully the skill and experience requirements.
☐ Make sure you have the necessary skills required for the position you are seeking.
(For internships I will focus on showcasing my potential)

Target Company—Visit Its Web site

☐ Carefully read the target company's mission statement and vision to understand goals and objective of the company.
☐ What are the products and services of the company, and how are they unique?
☐ What slogan or other statement is used to market its brand?
☐ Staff names and position—print copies, including pictures if available, to help remember names of people and what they do.
☐ What service or event do they use to showcase their company?
☐ Look for companies it partners with and learn more about them.
☐ Who is the competition?

The Job Posting

☐ Break down the duties and responsibilities and list what, by knowledge and/or experience, is in that area.
☐ For those areas I am not familiar with, I will research to gain basic knowledge of the area.

- ☐ Develop examples of how you experienced each of these responsibilities.
- ☐ With examples, I need to demonstrate that I am a team player, committed to servicing the needs of the client with exceptional quality experiences while ensuring there are appropriate business results.

Cover Letter

- ☐ Addressed to a person in the company.
- ☐ Include all my contact information.
- ☐ Write a letter with three paragraphs.
    - ☐ Show that I know something about the company.
    - ☐ Identify my agenda of what I am seeking.
    - ☐ Describe the call to action for moving to the next step.

Résumé

- ☐ Adjust the objective to reflect the position for which I am applying.
- ☐ Review that résumé and job posting to ensure there is a match.

Mailing Materials

- ☐ I will have someone proofread my resume and cover letter.
- ☐ I will use high-quality paper for all my written materials.
- ☐ I will place my materials in a quality full-size envelope (not Manila).
- ☐ The address label will be typed, as well as the return address.
- ☐ I will send as Priority Mail.

Send Via the Internet

- ☐ I will write an original letter and resume putting them in a PDF file.
- ☐ Compose a short message that informs the reader of what is attached.
- ☐ Choose the subject on the message such as: Peter Professional résumé and cover letter.

Phone Interview—Be Prepared

- ☐ I will keep materials with me at all times.
- ☐ I will always answer the phone in a professional manner.
- ☐ My answering machine message will be simple and professional.
- ☐ If not in a good location to speak, I will ask if I can call back in a few minutes or set a time for the call—the goal is to have the best possible interview.
- ☐ Remove distractions and focus on my sent materials, which is what the interview is reading.
- ☐ I will speak and act the same, as if we were in the same room speaking.
- ☐ I will speak deliberately to ensure I am understood.
- ☐ My energy and excitement must be heard in my voice.

DRESSING FOR MY INTERVIEW (WOMEN)

- ☐ I will have two outfits on standby for interviewing at all times.
- ☐ I will dress for a business setting rather than a social one.
- ☐ My business suit will be conservative.
- ☐ My blouse or other tops will not be low cut or revealing.
- ☐ Skirts will not too short or uncomfortable for me to sit.
- ☐ My jewelry will be simple.
- ☐ Perfume will be very light.
- ☐ I will dress in the matter in which I believe the company would want me to represent them in a business meeting with an important client.

DRESSING FOR MY INTERVIEW (MEN)

- ☐ I will have two outfits on standby for interviewing at all times.
- ☐ I will dress up rather than down.
- ☐ My business suit or sport jacket will be conservative.
- ☐ My tie will be simple, without a loud designs.
- ☐ My shirt will be ironed.
- ☐ Blue jeans, gym shoes, and sweat socks are not an option.
- ☐ My shirt will be buttoned except for the top one or two buttons without a tie.
- ☐ If not wearing a jacket, I will still wear an ironed dress shirt and my slack with be pressed.
- ☐ I will dress in the matter in which I believe the company would want me to represent them in a business meeting with an important client.
- ☐ I will be clean, including fingernails.
- ☐ My leather shoes will be polished, with no scuff marks.
- ☐ I will wear socks to match the color of my slacks and shoes.

FOR THE INTERVIEW

- ☐ I will bring copies of all information, including extra copies of my résumé.
- ☐ I will have a list of references that I have advised of my interest in this company.
- ☐ I will be very polite to everyone.
- ☐ I will shake hands firmly and smile, looking them in the eyes.
- ☐ When in a group, I will include everyone when answering questions.
- ☐ I will sit up straight, with hands in my lap or on a conference table.
- ☐ I will not cross my legs ankle on knee.
- ☐ If I do not understand the question. I will ask for clarification.
- ☐ When ask about myself, my focus will be about what I do, not who I am.
- ☐ I will practice my basic story of "this is what I have done in the past to bring me to where I am at this point and where I hope to be in the future."
- ☐ I will answer questions related to skills with an example of how I have used the skill—Example: Yes, I am very familiar with Excel spreadsheets, as we tracked all

expenditures on our recent event and used it extensively in my last position (or college program).

☐ I will use the recommended steps in answering questions and ask to give examples of past experience:

    ☐ Paraphrasing the question, making sure I understand the question

    ☐ Giving an example and the challenges faced with the example

    ☐ Explaining how I overcame the challenge

    ☐ Describing the results and what I learned from that experience

☐ If I do not know the answer to a question, I will not fake it or make up an answer but be truthful and say I do not know (but will get the information and share it in the recap/thank-you letter).

☐ Even if I feel I am not doing well in the interview, I will remain positive, knowing that I am establishing an impression.

☐ I cannot ask others to be excited about what I do if I am not excited.

☐ When answering questions, I will make sure that the interviewer knows I have completed my answer.

☐ I will not say anything negative about anyone—always take the high ground.

☐ If I have a question at the end of the interview, I will ask, but otherwise tell them I have no questions.

☐ I will thank everyone for my interview.

☐ I will have business cards to present, and will collect business cards from those involved with my interview.

☐ All business cards will be placed in a Rolodex file and become part of my network.

MY FOLLOW-UP

☐ I will have thank-you cards or a letter in the mail within 24 hours of the interview.

☐ I will write a recap of the interview, including all the questions I was asked and my replies.

☐ If there was an issue that needed additional clarification, my thank-you letter will address those issues.

ADDITIONAL FOLLOW-UP

☐ After ten days, I will send a follow-up letter expressing my continued interest in the position and a willingness for additional meetings.

☐ My mission is to keep the door open, even if the company does not hire me.

☐ After four weeks, I will request a short follow-up meeting, requesting feedback on my interview and advice on what I can do to improve.

☐ Send a recap and thank-you to the interviewer (now a coach) listing what I learned and request the opportunity to check in from time to time to demonstrate my progress.

☐ Request names of others in the industry that might be of assistance in finding a position.

☐ As I get more experience, I will send updated résumés approximately every six months.

REVIEW THE PROCESS

☐ I will review the recaps of my interviews, seeking to be better prepared for the next interview.

☐ If there are issues that continue to come up about my interviewing skills, I will find a career counselor to assist in developing the needed skills.

INDEX